A Season in the Sun

King of baseball, king of New York. *Courtesy of Getty Images.*

A Season in the Sun

THE RISE OF MICKEY MANTLE

RANDY ROBERTS & JOHNNY SMITH

BASIC BOOKS
New York

Basic Books
Hachette Book Group
1290 Avenue of the Americas, New York, NY 10104
www.basicbooks.com
Printed in the United States of America
First Edition: March 2018

Published by Basic Books, an imprint of Perseus Books, LLC, a subsidiary of Hachette Book Group, Inc. The Basic Books name and logo is a trademark of the Hachette Book Group.

The Hachette Speakers Bureau provides a wide range of authors for speaking events. To find out more, go to www.hachettespeakersbureau.com or call (866) 376-6591.

The publisher is not responsible for websites (or their content) that are not owned by the publisher.

Print book interior design by Brent Wilcox.

Library of Congress Cataloging-in-Publication Data

Names: Roberts, Randy, 1951- author. | Smith, John Matthew, author.
Title: A season in the sun : the rise of Mickey Mantle / Randy Roberts and Johnny Smith.
Description: First Edition. | New York : Basic Books, [2018] | Includes bibliographical references and index.
Identifiers: LCCN 2017038834 (print) | LCCN 2017041463 (ebook) | ISBN 9780465094431 (ebook) | ISBN 9780465094424 (hardcover)
Subjects: LCSH: Mantle, Mickey, 1931-1995. | Baseball players—United States—Biography. | New York Yankees (Baseball team)—History.
Classification: LCC GV865.M33 (ebook) | LCC GV865.M33 R63 2018 (print) | DDC 796.357092 [B] —dc23
LC record available at https://lccn.loc.gov/2017038834
ISBN 9780465094424 (hardcover)
ISBN 9780465094431 (ebook)

10 9 8 7 6 5 4 3 2 1

For Craig Roberts, the best brother and friend a man could have.—RWR

Few have ever loved baseball history and a good book more than Rod Eastin. This one's for him.—JMS

CONTENTS

Dubbed the "Year of the Slugger" by *Sports Illustrated*, 1956 was the year that Mickey Mantle fulfilled all the Yankee hype. Long compared to Babe Ruth, Lou Gehrig, and Joe DiMaggio, in his season in the sun he took his place in the record books beside the other Yankee greats. *Courtesy of Getty Images.*

INTRODUCTION

The Blue-Eyed Boy

"Jesus he was a handsome man . . . How do you like
your blue-eyed boy? . . ."
—E. E. CUMMINGS, "BUFFALO BILL," 1920

Look at the determination on Mickey Mantle's face—the resolve in
his fierce blue eyes, his flexed jaw, and the hardness around his
mouth. Look at the power—the prizefighter's cheekbones, the bull's
neck, and the hint of a slugger's shoulders. Is it the face of weakness,
the look of a man fragile enough to crack into a million pieces?

Mantle's chiseled physique looked like the ideal body of a power
hitter, a creation of Michelangelo sculpted out of marble. Wonder-
struck by his muscled, compact frame, sportswriters and teammates
tried not to stare when he ambled through the locker room, nearly
naked, wearing only a towel, his perfectly *V*-shaped torso, barreled
chest, hard stomach, and wide back on display. Built like a lead miner,
with broad, sloping shoulders, bulging biceps, and Popeye forearms,
Mantle was, in baseball parlance, country strong.

Hy Peskin's 1956 *Sports Illustrated* cover photo reveals the intensity
and rugged strength of baseball's most famous player. In that season—
branded the "Year of the Slugger" by the magazine—his career held

only great possibilities; baseball immortality itself was within his reach. His physical gifts—power, speed, and agility—made it seem like there were no limits to what he could do on a baseball field.

Yet, for all of his attributes, Mantle's biographers have emphasized his overriding weakness. Too often they have presented his life as seen darkly through a rearview mirror, interpreting many events during his baseball career as a way station along the road to alcoholism. "Mickey Mantle's life was spent waiting for a death that seemed just around the corner," biographer David Falkner wrote. Similarly, in her fine biography, Jane Leavy observed, "Mantle fit the classical definition of a tragic hero." By the summer of 1995, alcohol-induced cirrhosis of the liver, hepatitis C, and cancer had left him a shell of the man he had been in the 1950s, when, strong and tanned, he had graced the cover of American magazines and thrilled baseball fans on the diamond. Only later would his heavy drinking define the arc of his life.[1]

This approach ignores much of the joy of his life—the joy he discovered in the game and the joy spectators experienced watching him play. To fully understand the man, his impact on baseball, and what he meant to America, it is necessary to look at his life as he lived it, not as a study in retrospection. That means returning Mantle to the 1950s, when he became the most celebrated athlete in the country and reigned as the king of the National Pastime.

In 1956, only injuries stood between Mickey Mantle and greatness. The Mantle the fans knew—the one they saw at Yankee Stadium, watched on television, and read about in *Sports Illustrated*—was not a drunk. He was a latter-day legend.

IN THE LORE OF Mickey Mantle, it is an often-told tale. As well it should be. It's a story of two of the greatest players—and arguably the two most iconic—of the early post–World War II era, set against the backdrop of the excitement and pageantry of a Subway Series between the New York Yankees and the Brooklyn Dodgers, at a time when baseball was still the king of all American sports. It is fitting that virtually every book on Mantle pays homage to "the play."[2]

Before the 1952 World Series, Yankees manager Casey Stengel cornered his young center fielder for a lecture on the wily habits of Dodgers star Jackie Robinson. Jackie, Stengel explained, was the most aggressive base runner in the game. He was known for stretching a single into a double or blazing around second to turn a double into a triple. In a primal sense, he challenged the manhood of outfielders, calling into question whether they had the talent and the nerve to throw him out. Mickey listened, knowing he had the arm. But the nerve . . . that was another matter.

In the eighth inning of Game Three, with the Dodgers leading the Yankees 2–1, Robinson ripped a low line drive into center field. Charging down the first base line, he reached full speed in three strides. Rounding first, his spikes kicking dust, he challenged Mantle, who fielded the ball on one hop. Suddenly the game became a chess match, a test of wits between the young outfielder and an experienced, daring base runner.

Holding the ball shoulder high, Mantle eyed Robinson, who had slowed to a dance between first and second. Mickey cocked his arm as if he were going to fire it toward first, daring Jackie to make a move. Robinson hesitated, then streaked toward second. Mantle had conned him into running for the extra base and then threw him out by what seemed like half a city block. When it was over Jackie smiled and tipped his cap. Mickey grinned. He had outsmarted the great Jackie Robinson.

On the game's greatest stage, Mantle demonstrated that he had the intelligence, instincts, and ability to make "the play." No wonder he recalled it as one of his most treasured memories. No wonder his biographers and a legion of sportswriters have fondly recounted the episode. Some consider it one of his greatest World Series plays. As much as his tape-measure home runs, it signaled the arrival of Mickey Mantle, the Wonder Boy of the 1950s.[3]

It's a marvelous story. There is only one small problem with the tale. It never happened.

Mickey did not bait and trap Jackie. Robinson did not attempt to reach second. In fact, he advanced to third base on a single by Roy Campanella and then scored on a hit by Andy Pafko. The Dodgers won the game and took a 2–1 lead in the series. Anyone reading the New York newspapers the next day on October 4, 1952, would have seen it recorded that Robinson crossed home plate. The following spring, writing a magazine profile of Mantle, Milton Gross, an eyewitness reporter, noted that after Robinson hit the ball into center field and rounded first base, he "stopped, stumbled, got to his feet again, and then scrambled back to first."[4]

The significance of "the play" is not that it didn't happen but that it is remembered as if it did. Years later, Mantle confidently recalled throwing out Robinson. "I'll never forget it," he said. Perhaps Mickey confused the play with a similar one in another game. But a close inspection of every Yankees and Dodgers World Series contest that Mantle and Robinson played in 1952, 1953, 1955, and 1956 reveals that Mickey never threw Jackie out at second. It turns out that Mantle was an indifferent student of his own career. In that regard he was like his teammate Yogi Berra, who once commented, "I never said most of the things I said."[5]

Journalists and biographers have retold Mickey's tale, perpetuating a mythology that started with his own hazy memories. Discerning the truth of Mickey's world, especially during the 1950s, demands casting a skeptical eye on his many ghostwritten autobiographies and the popular reminiscences of the era. In reconstructing his public and private life, we visited his hometown, Commerce, Oklahoma, where the Mantle myth took shape; the Cooperstown Hall of Fame, where the legend is enshrined; and newspaper archives in New York and Washington, DC, where the story lies interred in hundreds of reels of microfilm. In Cooperstown we collected copies of team media guides, game programs, advertisements, and rare baseball magazines. Page after page, Mantle comes alive again, not brooding and pessimistic, as he is so often remembered, but hopeful and full of promise. We have sought not to judge Mickey Mantle but to reveal him as others saw him at the height of his career.

According to the conventional baseball narrative, Mantle played during a more innocent time. After he died in 1995, *Sports Illustrated*'s Richard Hoffer wrote, "Mantle was the last great player on the last great team in the last great country, a postwar civilization that was booming and confident, not a trouble in the world." In the introduction to Mantle's memoir of the 1956 season, coauthor Phil Pepe wrote of the era that it was "a wonderful time in this country when everyday life was much less complicated." Yet romanticizing Mantle's place in the "golden age" of baseball and the "happy days" of the 1950s distorts reality. Only when we ask how the Cold War and the culture of New York shaped American attitudes toward Mantle can we begin to understand why baseball needed a hero like him. In the making of Mickey Mantle, context was as important as his outsized talent.[6]

With the help of the very best sportswriters in New York—the capital of baseball—he emerged as an American icon. In the decade after World War II, when New York's three major league teams dominated baseball, the city was still very much a newspaper town. The papers connected baseball fans to Mantle throughout the day. Drinking their morning coffee, sports fans read Arthur Daley and Gay Talese at the *Times* or Red Smith of the *Herald-Tribune*; the *Daily News*'s Dick Young and the *Daily Mirror*'s Walter Winchell entertained readers on their subway rides to work; the *Post*'s great columnists, Jimmy Cannon and Milton Gross, absorbed their attention during the ride home; and Frank Graham at the *Journal-American* or Dan Daniel of the *World-Telegram and Sun* helped them relax after dinner, offering the latest gossip and baseball news. The most influential New York scribes shaped Mickey's popular image through their writing in *Sports Illustrated*, *Sport*, *The Sporting News*, *Baseball Digest*, *Saturday Evening Post*, *Newsweek*, *Time*, and *Look*. In 1956 Mickey

Mantle became baseball's cover boy, publicized and photographed from one coast to another.

Yet the writers did more than report feats; they fabricated baseball's myths and produced American heroes. "Most mythology," David Halberstam wrote, "is manufactured in New York about *American* virtues; thus the mythologists are from New York, but the mythologized are preferably from Commerce, Oklahoma, or"—in the case of Joe DiMaggio, the son of Italian immigrants—"Fisherman's Wharf."[7]

If Mickey Mantle had not existed, sportswriters and Yankees publicists would have invented him. And in a quite literal sense, they forged the Mickey Mantle Americans adored. Since 1920 sportswriters had helped create New York baseball legends. They transformed George Herman Ruth, a loud, boorish man, into the Babe, a jovial idol who loved children, candy, and soda pop as much as he did hitting home runs. They turned a distant, laconic DiMaggio into the incomparable Yankee Clipper, a reserved, classy paragon of excellence. They made Lou Gehrig, the reclusive son of German immigrants, into "the Pride of the Yankees," a sentimental favorite who battled a debilitating and ultimately terminal disease with unmatched and unwavering courage.

The Yankees and their supporters in the press promoted baseball stars because New Yorkers demanded excellence from the team that embodied the city's competitive values. In 1968, Mantle's final season, historian Bruce Catton recognized as much, writing, "The Yankees perfectly represented what might be called the New York Idea, which held that New York had and was the best of everything. No matter what line of work a man was in—finance, industry, communications, the arts, sports, or fashion—he was not really *in* unless he was in New York. New York made the pace; it led the way, and everybody else had to follow and like it."[8]

Mickey Mantle, the ball player from rural Oklahoma, was next in the assembly line of New York creations. It was all planned from his first glorious spring training camp when he began knocking the ball prodigious distances. That was in 1951, but his anointment was premature. Over the next four seasons, he struggled to fulfill the expectations thrust upon him by the city's hero makers. Instead of a wunderkind, he was an enigma. Fans questioned his character and determination. Then, in 1956, it all came together.

After years of disappointments, frustration, and a variety of injuries, in 1956 he confirmed his greatness. It was his best season ever. He performed magnificently, pounding tape-measure home runs into the bleachers of Yankee Stadium, making crucial plays during the World Series, and winning the Triple Crown, a rare achievement that marked his ascendance as the best player in the game.

That season Mantle joined Ty Cobb, Rogers Hornsby, Lou Gehrig, and Ted Williams as the only players who had led both leagues in home runs, batting average, and runs batted in (RBIs) in a single season. During their Hall of Fame careers Babe Ruth, Joe DiMaggio, Stan Musial, and Willie Mays failed to qualify for this elite club. This shortlist represents something more significant than the answer to a trivia question. The Triple Crown is at the very heart of baseball's hold on America. A testament of his greatness, Mantle's statistical feat garnered his permanent place in history. More than other sports, baseball, Halberstam observed, depends on statistics because they give meaning to the game's mythology. A player's "performance is not fulfilling enough," he wrote. "It must be shown in quantified heroics, records to be set and broken, new myths and heroes to replace the old."[9]

And in 1956 Mantle stepped out of the shadows of Ruth, Gehrig, and DiMaggio. For the first time in his career, the sun-bathed stage of Yankee Stadium truly belonged to him. There may have been a player who had a year close to Mickey Mantle's perfect season, but none had a more euphonious name or better looks or was so well suited for the television age. He was unlike any other baseball star in America, the realization of Bernard Malamud's protagonist in *The Natural*, a blue-eyed, blond-haired boy from the heartland whose raw power and mythical purity made him a hero.

Of course, there were always two Mickey Mantles—the man and the image—and New York's celebrity-making culture shaped and eventually eroded both.

OUR STORY BEGINS with three questions: How did Mickey Mantle come to be seen as a hero? Why did it happen in 1956? And what did he mean to America?

His emergence as an icon was a product of a particular moment when the country confronted the Cold War and baseball faced an array of problems. In the 1950s, Major League Baseball and its promoters created narratives about how the "Great American Game" expressed the nation's democratic character. Celebrated *New Yorker* writer Roger Angell commented in 1954, "Baseball is everybody's game, still the American pastime." From the sandlots to city stadiums to suburban Little League parks, baseball belonged to the masses, stitching together swaths of the American fabric at a time when many citizens believed that sports reflected and shaped the nation's values.[10]

World War II made sports integral to the "American way," an ideal based on the principles of democracy, equal opportunity, and, most importantly, winning. The war nationalized American sports, and baseball contributed to the arsenal of democracy. After President Franklin Roosevelt gave the green light to continue the games, major-league teams sold baseball as patriotic displays, promoting war-bond drives, raising money for military relief funds, and playing "The Star-Spangled Banner." The hundreds of players who interrupted their careers to serve in the army and navy were considered authentic heroes, courageous, selfless, and patriotic. They were part of "the greatest generation," men of action who stormed the beaches of Normandy, liberated Paris, marched into Germany, and raised the American flag at Iwo Jima.[11]

Yet, by the end of the Korean War—an unsatisfying stalemate that concluded in 1953—Americans had begun questioning the country's strength and influence abroad, wondering what happened to America's heroes on the battlefield. It was the season of the Red Scare, a troubling time when Americans worried about Communist subversion, Soviet spies, and the atomic bomb. Alarmed by the increasing protests over segregation, conservatives fretted that Communist agents were organizing civil rights demonstrations. Throughout the 1950s parents feared that "Pinkos" would recruit their children to the fifth column. Equally troubling, newspapers exaggerated an increase in juvenile delinquency, publishing stories about teenagers running wild in the streets, joining gangs, robbing old ladies, and smoking reefer.[12]

Yet sports, parents believed, offered an antidote to juvenile delinquency, and baseball formed the front line in the defense of the nation's youth. Team sports taught children the importance of building character, being a good teammate, fitting into a group, and playing fairly—democratic values that many believed made America exceptional. The success of the team, coaches reminded young players, mattered more than self-interest.

But these myths were shattered in 1951—the same year Mantle first joined the Yankees. Americans awoke to a series of scandals in their sports: Dozens of college basketball players had accepted bribes in exchange for shaving points and dumping games. Ninety cadets at West Point, half of them football players, had violated the honor code, many of them guilty of academic cheating. And the Department of Justice launched an investigation into the International Boxing Club for its monopoly on major championship fights: no boxer could rise through the ranks without selling his soul to gangster Frankie Carbo and the mob. Corruption tainted American sports, a troubling sign that young people could no longer look to athletes as role models—unless they played baseball.[13]

During the early years of the Cold War, baseball represented a model of Americanism. Adults believed that youths who played baseball would absorb its democratic virtues and resist communism. Idaho senator Herman Welker, a former miner and avid sports fan who scouted baseball players in his free time, feared that the country was losing the fight against the "Red Rats." For Welker, baseball was central to building consensus and unquestioned loyalty. "I never saw a ballplayer who was a Communist," he said.[14]

J. Edgar Hoover and other national leaders agreed. In 1950, the FBI director wrote a letter published in *Little League Hits*, arguing that youth baseball was an effective means of combating subversive forces and juvenile delinquency. Playing baseball, he wrote, prepared boys for the "rigorous competition of life" and bolstered old-fashioned "Americanism." In 1954, there were over 3,000 Little Leagues organized throughout the country, and Attorney General Herbert Brownell Jr. praised youth baseball in that year's Little League Official Program. "The Young Americans who compose Little League," he wrote, "will provide a hitless target for the peddlers of a godless ideology." The following year, schoolboys began reciting the Little League Pledge before every game: "I trust in God / I love my country / And will respect its laws . . ."[15]

Mickey Mantle was the perfect idol for the 1950s. A tabula rasa, he was complicit in letting others craft his image. Like Joe DiMaggio and Joe Louis, he was a malleable figure Americans shaped according to their own fears and desires. Mute on social and political issues, he was a hero suited for the age of Graham Greene's *The Quiet American*. He was strong and tight-lipped, a man of action respected solely for his deeds. Sportswriters and advertisers portrayed him as an exemplary role model, the great American athlete, a tough, clean-living family man who inspired youth to play the National Pastime.

Mantle personified the paradox of the 1950s, the tension between Cold War anxieties and burgeoning economic prosperity. By mid-decade, Americans embraced a "boom mentality," developing rising expectations of what they could accomplish. In the summer of 1956, Mantle challenged Babe Ruth's single-season record of sixty home runs. His chase fulfilled Americans' longing for heroes who epitomized unlimited potential, strength, and grand achievements. He appealed to younger Americans yearning to reach new frontiers. That season millions of fans bought tickets to see "Mighty Mickey," the quintessential hitter for the atomic age: a big, muscular, crew-cut slugger who embodied baseball's "big bang" style of offense.[16]

ALTHOUGH WE OFTEN THINK that Mantle played during baseball's "golden age," his breakout season occurred at a moment when the sport desperately needed a marquee player. In the early 1950s, game attendance began to slump. Owners and journalists speculated about the causes: suburbanization, television, and antiquated stadiums with few parking spaces at a time when more and more Americans owned cars. Others suggested that baseball had become a predictable, one-dimensional game that relied too much on hitters swinging for the fences.

Critics identified another cause: many of the best power hitters played outside the New York media's orbit. Few fans outside Kansas City, Philadelphia, and Cincinnati bought tickets to see Gus Zernial, Del Ennis, or Wally Post and Gus Bell play. Of course, baseball did not lack for great players, with Yogi Berra, Willie Mays, Duke Snider, Stan Musial, and Ted Williams, among others, giving fans reason enough to show up and cheer. However, as Roger Angell lamented, none of them possessed the drawing power of a "true star" like DiMaggio.

Two years before Mantle's historic season, Angell, a loyal Yankees fan, admitted, "Baseball has not quite been the same for me since Joe DiMaggio retired. Joe was my boy, my nonpareil, my hero." The Yankee Clipper "had the knack which almost all great stars have shared—the ability of making his every move on the field seem distinctive and exciting." DiMaggio was the kind of player who prompted schoolboys to read the newspaper and study box scores; he turned casual fans into devoted followers. In 1941, during his record fifty-six-game hitting streak, people across the country asked complete strangers, "Did he get one yesterday?" The question required no explanation. Everyone knew who "he" was.[17]

No player evoked that same kind of daily intrigue until Mickey Mantle in 1956. He differed from the other great players of his era. Unlike the spectacular Mays, he was white and so possessed mass appeal at a time when many white fans only grudgingly accepted the presence of black players. Unlike Ted Williams, he rarely expressed an opinion, let alone a controversial one. Unlike Berra, he hit towering home runs. And unlike Snider and Musial, he played in Yankee Stadium, which made him the natural successor to DiMaggio. *New York Post* columnist Jimmy Cannon recognized that the Yankees center fielder had become a unifying force in the city and a national attraction. "He has brought this town together and made other cities smaller, too," he wrote. "They hoot pitchers who walk him in parks where the Yankees are despised. When he bunts, they feel they have been swindled. But they talk about him all the time." While Mantle chased Ruth's home run record, New Yorkers riding the subway, sipping beer on a barstool, or buying a paper at the corner newsstand echoed a similar question from fifteen years earlier: "What did Mickey do today?"[18]

In 1956, Mantle moved to the center of America's imagination because he dramatized the daily struggle for individual achievement. Etching his name into the record books, he emerged as a symbol of American progress. His life bridged two worlds: the city's modern commercialized culture and the folklore of baseball's bucolic origins, a romantic ideal where country boys like Mickey played the game in unkempt fields. His success story promoted the myths around baseball's meritocratic values and shaped his heroic status. Mantle's hardscrabble origins reminded the country that anything seemed possible through baseball.

During Mickey's season in the sun, Yankees pitching coach Jim Turner sensed that a new hero had arrived. "That Mantle is something America has needed," he said, "and something America hasn't had since DiMaggio."[19]

CHAPTER 1

A Father's Dream

"There never was any talk about what I'd be in life.
Dad and I knew I was going to be a ballplayer."
—MICKEY MANTLE, 1953

A baseball weighs between 5.00 and 5.25 ounces and measures between 9.00 and 9.25 inches in circumference. For most of the twentieth century, it was covered by two horsehide strips tightly held together by 108 slightly raised double stitches. In the hands of an expert pitcher, the stitches determine the way the ball swerves, curves, and dips. The pitcher's power and technique account for the speed at which the ball travels the 60.5 feet from the mound to the plate. A good major-league pitcher can hurl it at 90 mph. An exceptional power pitcher can occasionally reach 100 mph. At that speed, the ball reaches the plate in 396 milliseconds.[1]

How does the batter experience this? Consider a voluntary blink, suggests physicist Robert K. Adair, which takes about 150 milliseconds. A major-league fastball reaches the plate in about three blinks of an eye. But to the batter, it feels faster than that, as the minimum time it takes to initiate a muscular response to a visual signal is about

150 milliseconds. Subtract that from the 396 milliseconds, and a batter has around two blinks to decide whether to swing and, if he chooses to do so, to calculate the relative speed of the ball and where it will cross the plate in the strike zone and to manipulate a two-pound bat so that the round barrel makes contact with it. Of course, the batter might anticipate a certain pitch and identify its speed and location from the angle of the thrower's arm, but even so, he faces a daunting task.

As Ted Williams, perhaps the greatest, most successful hitter in the modern game, insisted in 1970, "Hitting a baseball . . . is the most difficult thing to do in sport." What is there, he asked, that requires "a greater finesse to go with physical strength, that has as many variables and as few constants, and that carries with it the continuing frustration of knowing that even if you are a .300 hitter—which is a rare item these days—you are going to fail at your job seven out of ten times?"[2]

Because hitting a baseball is so difficult, and failure is so much more common than success, predicting which batters will make it to the major leagues has always been challenging. When Yankees scout Tom Greenwade first noticed him, Mantle was a skinny seventeen-year-old shortstop with remarkable speed and surprising power. Living out of a suitcase, Greenwade, "a gaunt, Lincolnesque man" who wore rimless bifocals, crisscrossed Arkansas, Colorado, Texas, Missouri, Kansas, and Oklahoma searching for the next great prospect. Retelling the story of how he "discovered" Mantle, he exaggerated his own talent for identifying future stars. "I knew he was going to be one of the all-time greats," he said. "The first time I saw Mantle I knew how Paul Krichell felt when he first saw Lou Gehrig."[3]

There's no way even a veteran scout could possibly predict that a scrawny teenager would one day become the most devastating slugger in the big leagues. In baseball most players spend their professional careers in the minor leagues and never even get "a cup of coffee," as the saying goes, in the majors. Even for the most talented players, there are no guarantees.

And if the odds of making it as a hitter are slim, they are even slimmer for switch-hitters. Only about 6 percent of professional baseball players, in the history of the major leagues, have batted from both sides of the plate, and very few of them have been .300 hitters. In addition, most of them have been lightning-fast single hitters, making it to first base more through foot speed than hitting prowess. Almost none have combined speed with the ability to hit with power. Before Mickey Mantle, no switch-hitter had amassed 150 career home runs, and only three had hit more than 100. None had won a Triple Crown. Mantle would finish his years with the New York Yankees with 536 home runs, and he remains the only switcher to win a Triple Crown. He was the rarest of the breed, the million-to-one-shot switch-hitting slugger who went all the way.[4]

THE LIVES OF THE Mantle men were stitched as tightly to the game as the two pieces of leather that form the cover of a baseball. Mickey's grandfather Charles had pitched left-handed on the sandlot squads in pre–Dust Bowl Oklahoma and Missouri, and his father, Mutt, had thrown right-handed from the mound of his Eagle-Picher Mining Company team. Even his mother, Lovell, had a passion for the game. She listened to the St. Louis Cardinals' afternoon contests on the radio and faithfully reported the exact sequence of the action to Mutt and Mickey at the dinner table.

The boy's name spoke to his father's plans for him. Mickey Charles Mantle: Charles after his grandfather, Mickey after Gordon Stanley "Mickey" Cochrane, the Hall of Fame catcher who played for the Philadelphia Athletics in the 1920s and early 1930s. Cochrane, Mutt's favorite player, had started in the 1931 World Series only a few weeks before Mickey was born. It is doubtful if Mutt ever knew the catcher's full name. In any case, "Gordon Stanley" was not the sort of tag a father would pin on a son in Spavinaw, Oklahoma, where Mickey was born on October 20, 1931.[5]

Likewise, a job at the Eagle-Picher Mining Company in Commerce, where Mutt worked when Mickey was old enough to begin swinging a bat, was not the sort of employment a father hoped to pass on to his boy. During Mickey's childhood in the 1930s, Oklahoma captured the imaginations of millions of Americans. It was not the dreamland of farmers and cattlemen portrayed on stage by the 1943 production *Oklahoma!*, unless one considered brooding, threatening, violent Jud Fry the protagonist of the show. Nor was it the Oklahoma that featured an impeachment of a governor during a "pajama session" of the legislature, a race riot in Tulsa, or the murderous exploits of "Pretty Boy" Floyd. Rather it was the Oklahoma of the Dust Bowl and John Steinbeck's *The Grapes of Wrath*, of thousand-foot tsunamis of grit washing across a godforsaken landscape and caravans of turtle-like jalopies, filled with Okies in search of phantom jobs, crawling across a harsh desert toward California.

Yet even that Oklahoma, that tale of human and ecological disaster and heartbreak, was not Mutt and Mickey's Oklahoma. The suffering in Mutt's Oklahoma took place under, not above, ground. At the end of the nineteenth century around Commerce, in the tristate region where Missouri, Kansas, and Oklahoma meet near Route 66, a farmer digging a shallow well discovered substantial lead and zinc deposits. Once rail lines connected the region to smelters in Galena, Kansas, and Joplin, Missouri, the rush commenced. Camp towns in Ottawa County, with names like Peoria, Quapaw, Cardin, Picher, and Commerce, boomed, drawing money and men into the region for much of the next half century. The nation's two world wars spurred the growth of the tristate mining industries. Munition manufacturers, the notorious "merchants of death" of the 1930s, and paint companies needed the lead for their products. And zinc was crucial in the production of galvanized steel and sink linings.[6]

The profits for the Eagle-Picher Mining Company swelled. So did the giant mounds of chat, the waste by-product of the hunt for lead and zinc. Mining towns like Commerce paid dearly for their mineral "blessings." Crisscrossing mineshafts left the land unstable, subject to periodic cave-ins and lurking sinkholes that swallowed homes and sections of road. The chemicals used in the mining process bled into the quarries, reservoirs, and streams like Tar Creek, which soon ran blood red. They also created singularly misnamed dry alkali "fields," smooth, lifeless, grassless places where Mickey and his friends played the game of baseball. Red-ringed eyes were a telltale sign for Mickey's mother that he had been swimming in a quarry or playing ball in a blighted field.[7]

If the mining process was slowly poisoning life above ground, work below ground was far more perilous. To the men who labored in the mines, life was so harsh and unforgiving that almost all of them were permanently marked by the job. It was grueling, backbreaking work. After blasting a rock face, miners had to load the shattered pieces into enormous steel buckets for transport to the surface. Imagine shoveling wet snow from a sidewalk. A good shovelful might weigh twenty pounds. A shovelful of lead-infused rock would weigh at least double that. Now imagine loading those buckets for nine or ten hours each day in a perpetual dusk, starved of good air, forced to breathe in the fumes produced by rocks lined with precious lead and zinc.

Accidents were almost as common as sore backs and scarred lungs. Deaths occurred with alarming frequency. Between 1924 and 1931 the Tri-State Zinc and Lead Ore Producers Association reported that 173 miners died in accidents, but that organization only represented about half of the operators. A violent end lurked in every step of the mining process. Rock crushed some miners, and machines mangled others. Some fell down shafts, and others died in cave-ins. And, of course, thousands of these men with muscles like steel cables worked for years and then started to find it increasingly difficult to breath, even outside the mines. They coughed blood, struggled to get oxygen into their lungs, and often died of silicosis or tuberculosis.[8]

"I always wished my dad could be something other than a miner," Mantle later wrote. "I knew it was killing him." He realized that underground, amid the toxic dust and debilitating dampness, his father was suffering a miner's fate. Mickey watched as Mutt "coughed up gobs of phlegm and never saw a doctor. What for? He'd only be told it was 'miner's disease.' He'd realize that if he didn't get cancer he'd probably die of tuberculosis." Seeing his two brothers die at thirty-four, sensing that he would be lucky to make forty, and adopting a fatalistic view of life, Mutt Mantle chain-smoked Camel cigarettes, did his time underground, and drew pleasure from the St. Louis Cardinals and his family.[9]

No miner in Commerce wished the same life for his son, and Mutt Mantle was a caring father, if not an outwardly compassionate one. He wanted something better for Mickey—a life aboveground, in the sun, free of "miner's disease." It was hard to fashion dreams in the worst years of the Great Depression, but Mutt managed to. His eldest son would be a ballplayer, not in the semipro sandlot leagues in the tristate region but in the major leagues. He would be like Mickey Cochrane, a splendid hitter with his name splashed on every newspaper in the country. Long before New York City sportswriters imagined what Mickey could do and might mean to the nation, Mutt Mantle had fashioned him in his own mind, a Frankenstein creation, a one-of-a-kind athlete. Mutt would forge Mickey into the ballplayer he had never been.

As A YOUNG BOY Mickey wondered why his father pushed him so hard. Mutt made baseball seem like a matter of life and death, because in some ways it really was. "Mickey," his father explained, "do you know what every miner wants most when he's down under? He dreams of fresh air and sunshine. It's not much—fresh air and sunshine. But when you're under the ground," risking your life, "it's the most important thing in the world." Mutt loved baseball because it was played outside in the "summer when the sunshine pours over you." Playing baseball relieved him of the stress, the daily uncertainty of working in the ground; baseball was the light in a life of darkness. It made him feel alive and hopeful that his boy would have a better life than him.[10]

Shortly after Mutt moved his family to Commerce in the mid-1930s, he and his father, Charles, began molding Mickey into a switch-hitter. The lessons took place in the side yard, between the modest four-room house and an all-purpose shed. It became a daily ritual: Mutt would return home from a grueling day in the mines, his overalls covered with soot, and he'd call for his boy. Arming Mickey with a "two-bit bat," he and Charles began lobbing tennis balls to him. As Mickey grew older they threw baseballs overhand, Mutt right-handed and Charles left-handed. They forced Mickey to bat left-handed against his father and right-handed against his grandfather. Mutt knew that right-handed batters hit better against left-handed pitchers and vice versa. So, he figured, learning how to switch-hit might increase Mickey's chances of making the big leagues.[11]

But it wasn't always easy for Mickey. Batting lefty felt unnatural and unnecessary to a boy who just wanted to play the game. He remembered that when his mother called him for dinner, Mutt would interrupt. "Your belly can wait," he'd say. And he'd continue pitching until Mickey satisfied him with a few more good cuts.[12]

As Mickey matured, Mutt became stricter. When he was just twelve Mickey defied his father during a game, batting from the right side of the plate against a right-handed pitcher—and striking out. Mutt's voice boomed across the field. He recalled his father saying, "Boy! You're in for it. Go on home and don't you put on a baseball uniform again until you switch-hit like I taught you." That was the last time Mickey ignored his father's instructions.[13]

Mutt only wanted the best for his son. He imagined that with practice and hard work, Mickey might just have a chance to become a professional ballplayer. He reminded Mickey that the men in Commerce had few opportunities and lived a meager, vulnerable existence. "Mickey," he said, "you know that our house is built over a mine. So are plenty of other houses in town. One day there could be a cave-in from a blast and the whole floor could fall right from under us." The odds of that happening, he said, were long, but it was possible. That's why Mickey had to practice. Every day. Committing himself to baseball could give him something Mutt never dreamed of having: a life on solid ground, a fine home, security, and peace of mind.[14]

Mickey had faith in Mutt's dream. So he swung hard from both sides of the plate, devoted countless hours to learning the fundamentals of the game, and mastered its nuances. Although he never became a true student of baseball, his father's instructions became a permanent part of his muscle memory. From age four to eighteen, Mutt and baseball determined the pattern of his life.

Mutt could not, however, control his son's health. In October 1946 Mickey was little more than a squirt, 130 pounds and a head shorter than many of his classmates, but he badgered his father to allow him to play football. Football, Mutt thought, was too dangerous, but he reluctantly consented. Sure enough, during a practice a teammate accidentally kicked Mickey in his left shin. At first it seemed like a dime-a-dozen football injury, hardly worth notice, and Mickey finished the practice. But the pain persisted and intensified. The next morning his ankle was swollen and bruised. Concerned, Mutt took off from work and rushed his son to the local hospital.[15]

The Commerce physician sent them up the road to the Picher hospital, which had an X-ray machine and superior facilities. There Mutt learned that Mickey had osteomyelitis, a serious bone disease that was often referred to as "cancer of the bone" or "TB of the bone." Modern antibiotics, especially the recently developed penicillin, had proven an effective remedy for the disease, and during the year after the injury, Mickey received a series of treatments at the Crippled Children's Hospital in Oklahoma City. It was a painful experience. Hobbled by osteomyelitis and hampered by crutches, Mickey recovered fitfully and slowly. Yet that same year, his body matured. He put on thirty pounds and by 1948 looked more like a young man than a kid, especially on the ball field. Everything his father had taught him, Mickey now seemed to do naturally. With the added muscle he now hit with power from both sides of the plate, threw runners out from deep in his shortstop's position, and ran the bases like an Olympic sprinter.

HIS TALENT AND PROGRESS, now packaged in a young man's body, impressed Tom Greenwade so much that in 1949 he signed Mickey to a modest professional contract to play the rest of the minor-league season for a $400 salary plus a bonus of $1,100. Mutt was surprised that the amount was less than what Mickey could earn playing Sunday semipro ball and working in the mines. Shrewdly, Greenwade had calculated that Mickey would earn about $0.87/hour in the mines and about $15 playing for a semipro team each Sunday. Add it up, Greenwade said, and Mickey would earn about $1,500—the same amount the Yankees could pay him. Unwilling to wait for other offers, Mickey signed the contract.[16]

Mantle played well in his first minor-league season, in Class D with the Independence team, which was part of the Kansas-Oklahoma-Missouri League. Then, in September of 1950, after an outstanding season with the Yankees' Class C team in Joplin, Missouri, during which he hit .383 and was named most valuable player (MVP) for the Western League, the Yankees called him up for a brief two-week major-league stint. Although he saw no action on the field, he found traveling with the team exciting. He began imagining joining the club for good the next season.

Returning to Commerce in the fall, Mickey worked alongside his father for the Blue Goose Number One mine, hoping that the Yankees would invite him to Phoenix for spring training. After the new year, as January turned into February and the cold ground hardened, Mickey grew anxious. When the Yankees didn't send him money for transportation, he figured that the team didn't want him anymore.

Perhaps, he thought, it was time to quit baseball and plan on working for the rest of his life in the mines just like Mutt.[17]

One afternoon a Yankees official called him at the mine. Where are you? Why haven't you reported for spring training? "I'm broke," he answered. "I don't have any money for transportation." Within a few hours the Yankees had wired him money for the fare. He stuffed his suitcase with clothes and his mitt and rushed to the train station, clutching the ticket to his father's dream.[18]

CHAPTER 2

The Commerce Comet

"Yankee rookie Mickey Mantle is hogging sport page headlines. They're calling him 'another DiMaggio.' Time will tell. Time will tell."

—WALTER WINCHELL,
Washington Post, March 25, 1951

"Wait till you see this kid from Oklahoma." Bill Dickey immediately recognized that the shortstop from Joplin was special. Watching Mickey Mantle swing a bat, the Yankees' hitting coach couldn't believe that he was only nineteen years old. Dickey, an old-timer, was not easily impressed. A Hall of Fame player, he had been teammates with every Yankee legend: Babe Ruth, Lou Gehrig, and Joe DiMaggio. And as an eleven-time All-Star catcher, he had scrutinized the hitting prowess of Jimmie Foxx, Hank Greenberg, and Ted Williams. But Mantle was the best prospect he had ever seen. He told Yankees second baseman Jerry Coleman that Mickey had unprecedented power from both sides of the plate and was faster than anyone else in camp. "Just wait till you see this kid," he repeated.[1]

Mickey excited his teammates too. "When he gets up to hit," Yankees coach Jim Turner noticed, "the guys get off the bench and elbow each other out of the way to get a better look." The same thing happened in the opposing dugout. Every time Mantle approached the batter's box, everyone in the ballpark focused on him. "Here's one sure tip-off on how great he is," Turner added. "Watch DiMag when Mantle's hitting. He never takes his eyes off the kid."[2]

Throughout spring training, reporters peppered DiMaggio with questions about his future—and about the kid from Joplin who seemed destined to become the next great Yankee. After twelve seasons, DiMaggio was recognized as the best player of his generation. He was, the *New York Post*'s Jimmy Cannon opined, "a whole ballplayer, complete and great." There were players who hit with more power or ran faster, but none had DiMaggio's grace. He did not sprint across the outfield; he glided. He didn't swing the bat; he stroked it with ease, like a smooth serve from Jack Kramer. "Never satisfied with anything less than perfection," the *New York Times*'s Arthur Daley noted, DiMaggio competed as though every game were his last. As he was nearing the end of his career, his legs ached constantly, and yet he doggedly played through pain. After one late-season game, when the Yankees held a comfortable lead in the pennant race, Cannon asked him why he played so hard. "Because there might be somebody out there who's never seen me play before," he answered.[3]

DiMaggio was more than the greatest player of his era. He was the most famous athlete in America and arguably the biggest celebrity too. Throughout his career, he had appeared on countless magazine covers and movie screens, in newsreels and newspaper headlines across the country. Sportswriters exalted him as a "demi-god who could do no wrong."[4]

Regally aloof, DiMaggio guarded his privacy and offered little during interviews. Reporters frequently replaced his monosyllabic answers with fabricated lines that they imagined a heroic player would say after a ballgame, always making sure that the Clipper sounded better than he really did. W. C. Heinz, one of the most talented writers of the age, noticed that his colleagues treated Joe with a kind of reverence never accorded to other players.[5]

On March 2, 1951, the second day of spring training, DiMaggio met with three reporters at the Adams Hotel in Phoenix. Nagging injuries—bone spurs in his heels, an aching throwing shoulder, and sore knees—were leading the thirty-six-year-old center fielder to consider retirement. "I want to have a good year," he announced, "and then hang 'em up." When Yankees manager Casey Stengel heard the news, he instructed Mickey to talk to Joe about learning how to play center field. Someday, Stengel planned, the kid would replace the Clipper. The only problem was that DiMaggio had no interest in mentoring the rookie.[6]

When he first met Joe, Mickey barely said a word. He was too shy and intimidated to initiate conversation. Afraid of saying the wrong thing, he avoided even glancing at DiMaggio. Cold and distant, Joe occupied the Yankees clubhouse with majestic authority. He "had this aura," Mantle recalled. "It was as if you needed an appointment just to approach him." Unless DiMaggio spoke first—and he rarely did—Mantle didn't dare interrupt him with a question or comment. Usually, he just said good-bye as Joe exited the clubhouse.[7]

DiMaggio's cool disposition made Mantle even more insecure than he already was. He began to wonder if he belonged in the same room as the Yankee Clipper. And although Joe may have praised Mickey publicly, calling him "the greatest prospect I can remember," in private he derided Mantle as "a rockhead" who wasn't worth his time.[8]

Nervous around the Yankee veterans, Mickey let his bat do the talking. As he stood in the batter's box during hitting practice, his cap pulled down over his cropped blond hair, his muscles stretched the flannel jersey across his broad back. Swinging the bat, Mantle crushed ball after ball over the outfield fence. His towering shots seemed to climb above the clouds, disappearing into the distance, landing somewhere in the Arizona desert.[9]

Sportswriters quickly took note of Mickey's natural talent. During an exhibition tour in California, riding in smoke-filled train cars, Yankees beat writers traveling with the team argued deep into the night about his ability. For hours, one columnist recalled, they "talked about nothing but Mickey Mantle." Every day writers wired hyperbolic reports back to New York proclaiming Mantle as the "next DiMaggio." In packed press boxes, scores of reporters wearing fedoras with their shirtsleeves rolled up leaned over their portable typewriters, churning out copy about "one name" only. "No matter what paper you read, or what day," *New York Daily Compass* writer Stan Isaacs observed, "you'll get Mickey Mantle, more Mickey Mantle, and still more Mickey Mantle."[10]

The fact that Mantle had become the story of spring training surprised Isaacs. No one expected him to make the big leagues in 1951. Only two years out of high school, before he was even old enough to vote, Mickey was attempting something never done in Yankees history. In fact, before 1951, only three players in the history of baseball had ever jumped five classes from the minor leagues to the majors. Reading the New York press, however, Mantle's spot in the Yankees' opening-day lineup seemed a foregone conclusion.[11]

Sportswriters lionized the "Wonder Boy," constructing an image of "the perfect rookie." Raving about his power and speed, writers ran out of superlatives to describe "the infant prodigy." They wrote about the "Colossal Kid's" rapid ascension, fabricating a legend faster than Mickey ran to first base. He was the "future of baseball," a "one-man platoon," the "rookie of the eons." Reporters saw in the speedy switch-hitter the skills of the greatest players in history all rolled into one. "Mighty Mickey" was "another DiMaggio," "faster than Ty Cobb," with "more power than Ted Williams." In the New York dailies, the "Commerce Comet" was faster than a speeding bullet, more powerful than a locomotive, able to leap tall buildings in a single bound. Sportswriters made him into Superman, but not even the Man of Steel could hit from both sides of the plate and live up to their expectations.[12]

Every time Mickey buttoned his jersey during spring training, he was reminded that he had inherited the responsibility of becoming a Yankees legend. Everyone involved with the team, from the front office down to the playing field, built him up as the next star of the sport. Stengel gushed about him: "He's the greatest switch hitter who has ever played baseball," adding, "The kid runs so fast in the outfield, he doesn't bend a blade of grass." Yankees publicist Red Patterson sold writers on Mickey's destiny. "It's the law of mathematical progression," he proclaimed. "Babe Ruth wore No. 3 and was succeeded by Lou Gehrig, who wore No. 4. Gehrig was succeeded by Joe DiMaggio, who wears No. 5." He asked a writer, "Have you noticed that Mantle wears No. 6?"[13]

By the end of spring training, Mantle's life had changed in ways he had only dimly perceived. Two months earlier he had been working for Eagle-Picher, wondering if the Yankees would someday invite him to try out for the team. Now he was on his way to New York, a successful spring training behind him, yet still unsure if he would make the opening-day roster or be sent to the team's Triple-A club in Kansas City.

Every day he heard people tell him that his potential was boundless. Stengel proclaimed it. DiMaggio said it. And so did every New York scribe who owned a typewriter. One voice, however, drowned out all the noise. His father reminded him not to believe everything he read in the newspapers. "You've made the headlines," he said. "Now make the team."[14]

FOR ALL THE HYPE during spring training, Mickey still had doubts about his ability to play for the Yankees. Could he hit big-league pitches? Or would he fail and return to the mines? He knew that he had talent, but he also knew that might not be enough. He admitted to a writer from *The Sporting News*, "I somehow get the feeling that I hadn't ought to be here."[15]

For a time he figured he'd be wearing a khaki uniform, not Yankee pinstripes. On April 4, when Mickey was in Phoenix, his father called to notify him that his local draft board had sent a notice to report for a physical. As Mutt said, "A lot of people were wondering why [Mickey] was not soldiering in Korea." In 1950, the army had classified him 4-F, physically disqualified from service owing to his history of osteomyelitis. In the past year, Mantle had hardly thought about his draft status or the Korean War.[16]

By the time he received his draft board notice, the war had devolved into stalemate. After General Douglas MacArthur pushed north of the 38th Parallel, moving toward the Yalu River, Communist China intervened and repelled the Americans at the Chosin Reservoir. Holding the line at the 38th, American forces suffered mounting casualties. Frustrated with President Harry Truman's "limited war," MacArthur believed that the United States should bomb critical targets in China and use atomic weapons if necessary. When MacArthur learned that Truman intended to negotiate a peace settlement, he argued that the president's policies would only appease the regimes in China and North Korea. "We must win," the general had recently written to Republican House minority leader Joseph Martin. "There's no substitute for victory."[17]

Many Americans agreed with MacArthur. Winning was everything. And it was the duty of every able-bodied American man to serve his country in a time of war. During the early years of the Cold War, patriotic baseball fans could not comprehend why a stellar young athlete like Mickey Mantle was not fighting in the army. *Sports Illustrated*'s Robert Creamer recalled, "The superpatriots came out in force demanding to know why Mantle hadn't been drafted." Mantle insisted that he was willing to serve in the military, even if in a limited capacity. "I'll play baseball for the Army or fight for it, whatever they want me to do," he said. "But if I don't go to the Army, I want to play baseball."[18]

On April 14, a day before the Yankees departed Grand Central Station for opening day in Washington, the *New York Times* announced, "Mantle, Rejected for Army Duty, Flying to Rejoin Bombers Today." Once again, army physicians had dismissed him because of his anklebone infection. Relieved, he couldn't wait to reunite with the

Yankees. Yet some Americans, including some Yankees fans, grumbled over his draft status, while others questioned his patriotism. After all, more than five hundred baseball players had served in the military during World War II, including Joe DiMaggio, Ted Williams, and Stan Musial, and many players were serving in Korea. In an age of national consensus over foreign policy, Americans expected baseball players to interrupt their careers for the good of the country.[19]

Mantle's fame turned his draft status into a cause célèbre. Had he performed like an ordinary prospect, destined for the anonymity of the minor leagues, few would have cared about his military disqualification. But because his name appeared in newspapers every day for over a month, he became the most famous 4-F in America. Yankees general manager George Weiss supposedly requested that military physicians reexamine Mickey. Although Weiss denied having any contact with Mantle's draft board, he admitted that his office received angry letters from fans. Certainly he understood the political implications of signing Mantle to a major-league contract. Despite failing the army's physical, critics still demanded that Mickey put down his bat and pick up a rifle. Swept up in the anti-Communist hysteria, "armchair generals" argued that soldiers with flat feet were marching through Korea. Why couldn't Mickey do the same?[20]

Before he had even played his first game in Yankee Stadium, Mickey found himself at the center of a political debate that prompted Americans to question his character. In that unforgiving city, Mantle would have to prove that he was a true Yankee, a loyal American who possessed the kind of courage that made DiMaggio a hero. Yet, while DiMaggio may have enlisted in the army in 1943, he never got deployed overseas or saw combat, and he frequently complained that the war had cost him part of his prime and tens of thousands of dollars. Playing exhibitions in the Honolulu sunshine for the Seventh Army Air Force team, Sergeant DiMaggio found little satisfaction in entertaining the troops. Nonetheless, baseball fans considered him a patriot for his service and expected Mantle to make the same sacrifice.[21]

As the team train rolled toward the nation's capital, Mickey recalled Casey Stengel tapping him on the shoulder. The manager wanted Mickey to meet Weiss and owners Del Webb and Dan Topping in the smoking lounge. Mickey nervously asked Stengel about his chances of making the team. Casey told him that he had a good shot. After Mantle and Stengel greeted Weiss and the team owners, Casey did all the talking, arguing that Mickey should start the season with the club. Weiss disagreed. Mickey needed more seasoning, he said. The youngster wasn't ready for big-league pitching.[22]

As Mickey later recalled, Casey insisted: "I don't care if he's in diapers. If he's good enough to play for us on a regular basis, I want to keep him."

It was hard for anyone in the drawing room to argue against Stengel. In just 102 at bats, Mickey had finished spring training with a .402 average, nine home runs, seven doubles, and thirty-two RBIs. The owners recognized that he was more than a talented prospect; he had become a commodity, a ticket-selling attraction. The Yankees had just set a spring training attendance record, mostly because of public curiosity around Mantle. Webb and Topping were convinced that the publicity around Mantle would generate profits for the club.

Stengel agreed. He was so confident that Mantle would perform that he suggested Weiss pay the rookie $2,500 above the minimum. Mickey could hardly contain his excitement. He knew the minimum was $5,000. After making only $225 each month playing minor-league ball in Joplin, $7,500 sounded like ransom money. He wanted to shout, "I'll take it!"

Weiss hesitated, looking at Mickey as though reading a balance sheet. A stout, middle-aged man with thinning black hair and a pulpy face, he looked like the shrewd, ruthless businessman that he was. In New York—and baseball generally—the Brooklyn Dodgers' long-winded president Branch Rickey overshadowed him with his gregarious personality. "Deacon Rickey" charmed reporters, seducing them with a combination of sanctimonious philosophy and Barnumesque salesmanship, convincing journalists and baseball fans that he believed in more than the bottom line. Weiss, on the other hand, was stolid and colorless, known as a calculating and efficient executive. Before he became general manager in 1947, he had been the director of the Yankees' farm system, and in that position he shrewdly stockpiled talent, planting the seeds for an unprecedented run: in eight seasons, between 1936 and 1943, the Yankees won seven pennants and six World Series.[23]

After his promotion to general manager, he continued shaping the roster, buying and selling players like an aggressive day trader at the New York Stock Exchange. Following a strict philosophy for team building, the "Yankee Kingmaker" was determined not to let the team grow old. Securing young talent, he argued, was the key to sustaining the franchise. Each season, he called up three to four promising prospects. Perhaps, Stengel suggested, he should take a chance on Mickey Mantle. If the kid failed to stay with the team for the entire season, Casey said, then Weiss would only have to pay him the minimum.[24]

Weiss finally relented and agreed to promote Mickey to the majors.

Mickey couldn't wait to call his father. The following day, when Mutt learned that Mickey had signed a contract with the Yankees, all his friends at Eagle-Picher congratulated him. Mutt had never been prouder of his son.

NEW YORK, E. B. WHITE observed, "can destroy an individual, or it can fulfill him, depending a good deal on luck." It was a truism Mickey would soon experience. He arrived in Manhattan carrying his father's dreams, as well as his entire wardrobe in a cardboard suitcase. He was, teammate Hank Bauer recalled, "a hayseed." Wearing cuffed blue jeans that exposed his long white socks, rubber-sole shoes, a tweed sport coat, and a wide tie decorated with a peacock, Mantle looked unfashionably out of place, a country bumpkin lost in the big city. Bauer, a decorated marine who had fought at Guadalcanal, Guam, and Okinawa, had learned more about life on the battlefield and between the chalk lines of Yankee Stadium than he ever had in eight years of school. Yankees, Bauer taught the rookie, didn't travel in blue jeans and tweed jackets. He took Mickey to Eisenberg & Eisenberg and bought him a tailored suit. Years later, Mantle often joked about his shoddy wardrobe, but in truth he was painfully insecure about his appearance. For the first time, living in New York, he realized just how poor he had grown up.[25]

Mantle's experiences were not unique. John Steinbeck may never have met Mickey, but he would have understood him well. In 1925, when the struggling writer first moved to New York from a small farming town near Monterey, California, he found work as a day laborer, hauling cement at the new Madison Square Garden. Eventually, after leaving New York and publishing *The Grapes of Wrath*, he returned to the city in 1941 as a prominent national voice for the downtrodden and the dispossessed. In New York, an expansive, tireless metropolis, Steinbeck observed ordinary migrants who aspired to a better life but discovered that the city was "a dark hulking frustration," a hard lesson Mantle learned early in his career. "The transition from small town to New York," Steinbeck wrote, "is a slow and rough process."[26]

"I was a country boy," Mantle said years later, "not the least prepared for [New York]." When he first moved to the city, he stayed in a room by himself at the Concourse Plaza Hotel in the Bronx. Located at the top of a hill where 161st Street intersected the Grand Concourse, the eleven-story redbrick building, with its limestone facade, looked like a grand Parisian resort. Since the 1920s, numerous Yankee players, including Babe Ruth, Lou Gehrig, and Joe DiMaggio, had called the Plaza home.[27]

At the time, the Bronx consisted of lower-middle-class ethnics, mostly Italians and Jews, but to Mickey it seemed as fashionable and exciting as Manhattan. Wandering along the Grand Concourse, the busiest thoroughfare in the Bronx, he absorbed the colorful scenery:

the wide, tree-lined streets dotted by bright yellow taxicabs and red-and-white buses, the sidewalks packed with shoppers, the storefront windows, fruit markets, delis, and soda parlors. To Mickey, the contrast between Commerce and the Bronx could not have been starker.

After playing afternoon games at the stadium, Mantle would walk up the hill toward the Plaza with little to do except replay every at bat in his head. Sometimes he stopped at a diner for a quick bite. Sitting at a crowded counter, he often heard factory men arguing about baseball in nearly incomprehensible New York accents. The Yankees, he quickly learned, were the pride of the borough. When he reached his cramped hotel room, he would sit in his bed reading the newspaper while roaring El trains interrupted the silence. He later claimed that he often stared at the walls, thinking about how much he missed his friends and family.

Later that season, Mickey moved into a Manhattan apartment above the Stage Deli on Seventh Avenue near West 54th Street. Rooming with teammates Hank Bauer and Johnny Hopp made the nights less lonesome, though he frequently spent afternoons by himself, sitting in dark movie theaters watching Westerns. At night, he absorbed the sights and sounds of Times Square, "a glittering cityscape lit by the world's most elaborate advertising signs." Looming skyscrapers, massive structures made of concrete and steel, and those "Broadway lights, the neon glowing," mesmerized him. Broadway, wrote theater critic Brooks Atkinson in 1951, was unlike any other strip in America. Crowds of people trudged up and down the streets, gazing "with a kind of bemused curiosity at the blazing signs that surround[ed] them—flashes of news nervously whirling around the slender Times Tower, a sheet of water pouring down the luminous wall of the Bond store's sign, rings of steam puffing out of the face of a stupendous Camel cigarette smoker." Atkinson observed that "nothing like this ever went on night after night and year after year on such a monstrous scale."[28]

Mantle had encountered a new world. He was living in the largest city in America, the epicenter of everything: television, theater, art, advertising, publishing, writing, banking, business, and, of course, baseball. Every morning millions of people poured into Manhattan Island, packing its skyscrapers, factories, department stores, offices, and restaurants. The pace of the city startled him. Tourists and traveling salesmen rushed to Grand Central and Pennsylvania stations, while commuters hustled to the subway, pushing, shoving, and cramming their way into cars.[29]

E. B. White observed that New York drained people faster than other cities did. "The normal frustrations of modern life are here multiplied and amplified—a single run of a crosstown bus contains, for the driver, enough frustration and annoyance to carry him over the edge of sanity: the light that changes always an instant too soon, the passenger that bangs on the shut door, the truck that blocks the only opening, the coin that slips to the floor, the question asked at the wrong moment." New York, White wrote, had "greater tension and greater speed," less tolerance and less patience.[30]

New Yorkers' impatience, combined with the immediate success of previous Yankee stars, created unrealistic expectations for the team's rookie right fielder. When twenty-five-year-old Babe Ruth first joined the Yankees in 1920, he led the major leagues with 54 home runs—crushing his own single-season record of 29—and 135 RBIs. In his first season in New York, the Sultan of Swat not only redefined the importance of the home run, hitting more of them than fourteen of the other fifteen big-league clubs, but inspired new attendance records. In 1936, a year after the Bambino retired, DiMaggio broke in with the Yankees and was anointed by beat writer Dan Daniel as "the replacement for Babe Ruth." Despite missing a few weeks of the season with a foot injury, DiMaggio managed to hit .323 with forty-four doubles, twenty-nine home runs, and a league-best fifteen triples. In his first season, he made the American League (AL) All-Star team, appeared on the cover of *Time*, and led the Yankees to a World Series victory over the New York Giants, the first of four straight titles. If Mickey was ever to overcome his reputation as a hayseed and replace

Ruth and DiMaggio, then just as they had, he would have to win New Yorkers' admiration right away.[31]

DiMaggio's experience with fickle New York fans was not dissimilar from Mantle's. He may have won respect soon after arriving, but New York reporters and fans did not totally embrace him at first. During a time of intense ethnic prejudice, writers emphasized his Italian heritage, dark features, and supposed indolence. "Instead of olive oil or smelly bear grease," a *Life* profiler wrote, "he keeps his hair slick with water." Surprised, the writer noted that DiMaggio didn't smell like garlic. Photographers posed him at the dinner table eating giant plates of spaghetti. Before he became the esteemed "Yankee Clipper," writers called him "the Walloping Wop" or "the Daig."[32]

Then, in the summer of 1941, a half year before Benito Mussolini declared war against the United States, native-born Americans began questioning the loyalty of Italian immigrants. In New York, even though the city had an Italian American mayor, Fiorella LaGuardia, Italian nationals were scrutinized like criminals, fingerprinted, photographed, and forced to register with the government. The New York Police Department and the FBI raided Italian homes and businesses, arresting "aliens" suspected of sabotage.[33]

Against this backdrop of nativism and political turmoil, DiMaggio distracted the country with his record fifty-six-game hitting streak, and Americans came to see him as one of their own, a symbol of assimilation. DiMaggio, like Babe Ruth and Lou Gehrig before him, affirmed that baseball was a melting pot—the meritocratic notion that the game welcomed white men from the old country. As the son of an Italian fisherman, DiMaggio could easily be seen as embodying old-fashioned Americanism. Unlike gangster Al Capone, he didn't break the law; unlike anarchists Nicola Sacco and Bartolomeo Vanzetti, he expressed no political opinions; and unlike boxer Primo Carnera, a giant circus strongman controlled by the mob, he played "that clean American game" for "the team whose very name stood for America."[34]

DiMaggio's ascendance as a great American culminated that summer, when Les Brown's band recorded a hit song played on radio stations from New York to San Francisco. "Jolting Joe DiMaggio" was more than a popular tune celebrating the achievements of the Yankee Clipper. It announced his arrival as a real American. Now he belonged to everyone, not just Italians. "Joe . . . Joe . . . DiMaggio . . . we want you on our side."

Our side. If war broke out, the United States would need DiMaggio, a man who reminded the country that he and his Italian American brethren were nothing like the fascists fighting for Il Duce.[35]

KNOWING HOW HARSH New York could be to the most innocent newcomers, sportswriters wondered if Mantle would survive. Could he withstand the competition? Would he wither under pressure? How would he respond when he struggled? Could he adjust to life in the Big Apple?

Local writers crafted a narrative based on the tension between his country roots and his new urban life. Initially, they portrayed him as the "typical All-American boy," modest and innocent, unfazed by the demands of playing for the Yankees. "His physical appearance," Gilbert Millstein wrote, "serves to evoke the image, traditional and dear to Americans, of the clean-living country boy grappling, at great odds but ultimately in triumph, with the big city and its perils." In May, the *New York Post*'s Arch Murray wrote that Mickey was "completely untouched by the surging tide of publicity that has all but completely engulfed him."[36]

But that wasn't really true. Every day reporters huddled around his locker, asking questions about every game, every hit, and every strikeout. There were so many writers that—even if he tried—he could hardly tell them apart. Interviews made him uneasy and self-conscious. Mantle could play baseball far better than he could talk about it. "I'm no good at answering questions," he admitted in a sharp country twang. Curious what the writers had to say about him, he couldn't resist reading the newspapers. Knowing that reporters evaluated him daily added more pressure. So did the photographers who snapped his picture without asking. Publicists and booking agents approached him about appearing on radio and television shows, making all sorts of promises.[37]

Posing as an agent, a conman straight out of Damon Runyon's *Guys and Dolls* named Alan Savitt duped Mickey into signing an exploitive contract that gave Savitt's "Hollywood Enterprises" half of Mantle's income from endorsements, testimonials, and appearances. After meeting Mickey at the Grand Concourse, Savitt knew that he lacked an instinct for business. He could have offered Mantle shares in the Brooklyn Bridge, and Mickey would have bought them. Shortly after Mantle signed the first contract, Savitt had him sign another, which he claimed superseded the first, giving the agent 10 percent of Mantle's outside earnings for ten years. When Yankees officials learned about the arrangement, the team's lawyers advised him to cease contact with the hustler. The deal, they argued, would not hold up anyway, since Mickey had signed it as a minor. In the future, the lawyers suggested, he should not enter into any formal business agreements without the team's approval. Although he did not honor the contract with Savitt, it would later jeopardize his all-American image.[38]

Sometimes Mantle felt as if his life no longer belonged to him. Everywhere he went—the ballpark, train stations, restaurants, movie theaters, and hotels—strangers wanted to talk to him, shake his hand, or ask for his autograph. The fans meant well, but they always seemed to remind Mickey what they expected from him. There was hardly a moment when he could get away from it all. "I was surrounded," he told reporter Charles Dexter.[39]

Gradually, the Yankees' front office realized that Mickey's ascent from Class C to the big leagues had been too quick. After his strong first month at the plate, pitchers soon discovered the holes in his swing, exploiting his penchant for chest-high fastballs. Mickey struck out with increasing regularity, about 20 percent of the time. Trembling, he would erupt in the dugout, smashing bats against water coolers, and pounding his fists against concrete walls. Embarrassed, he tried to hide his tears, shrinking in the corner, his face turning tomato red. He could hardly bear to go back onto the field, standing out there all alone, hearing the fans curse his name: "Go back to Oklahoma you big bum!"[40]

Mantle started to brood, and his mood darkened. One time, when he returned to the dugout after a failed at bat, cursing and yelling, a season-ticket holder Mickey knew only as "Mrs. Blackburn" chastised him. Sitting near the Yankees' on-deck circle, she scolded, "Stop that talk." Seething, Mickey snapped, "Shut your goddam mouth!"[41]

Trying to compensate for his frequent strikeouts, Mickey seemed to swing even harder. By mid-July he had fifty-two strikeouts in sixty-nine games. He also had the third-most hits on the team and the second-most RBIs, but it wasn't enough. He had become a liability in the lineup, hitting only .260. Mickey sensed what was coming. On a train ride to Detroit to play the Tigers, he overheard Stengel talking to the coaches about sending him down to the minors. Perhaps, he thought, his major-league career had already ended.[42]

On July 15, Stengel called him into the visiting manager's office at Detroit's Briggs Stadium. Mantle could see the concern on the skipper's wrinkled face. Stengel told him that he looked uncomfortable at the plate. Mickey was swinging at too many bad pitches, but someday, he said, "you're gonna develop into a big league star."

Mickey feared what Stengel might say next.[43]

Finally, the skipper delivered the news, telling Mantle to pack his bags. Mickey was going back to the minors.

Heading to the airport with Red Patterson, Mantle didn't know what to say. He only knew that he was joining the Yankees' minor league club, the Kansas City Blues, in Milwaukee. Patterson handed him his one-way ticket and offered words of encouragement: "You'll be back to play in the next World Series," he predicted. But Mantle wasn't so sure.

THE DEMOTION MADE MANTLE miserable. After bunting for a single in his first plate appearance, he went hitless in nineteen straight at bats. A reporter described him as a "dejected and harassed young man" who had lost all joy in playing the game. He lacked confidence and was ready to give up. It seemed like he had forgotten how to hit a baseball. With every flailing swing, his frustration grew. He feared letting everyone down in Commerce: his friends, his family, and especially his father.[44]

On July 22, he called home from Kansas City. He had not spoken to his dad since being reassigned to the Blues. When Mutt answered the phone, Mickey sounded defeated, explaining that he just couldn't hit anymore.[45]

Mutt interrupted him. He explained he wouldn't listen to any more of this "can't" business from his son. "Hell you can't. Where are you staying?"

"The Aladdin Hotel," Mickey answered.

"Okay. I'll be there," his father said, hanging up the phone without saying good-bye.

About three hours later, after a long drive north, Mutt arrived at the hotel with Mickey's mother, brother Larry, sister Barbara, and girlfriend Merlyn. Mickey hoped Mutt would cheer him up with some fatherly encouragement. "I guess I was like a little boy, and I wanted him to comfort me," he said later. Instead, he recalled, Mutt entered the room and gave him a sharp stare that "cut me in two." Then Mutt asked everyone to step outside while he spoke privately to his son.

Mickey began complaining about how he couldn't hit. He said he just wasn't good enough to play professional baseball. It was time, he said, for him to come home and work in the mines.

Mutt wouldn't accept that. He'd listened to everything Mickey had said, and now it was time for him to speak his mind. Mickey recalled that his father told him to grow up. Mutt reminded him that he wasn't a child anymore. It was time to be a man in a man's world. He didn't raise his son to be a quitter. "You don't get nothing without fighting for it."

Mickey felt guilty. His father looked haggard and underweight, his shirt dangling loosely around his lean frame. He wasn't quite sure what was wrong with his dad, but he knew that Mutt lived in misery from the backbreaking work in the mines. "Deep down," Mickey thought, "my failure pained him more than that ache in his back."

Mutt's tough talk inspired Mickey to return to the ball field. Looking back, Mickey believed that evening at the Aladdin Hotel turned out to be the "greatest thing my dad ever did for me. All the encouragement he had given me when I was small, all the sacrifices he made so I could play ball when other boys were working in the mines, all the painstaking instruction he had provided—all of these would have been thrown away if he had not been there that night to put the iron in my spine when it was needed most."[46]

By challenging his son's manhood, Mutt had motivated him. Mickey soon found his confidence again at the plate. Over the next forty games, he hit eleven home runs and drove home fifty RBIs, bringing his average with the Blues up to .364. Yankees scouts were so impressed that on August 20, George Weiss recalled him for the stretch run. When he returned to the Bronx, a crisp, clean jersey with a new number hung from his locker. Wearing number seven, Mantle hit consistently as a regular starter for the rest of the season. And on September 28, the Yankees clinched the American League pennant.[47]

Red Patterson was right: Mickey Mantle played in the next World Series.

IN THE FIFTH INNING of Game Two of the 1951 World Series, with the Yankees leading the New York Giants 2–0, Willie Mays, then a sensational twenty-year-old rookie outfielder, strode to the plate. Mickey positioned himself in deep right field, while Joe DiMaggio shaded toward left center, anticipating that Mays would pull the ball. Mantle never really felt comfortable sharing the outfield with DiMaggio. Yankees coach Tommy Henrich had drilled him repeatedly: "You play off DiMaggio." The code among outfielders required that they defer to the man playing center field, which meant that Mickey had to react to the ball and to DiMaggio. But Stengel had instructed him to pursue any ball that he thought he could catch. DiMaggio, nursing a sore Achilles tendon and an aching heel, could not glide the way he used to. "The dago's heel is hurtin'. Go for everything."[48]

Facing "Steady" Eddie Lopat, a junk pitcher, Mays sliced a looping drive into the gap between center and right field. As the ball took off, DiMaggio and Mantle bolted toward it. Second baseman Gil McDougald drifted into the outfield, figuring that the sinking ball was Mantle's since it was closer to him than anyone else. But when Joe yelled, "I got it!" Mickey took his eyes off the ball and saw Joe charging near him. "Oh, shit!" he thought to himself, "I'm gonna hit DiMaggio!"

As Mantle broke hard, his right shoe caught the rubber cover of a drain, his right knee buckled, and he crumpled to the ground. Sitting a few rows above the Yankee dugout, Mutt watched his son collapse onto the grass. After DiMaggio caught the ball everyone in Yankee Stadium turned to Mickey. Mutt knew that his son was hurt, but he did not know how badly. His mind raced back to Oklahoma. He could only imagine how scared Mickey's mother felt listening to the game on the radio.

Writhing in pain, Mantle lay sprawled on the field, his right leg folded beneath his body. "What happened, kid?" DiMaggio asked, kneeling beside him. "Mickey, what happened?" Face down, Mantle groaned, burying his head between his arms.

Panicked, DiMaggio told him not to move and waved for help. "They're bringing a stretcher, kid." A group of teammates ran from the

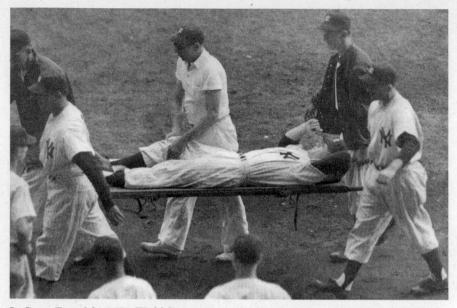

In Game Two of the 1951 World Series against the New York Giants, Mantle streaked after a Willie Mays fly ball, venturing into Joe DiMaggio's center-field territory. When, at the last moment, DiMaggio hollered, "I got it!" Mickey "slammed on the breaks." His spikes caught on a rubber drain cover, and the ligaments in his right knee twisted and tore. When his teammates carried him off the field on a stretcher, Yankee fans feared that the promising rookie might not fully recover. *Courtesy of the National Baseball Hall of Fame.*

bullpen toward Mickey. Coach Frank Crosetti placed a towel under his head while Mantle curled up in a fetal position. Mutt anxiously watched four of Mickey's teammates carry him off the field. After they reached the clubhouse, the trainer, Gus Mauch, wrapped his knee with ice and placed splints on both sides of his leg.

The New York newspapers announced that Mantle was done for the rest of the series due to "a sprained muscle on the inside of the knee." But the injury was much worse than a knee sprain. Mantle had shredded the ligaments, cartilage, and tendons in his right knee. He worried that he would never fully recover his speed and strength and that his career might be over. Years later Mantle said, "I was never right again. . . . So far as I'm concerned that was the worst thing that could ever have happened to me."[49]

When Mickey woke up the following morning, his knee had swollen into the size of a watermelon. He needed crutches just to stand. When a taxi dropped him and his dad off at the Lenox Hill Hospital, Mutt stepped out first. Easing out of the cab, Mickey placed his hand on his father's shoulder for support. But when he leaned on him, his dad collapsed onto the sidewalk. His father had always been a strong man, so something was clearly wrong with him, as Mickey had suspected. Gaunt and hollow cheeked, he looked like he had not eaten anything for days. Mutt was never one to complain, but he could no longer bear the excruciating pain in his back.[50]

Mutt checked into the hospital and spent the next few days in the same room as his son. While Mickey rested in his hospital bed, doctors performed a battery of tests on Mutt. During Mickey's recovery, father and son watched the Yankees win the World Series on a rabbit-eared black-and-white television set. Occasionally, Mutt reminded Mickey that he needed to improve if he was going to become a trusted regular on the team. Even when he was laid up in a hospital bed, Mickey's baseball career consumed his father.[51]

Mantle recalled Mutt's doctor knocking softly on the door and entering the room. He told Mickey that he had some bad news. "Your father is dying of Hodgkin's disease," he said. Mickey was certain that his father had suffered a miner's fate. There was nothing the doctor could do to save his dad and nothing he could say to console Mickey. Mutt had always been at his side. But for the first time in his life, Mickey confronted the reality that someday soon his father wouldn't be there.[52]

CHAPTER 3

The Natural

"I am retiring from baseball. The game is no longer
fun. The aches and pains aren't worth it."

—JOE DIMAGGIO,
December 11, 1951

The great DiMaggio left the biggest stage in baseball, retiring a nine-time World Series champion. Without him Yankee Stadium lost much of its aura.

His presumed replacement limped into spring training. In late February 1952, when Mickey Mantle arrived in St. Petersburg, Florida, his coaches and teammates doubted he would be ready to play at full strength by opening day. In December, team physician Sidney Gaynor had examined him in New York and declared that there was no damage to his knee cartilage and that the torn ligament on the inside of his right leg had fully healed. Mantle was relieved, but he still felt soreness in his thigh. Gaynor prescribed a series of exercises to strengthen the leg, which Mickey promptly ignored.

It didn't matter though. No amount of exercise could prevent the degeneration of his right knee. In an age before magnetic resonance imaging and arthroscopic surgery, Mantle's doctors could not see that he had a torn anterior cruciate ligament (ACL). As long as he played baseball, running and cutting across the field, his knee would continue to deteriorate, and the pain would linger.[1]

He had spent the winter in Commerce, sulking around the house, wearing a heavy brace on his right knee. His father's terminal diagnosis weighed on him. Mutt's cancer sapped his strength, forcing him to quit work. Seeing him languish, Mickey felt helpless. He recalled spending most nights lounging on the couch, staring at the television with a beer in his hand. He gave little thought to his rehab exercises, figuring his body would recover naturally. "I was twenty years old," he said later, "and I thought I was superman."[2]

In Florida, he worked with the team trainer and gradually regained stability in his leg. Still, on opening day against the Philadelphia Athletics, Casey Stengel questioned Mickey's ability to cover the gaps, so he sent him back to right field. Yet Mantle played with confidence and vigor, notching three hits in four at bats, knocking in two runs, and stealing a base. He performed so well early in the season that the Yankees traded Jackie Jenson, Mantle's primary competition to replace DiMaggio in center field.[3]

Three days after the trade, on May 6, 1952, Stengel called Mickey at the Grand Concourse where he stayed with Merlyn, now his wife of hardly four months. Casey had just finished speaking to Mickey's mother, Lovell, on the phone. She asked Stengel to forward a devastating message to her son: Mutt had died earlier that morning in a Denver hospital. He was only forty years old.[4]

Merlyn would never forget that painful moment, watching Mickey hammer his fist against the wall. She tried to console him, but he rejected her embrace. She asked when they would leave for Oklahoma, but he shook his head and told her that she didn't need to go with him. He just wanted to be alone.[5]

Merlyn was crushed. She could not understand why her husband did not want her at the funeral. Offering no explanation, Mickey suppressed his emotions, just as his father had. He didn't know how to be

Frequent leg injuries and haphazard attention to rehabilitation made spring training an ordeal for Mantle. Occasionally it felt like he had to learn to run and slide on new, but not improved, legs. *Courtesy of the National Baseball Hall of Fame.*

vulnerable with his young wife. He couldn't allow her to see any weakness. His father had told him to marry Merlyn, but he never taught him what it meant to be a husband. "She's your kind," he said, implying that Mickey should avoid getting involved with a showgirl from the city who might distract him from his single priority: baseball. Merlyn, Mutt reminded him, was wholesome and loyal, a woman who loved Mickey unconditionally and understood where he came from. And so he had married her.[6]

Overwhelmed by grief, Mickey felt guilty that he wasn't at Mutt's side when he died, that he had never said good-bye or told his father that he loved him. He escaped to the ballpark, his sanctuary, leaving Merlyn alone at the hotel. He dressed for the game against the Cleveland Indians but never left the dugout. It's hard to imagine that he could have concentrated on the game. His father's death left him feeling empty. Mutt had been everything to him: his mentor, coach, and best friend. He was irreplaceable.

On May 11, two days after the funeral, Mantle returned to Yankee Stadium a changed man. He was only twenty years old, but baseball was no longer just a boy's game. It was his profession. His father's death meant that he had to step up as the man of the family. It also meant that he could not fail. Too much was at stake. He carried the burden of supporting Merlyn, his mother, and his four younger siblings. And in a year he would be a father himself.

Playing on a fragile knee, Mantle wrestled with self-doubt. Struggling early in the season, he must have wondered if he was damaged goods. In a time before sophisticated knee surgeries, there were no guarantees that he would recover the speed and power he had displayed a year earlier. For all his talent, he understood that life promised him nothing.

MICKEY MANTLE'S ROOKIE season had ended with his teammates carrying him off the field on a stretcher. The sight of him collapsing was etched into the minds of everyone in Yankee Stadium that day. The club had great plans for him in 1952, banking that he would "move into the king's row reserved for the Yankee greats." Yet his career—and the Yankees' season—was in question. If the Yankees were going to win another World Series, Mickey would not just have to recover. He would have to deliver a sensational sophomore campaign. And he did.[7]

Mantle finished the season rated among the best hitters in baseball. In 142 games, he hit .311—good for third in the American League—with twenty-three home runs and eighty-seven RBIs. He also ranked among the top ten American League batters in hits, total bases, home runs, doubles, runs, walks, and slugging percentage. His 111 strikeouts—the most by any American League hitter not named Larry

Doby—proved that the first-time All-Star had not yet mastered the strike zone. Nonetheless, in July the *Washington Post*'s Shirley Povich, one of the many impatient writers of the era, declared that Mantle—playing in just his first full season—was "*finally* coming of age as a big leaguer." Most importantly, when the Yankees competed against the Cleveland Indians in a tight pennant race, Mantle demonstrated great composure, batting .362 over the final three weeks of the season.[8]

In October, the Yankees met the Brooklyn Dodgers in the World Series. After the Yankees lost Game Five, they returned to Ebbets Field down 3–2 and on the brink of failure. However, in the eighth inning of Game Six, with the Yanks leading 2–1, Mantle launched a fastball into the deepest part of the left-center-field grandstand, boosting the Yankees lead by another run. After the Yankees tied the series with a 3–2 victory, *New York Post* columnist Jimmy Cannon wrote that Mantle had become the idol of every boy in New York. "How many kids," he wondered, "pretended they were Mickey Mantle last night[?]"[9]

In the crucial final game of the series, Mickey inscribed his name into Yankees lore. In the sixth inning, he settled into the left side of the batter's box, facing Dodgers hurler Joe Black. With the game tied at two, Black knew he could not afford to make a mistake. His first two pitches fell wide of the plate, and his third nearly grazed Mantle's jersey. On a 3–0 count, he finally threw a strike, as Mantle squared late, threatening to bunt. On the very next pitch, Black fired a fastball. Mantle uncorked his body and slugged it skyward. Calling the game for NBC, Mel Allen, his sweet southern voice rising with excitement, announced, "There's a fly ball out to right field. That ball is going, going . . . it is gone!"[10]

The next inning, batting from the right side of the plate against Preacher Roe, Mantle smacked a single into center field, driving home Gil McDougald. In the end, the Yankees won Game Seven 4–2 on Mantle's decisive swings. The Yankees, Jackie Robinson said, "didn't miss Joe DiMaggio." "It was that Mantle, that Mickey Mantle killed us," he added. "Mantle was the difference."[11]

Three years before reporters began naming a World Series MVP, Mantle was undoubtedly the most valuable Yankee. In each of the team's four victories, he made critical, game-changing plays. It appeared that he had seamlessly replaced DiMaggio. "There may be no ceiling on the lad's skills," Povich concluded after the series. An intimidating slugger, the "golden boy," Roger Kahn wrote in the *New York Herald-Tribune*, had become a bona fide star, a true "hero." And he already seemed poised for an encore.[12]

YANKEES PUBLICIST RED PATTERSON had been waiting for this moment. On April 17, 1953, World Series winner Mickey Mantle, batting right-handed, dug his cleats into the dirt around home plate, concentrating on Washington Senators southpaw Chuck Stobbs. Mantle's eyes scanned the field as a brisk wind unfurled the American flag above the center-field wall. With the Yankees leading 2–1 in the top of the fifth inning and a runner on first base, Stobbs ran his fingers over the seams of the baseball. When he delivered a high fastball right over the heart of the plate, Mantle punished him, crushing it high into the cloudy gray sky. Senators second baseman Wayne Terwilliger swore that the ball flew so high that Mantle had already rounded second when it eclipsed the left-center-field bleachers of Griffith Stadium. After it clipped the National Bohemian Beer sign—about 460 feet from home plate and nearly 60 feet above the outfield grounds—it bounced onto Fifth Street. According to baseball lore, Patterson bolted out of his press box seat and declared, "That one's got to be measured!"[13]

A former sportswriter who had covered the Yankees for the *New York Herald-Tribune*, Patterson knew a good story when he saw one. He later claimed that a boy named Donald Dunaway had retrieved the scuffed baseball and led him to the exact spot where he found it: the backyard of a modest two-story redbrick row house at 434 Oakdale Street. According to Patterson's exaggerated calculations, Mantle had hit the ball farther than any previous home run: 565 feet. Patterson rushed back to the stadium's broadcast booth, nearly out of breath, and convinced radio announcer Bob Wolff to report the record. "He was the Yankee PR man," Wolff said years later. "You accepted what he said."[14]

The following morning, newspaper headlines trumpeted Patterson's tall tale. "Ruth Never Slugged a Baseball Farther Than Mantle's Homer," the *Washington Post* declared. That day Patterson popularized the "tape-measure home run." He told reporters that he paced 105 feet from the spot where Dunaway found the ball to the edge of the stadium—failing to mention that the houses on Fifth Street and the backyard fences would have prevented him from walking in a straight line—and added the 460 feet from there to home plate. Based on his "scientific calculations," he concluded that the ball had traveled 565 feet. Padding the distance from home plate to the house on Oakdale Street, he labeled Mantle as the greatest power hitter in history. "It was my job," he reflected, "to make Mickey look good."[15]

Patterson understood that the Yankees were not just selling baseball; they were selling entertainment in a big city that offered customers plenty of options. "Look," he said years later, "I saw that the Yankees were not just competing against the Giants and Dodgers. They were competing against every leisure-time activity that you have in summer. If you decided to go to Jones Beach, you didn't go to Yankee Stadium. You didn't buy our tickets, pay our parking charge, eat our hot dogs, or drink our beer. I was trying to make the Yankees more interesting than the Giants *and* Jones Beach as well."[16]

He succeeded. In 1953, Brooklyn Dodgers outfielder Duke Snider hit forty-three home runs, third overall in the major leagues. Yet nobody expected him to fulfill the same grand expectations foisted onto Mantle. Snider literally played on a smaller stage. Ebbets Field was a mom-and-pop ballpark, and Yankee Stadium was baseball's equivalent of vaudeville's Palace Theater. Writers and fans presumed Snider would perform like a regular All-Star, but they didn't view him as a legend in the making, as they did Mantle. Both men were among the most talented power hitters in the sport, but only Mantle had Red Patterson magnifying his achievements. When he hit home runs, Patterson recalled, "I made a point of leaving the ballpark and measuring them down to the last inch. Or so I told the writers. Duke Snider hit very long home runs, but nobody in the Brooklyn organization realized the extra press mileage they could get with a two dollar tape-measure."[17]

From the moment Patterson paced the distance of Mantle's dinger in Washington, fans and sportswriters expected Mickey to continue hitting spectacular home runs. It was no longer satisfying simply to count his homers; each one had to be measured, not only in distance but also against the stars from the past. Baseball's mythical timelessness—the idea that the game and the players themselves remained essentially the same—led writers and fans to compare the very best players to former legends without considering the context in which each man played. For many, Mantle was so outrageously talented that his performances could only spark new interest when he challenged records set by the greatest players who came before him. And now, it seemed, the twenty-one-year-old had satisfied the Yankees' expectations. "Only Ruth and Lou Gehrig, left-handers, and [Jimmie] Foxx, a right-hander, compare with Mickey in hitting long ones," Casey Stengel contended. "He might go on to become the greatest left-handed hitter and the greatest right-handed hitter."[18]

Mantle's power evoked the protagonist of Bernard Malamud's novel *The Natural*, a Herculean figure who could knock the cover off the ball. Like Malamud's Roy Hobbs, a prodigy plucked out of the plains by a lucky scout, Mickey appeared divinely gifted. Yet, unlike Hobbs, his preternatural strength didn't come from a baseball bat hewn from the pure white ash of a tree "split by lightning." Rather, his power came from swinging a sixteen-pound sledgehammer as a "screen ape" for the Eagle-Picher mine, crushing large rocks. As a teenager, during long, hot summer days, Mantle built up his back, shoulders, and arms working in the mines, digging graves, and carrying tombstones for a friend who owned a cemetery. When he first joined the Yankees, Casey Stengel started calling him "the boy with the man's back."[19]

Mantle's incredible performances early in the 1953 season convinced writers that he was on the verge of canonization. He was batting so well in early June that *New York Times* columnist Louis Effrat suggested that he might become the youngest player in history to win the Triple Crown. As the next great superstar, however, he was obligated to do more than perform on the field. Charles Dexter wrote in *Baseball Digest*, "He must be an example to American youth, a public speaker and TV personality, one of the nation's ten best-dressed men, a husband, father, and friend of the small fry everywhere." But Mickey was made to swing a baseball bat, not to play these roles. Although he became a spokesman for Wheaties, Camel cigarettes, Gem razor blades, Haggar slacks, and Louisville Slugger bats, off the field he appeared uncomfortable standing in front of photographers and television cameras. Embarrassed by the attention, he squirmed in front of reporters. He wasn't any more relaxed around the beat writers than he had been during his rookie season. He simply couldn't understand why they asked him so many questions. "What's so special about me?" he wondered. Before joining the Yankees, he'd never had to explain himself, and now the reporters were asking him to do just that. He thought that his performance spoke for itself. [20]

Just when Mantle seemed on the top of his game, injuries dashed his hopes for another spectacular season. In late June he sprained his left knee and missed six games. Then, on August 8, in the fifth inning of a game against the Chicago White Sox, Bob Boyd drove a ball into the left-center-field gap. Mantle charged toward it, halting to scoop it up. Breaking hard, he pivoted to make the throw to second base and wrenched his knee, the same one he had injured in the 1951 World Series. After the game, the team physician reported that Mickey had sprained his knee, but he had actually torn ligaments again.[21]

Somehow Mantle limped back to the field later that month, wearing a knee brace. Since the All-Star break, injuries had cost him twenty-seven games, but even before he twisted his right knee, he had already started unraveling at the plate. "Muscles," reporters affectionately called him, seemed to swing for the fences during each at bat. His strength, however, could not help him catch up to shoulder-high fastballs. The more he struck out, the harder he swung. And the harder he swung, the more he missed. From July 10 until the end of the season, he hit only .269, an abysmal average for a player anointed as the premier batter in the game. He finished the season with a respectable batting average (.295), but reporters couldn't ignore that he had slipped sixteen points from the previous year and finished second among American League batters in strikeouts (ninety). And he had hit fewer home runs (twenty-three to twenty-one), triples (seven to three), and doubles (thirty-seven to twenty-four) than he had in 1952 (albeit in nearly ninety fewer at bats). By the end of the regular season, critics considered Mantle "the bust of the Yankees, merely because so much has been expected of him."[22]

Despite Mantle's injuries, the Yankees met the Dodgers in the World Series again. Playing in his third straight Fall Classic, Mantle struggled miserably against the Brooklyn pitching staff. In twenty-four at bats, he managed only five hits, though he did smack two important home runs. In Game Two, with the score tied 2–2, Mantle thumped a two-run homer in the eighth inning off Preacher Roe, giving the Yankees the lead and ultimately the win. In Game Three, Dodgers ace Carl Erskine struck him out four consecutive times. The next day, he fanned twice more. Humiliated, he returned to the dugout each time with his head down, his cap pulled low over his eyes.[23]

In the third inning of Game Five, Mantle stepped into the batter's box with the bases loaded, two outs, and the Yankees leading 2–1. Facing Russ Meyer from the left side of the plate, he clubbed a grand slam into the left-field upper deck of Ebbets Field. His homer proved the difference in the Yankees 11–7 victory and momentarily relieved the pressure of being Mickey Mantle.[24]

He hardly enjoyed the moment. Failure, he feared, would reduce him to an ordinary, meager existence. Even after playing in two All-Star games, he felt insecure about his career. "That grand slam was a big moment in my life because baseball wasn't a game to me as the spectator understands it," he said. "It was my job and my living and all I knew. Without it, I was going to be digging fence posts back in Commerce or carrying a pick down to the zinc mines."[25]

Although the Yankees won their fifth consecutive World Series, Stengel remained disappointed with Mantle. He fixated on his short-comings. "They had the kid cold," he said, "and we knew it and we kept telling him he had to cut down on his swing and hit down on the ball." He reminded Mickey that he didn't have to knock the leather off the ball. Stengel yammered in his ear, but Mantle just tuned him out.[26]

By the end of the 1953 season, most baseball writers concluded that Mickey lacked maturity and ambition. After only three seasons, they questioned whether he could overcome persistent injuries and his weaknesses at the plate. Perhaps he had already reached the ceiling of his talent. "If Mantle never achieves greatness," Joe Trimble wrote in the Saturday Evening Post, "it will probably be because he's willing to settle for less."[27]

"I'M NOT HAVING ANY operation," Mickey insisted. "That's final." The thought of surgery paralyzed him. But when Dr. Dan Yancey, an orthopedist in Springfield, Missouri, showed Mickey his X-rays, he reluctantly agreed to the procedure. On November 2, 1953, Yancey successfully removed part of the cartilage in Mickey's right knee, but without reconstructive surgery his ACL would never fully heal.[28]

For the rest of his career—another fifteen seasons—Mickey played with a partially torn ACL. Every day during the season, he bandaged his right leg from ankle to thigh before putting on his uniform. Yankees trainer Joe Soares explained, "His muscles were so large, but his joints—wrists, knees, ankles—were frail. This discrepancy between the awesome muscles and the weak joints caused the vast majority of his muscle tears and injuries." From the moment he wrecked his right knee in 1951, he favored his left leg, the one weakened at the ankle by chronic osteomyelitis.[29]

He struggled just to get dressed before games. Cleveland Indians pitcher Early Wynn recalled seeing a trainer wrap Mantle's legs and ankles with several rolls of tape before an All-Star game. "I watched him bandage that knee—that whole leg—and I saw what he had to go through every day to play," he remembered. "He was taped from shin to thigh." Wynn and Mantle's teammates respected him for playing through throbbing knees, strained hamstrings, and sore ankles. "I'll tell you who I admired most on the team—Mantle," Yankees first baseman Bill "Moose" Skowron said years later. "He played when he was hurt."[30]

In late 1953, Mantle could not have known that the injury, and the pain, would dog him for the rest of his playing days. After spending eleven days in the hospital and departing on crutches, he anticipated only a long, dull winter. He was supposed to recuperate at home, but when his teammate and friend Billy Martin surprised him in Commerce, Merlyn worried they would get into trouble. She blamed Martin for her husband's late-night drinking and carousing. Merlyn resented his intrusion, especially since she was nursing her first baby. But Martin didn't know where else to turn. His wife, Lois, had recently served him with divorce papers, taking their daughter away from him. And his draft board, after reviewing his hardship case and reclassifying him 1-A, called him into service. The thought of not playing baseball with the guys—his second family—devastated him.[31]

Merlyn was not the only one concerned about Mickey's friendship with Billy. George Weiss was convinced that Martin corrupted Mantle. The general manager heard rumors that the "M&M boys" stayed out all night like a couple of fraternity brothers. One evening during the 1953 season, they returned to the Kenmore Hotel in Boston a few minutes past midnight. Hurrying toward the lobby entrance after curfew, they noticed Stengel holding court with a group of writers, so they slinked behind the hotel, searching for another door. Prowling down an alley, they spotted a locked door and an open transom window. That gave Martin an idea.[32]

"I'll get up on your shoulders," Billy suggested, "and climb through the window, then I'll come around and open the door for you." Wearing a brand-new sharkskin suit, Mickey grudgingly agreed to Billy's plan. Standing on a garbage can, Mantle boosted him up as Martin stepped onto his shoulders. Billy climbed through the first floor window and momentarily disappeared. When he returned to the window, he poked his head out and explained that he could not unlock the backdoor. "Nighty night, Mickey," Billy said with a sly grin. "You're on your own."[33]

Fuming, Mickey started stacking garbage cans, but each time he lost his balance, toppling the cans as he fell onto the pavement. Finally, after three or four tries, he pulled himself through the window, covered in garbage. His suit, soiled with rotten lettuce and tomatoes, was ruined. It was a typical Billy and Mickey story, straight out of an Alphonse and Gaston routine. Martin, the city slicker, shrewdly avoids trouble, while Mantle, the overwhelmed rube, stumbles after him.

Later that season, after the Yankees clinched the pennant, Billy, Mickey, Whitey Ford, and a few other players celebrated at the Latin Quarter, a Times Square nightclub known for its brass bands, beautiful chorus girls, and shady clientele. After enjoying drinks and a show, the players and their wives ran up a staggering bill. Feeling generous, Martin tossed a roll of cash onto a table. His teammates refused to let him pay the check, and one of them suggested that they let team owner Dan Topping cover it. "He's got a million bucks," the player said, as he signed the check under Topping's signature. Topping wasn't amused when he received the bill. Convinced that Martin was behind the prank, he ordered Weiss to punish each of the players who were with Billy at the night club. with a $500 fine. From that moment forward, the Yankees' front office scrutinized every move Martin made.[34]

Mantle and Martin misbehaved everywhere they went. And in the boredom of a Commerce winter, they sought a break from their sorrows: Mickey, still mourning the death of his father, feared his damaged knee might never fully recover, while Martin lamented the end of his marriage and the loss of the upcoming baseball season to military service. Cruising around the icy dirt roads of Commerce, they listened to country music and drank Jack Daniel's. They lived recklessly, drag racing like two teenagers in a James Dean movie. One time, they were racing so fast that Martin lost control of his Cadillac and crashed it at the bottom of a hill.[35]

That winter, Mickey rarely stayed home. Merlyn hardly knew when he was coming or going, and she became increasingly concerned about his drinking. Years later he admitted, "The drinking escalated after the '53 season, when Billy came to live with me and my wife." For them, drinking became a competition to see which could chug harder and longer than the other. "Billy and I were bad for each other," he said. "We were always on the go—rushing out the door, telling Merlyn we were going fishing but, instead, heading straight to a bar."[36]

Feeling suffocated by the responsibilities of marriage and fatherhood, Mantle often left Merlyn at home alone with the baby while he drank away the day with friends at a local watering hole. Unlike Mutt, who was a constant presence in his son's life, Mickey was almost indifferent to fatherhood. "I wouldn't even think about going home," he said later. When spring training started, he cut back on the booze while he worked off his winter weight. During the season, Mickey, Billy, Whitey, and the guys spent their evenings bar hopping around town.[37]

When Mickey reported for spring training, he was still recovering from a second surgery performed three weeks earlier. On February 3, 1954, Dr. Yancey had removed a cyst behind his swollen right knee. By the time the Yankees started drills on March 2, Mickey could hardly straighten his leg. Exasperated, Stengel scolded him. "If he did what he was told after the first operation he would be able to play now," he told a reporter. "This kid—you can't ever teach him nothing in the spring because he's always hurt."[38]

Mickey's season began poorly. By the end of April, he was only hitting .175. His frustration at the plate turned into fits of rage. When he returned to the dugout, he unleashed his anger on bat racks. His tantrums infuriated Stengel. One time the skipper lost his temper and grabbed Mickey by the back of the neck, squeezing hard as he yelled, "Don't let me see you do that again, you little bastard!"[39]

Mantle's troubles consumed him. Brooding after a miserable day at the ballpark, he ignored reporters who crowded around his locker. In dark moods, he didn't hesitate to tell writers to scram. "Get the hell away from me," he barked. "What the fuck are you bothering me for?" He had no use for the men who followed him every day, the writers who had built him up only to tear him down. Sometimes Mickey answered questions with silence. A cold glare was enough to end an interview before it even started.[40]

In May Mantle broke out of his slump. He finished the 1954 season hitting .300 with 27 home runs, 102 RBIs, and a league-best 129 runs. But in New York it didn't seem to matter, since the Yankees had failed to win the pennant for the first time in six seasons. Although the team won 103 games, its best regular season total under Stengel, the Cleveland Indians won 111—the most ever by an American League club at that time. Perhaps even more troubling for Yankees fans, it appeared that the best hitter in the city—and the best center fielder in all of baseball—wore a Giants uniform. If New Yorkers wanted to see the man who was arguably the premier player in the league, they had to visit the Polo Grounds to watch Willie Mays.[41]

In New York, everyone had an opinion. Like most writers, *New York Times* columnist Arthur Daley rated Mickey as the third-best center fielder, behind Mays and Brooklyn's Duke Snider. On the eve of the 1955 season, Daley wrote, "Thus far Mantle has displayed only the physical requisites of greatness. He has shown none of DiMaggio's fierce inner pride." Shirley Povich agreed. "Mickey Mantle, the lad who appeared destined to make it, has been a disappointment, which is the greater because he has the native talent to be a tremendous ball player. He hits the ball farther, runs faster, bunts better than anyone in baseball, but apparently lacks the high resolution to make the most of his skills."[42]

The press wrote off Mickey as a lost cause, a player who had entered the big leagues with too much fanfare, failed to perform in the clutch, and proved incapable of getting through the season without debilitating injuries. Writers complained that he was a dull country bumpkin, moody and colorless. He lacked Babe Ruth's charisma, Lou Gehrig's fierce resolve, and DiMaggio's impeccable style. He had tried to live up to the hype, to be the star that New York desired, but the "poor kid from the slag hills of Oklahoma" seemed out of place in the Big Apple. "The bright lights," a *New York Daily News* writer concluded, "are not for Mantle."[43]

NOTHING MICKEY DID SATISFIED Yankees fans. He "should be the popular hero of the standard baseball success story," Milton Gross wrote. "He is the walking realization of the childhood dreams of untold numbers of our country's youth. He has never had a truly bad season with the Yankees. He is one of the most feared hitters in the American League." And yet, Gross noted, he was "also the most booed."[44]

Late in the 1955 season, on a balmy August day, Mantle entered the batter's box, preparing to face Red Sox pitcher Willard Nixon. Sitting in a cramped booth next to the Yankee Stadium press box, public address announcer Bob Sheppard introduced Mantle in his deep, resonant voice. "Batting third and playing centerfield, No. 7, Mickey Mantle." A chorus of boos "rolled across the huge ball park," as if the Yankees were playing at Fenway. Mantle had done nothing that day to draw the crowd's ire. It was only the bottom of the first inning. In fact, he was having a great season, the best of his career. The next inning, after popping out to the shortstop, Mantle jogged to center field, while the boo birds sang. It had become a regular scene at the stadium, one that confused Mantle as much as his teammates.[45]

As he stepped into the batter's box or trotted onto the field, Yankees fans—his hometown crowd—booed, jeered, and cursed his name, a cruel reminder that while he might play for the Yankees, New Yorkers had not yet embraced him as one of their own. Interviewing "bleacher bums," those blue-collar fans who regularly watched games from the cheap seats, Gross heard them grumble that Mickey was lazy, thoughtless, and overrated. The common man resented that he had not earned his place in the game, complaining that his work ethic didn't match his talent. Worse, he didn't seem to care about the people who paid to see him play. "He never waves out here or smiles or anything," one man complained. Why, the fan wondered, couldn't Mantle "show his appreciation?" Ignoring Mickey's history of injuries, the man groused, "He got all the breaks and what did he do with them? Nothing."[46]

Some New Yorkers wondered whether Mantle lacked the intelligence required to be a great ballplayer. In their view, Mickey was no brighter than Lil' Abner. "It's too bad that Mantle is a bit of a rockhead," a writer lamented in the Yankee Stadium press box. Ever since Mantle joined the club, New York writers mocked his country dialect. Fans laughed at him standing in center field with his hands on his hips, blowing bubbles with his gum, like a bored schoolboy mindlessly staring out a classroom window. When asked about his intelligence, Mickey just shrugged. "Well, I never did claim to be smart and never was much, I guess. I'm sorry some of 'em call me a dummy. But to tell you the truth, it doesn't bother me anymore and I'm not going to holler."[47]

He remained underappreciated until the 1955 World Series, when Yankees fans were forced to confront the reality of competing for a championship without him at full strength. When his team needed him the most, when everything was on the line, a hamstring injury effectively crippled him. Since late September, when he pulled a leg muscle running out a bunt against the Red Sox, Mantle had limped around the clubhouse, hoping that he would be ready for the series. But when Stengel asked if he could play through the pain, Mantle admitted that he would be a liability in the lineup. Stengel had grown impatient with his star's frequent injuries. It was always something: a hamstring, an ankle, a knee. It seemed that Mickey could never live up to his manager's standards.[48]

The problem with Mickey, Stengel concluded, was that he had never fulfilled his promise. In some ways, his disappointment in Mantle derived from his frustrations with his own career, managing in the shadow of Yankee legend Joe McCarthy. When Mickey arrived in 1951, the Ole Professor determined that "the boy" would become the greatest player in history, and consequently he would be remembered as the greatest manager of all time. In order for Stengel to realize his ambitions, he needed Mantle to be as consistently great as DiMaggio had been. Every pulled hamstring, every game missed threatened Stengel's legacy.

After missing the first two games of the series against the Dodgers, Mantle started in center field for Game Three. In the second inning, he hit a solo home run off Johnny Podres. However, when Junior Gilliam hit a routine fly ball into right-center field, Mantle gingerly chased the ball, barely snagging it. Everyone in Ebbets Field knew that he was in no condition to play center, so Stengel moved him to right for the rest of the day and for Game Four.[49]

It was impossible to boo Mickey Mantle during the World Series. He gave everything he had to Stengel, his teammates, and the fans. During Game Four, he faced pitcher Clem Labine from the left side of the plate, shifting all of his weight onto his sore plant leg as he unleashed his swing. He appeared helpless, robbed of any real power. He struck out twice, tapped a weak grounder to the mound, and flipped a single into right field. Stengel had no choice but to bench him for the last two games of the series.

For Mickey, the season ended with great disappointment. As a pinch hitter in Game Seven, he hit an impotent popup. That was his final contribution. After losing five championships to the Yankees, the Brooklyn Dodgers finally beat them to win the World Series. For the first time in Mantle's five-year career and on his fourth series appearance, the Yankees failed in Game Seven. Mickey Mantle, a writer from *Baseball Digest* concluded, "was practically useless in the Series."[50]

Mantle had reached the nadir of his career, blaming himself for the Yankees' failures. But something happened to him during the Fall Classic that would change the way people viewed him the following season. Suffering on the field, sacrificing his body as he hobbled across the grass and flailed at the plate, he finally earned the respect of writers and fans. By the end of the championship, Gross suggested, Mantle "was loved by the customers more than at any other time." It appeared that Stengel had pressured him into playing when he was physically incapable. The fans could see that Mantle was human, flawed even, "not a young god who would pull lightning from the sky."[51]

After Game Seven, Mantle sat alone on a stool in front of his locker, hunched over with his hands covering his face. Not even a kiss from Grace Kelly could have cheered him up. When Stengel noticed Mantle sitting in the corner, staring at the floor, the skipper walked over and put his arm around Mickey's shoulder. "Son," Stengel advised, "I want you to be a tough loser. That shows that you want to win, but don't go blamin' yourself for losin' the Series." He reminded Mickey that no one player lost the championship. One day, he predicted, Mickey would "bust out and be the big man of this here team." "I wouldn't be surprised," the manager said, "if it happens next year."[52]

DESPITE THE DISAPPOINTING ending to the 1955 season, Mantle remained the best hitter in the American League. That year he hit .306 and led the league in five batting categories: home runs (37), triples (11), walks (113), on-base percentage (.431), and slugging percentage (.611). And yet he finished fifth in MVP voting. He could not understand why teammate Yogi Berra won the MVP again—for the third time in five years—when he had better statistics in most hitting categories.

In early 1956, before spring training began, he talked to Bill De-Witt, the Yankees' assistant general manager. Mickey said that he was happy for Berra's success, but he wondered, "What's a guy have to do to be considered Most Valuable?" "Maybe," DeWitt suggested, "a ballplayer has to do more than have a good season on the field. Maybe he has to win a little personal popularity."[53]

Few players had ever been more popular than Berra. "Everybody," the *New York Journal-American*'s Frank Graham wrote, "loves Yogi." Berra was "the best, the most consistent, [and] the hardest working player on the club." While Mantle remained sidelined during crucial stretches, Berra was durable and reliable, catching doubleheaders without complaint. If Yankees fans booed Mantle for underperforming, they admired Berra for overachieving. Yogi made up for his lack of an athletic physique with alertness, skill, and industriousness. Built like a gnome with a "homely face," Yogi, according to the press, did not look like a Yankee. Writers turned the stout catcher, known as much for his verbal gaffes as for his exceptional play, into a cartoonish figure, a halfwit who read comic books in the clubhouse because the pictures made the stories easier to follow.[54]

Reporters loved to tell stories that affirmed Berra's image as the comical catcher. When he first joined the Yankees in 1947, manager Bucky Harris reminded him not to chase pitches off the plate. "You've got to think when you're up at the plate," Harris instructed. "Think!" Predictably, Berra struck out and returned to the bench, muttering, "Think! Think! How the hell are you supposed to think and hit at the same time?"[55]

It was a classic Yogi tale. Yet it never happened. The story—like most Yogisms—was the creation of a sportswriter who most likely fashioned it out of something he heard near the batting cage or in the press box. The story became funnier when the punch line came from

Yogi. But Berra was not the endearing character the writers made him out to be. David Halberstam recalled that his colleagues who covered the Yankees found the real Berra to be "a crude and dull man, as apt as not to yell something foul from the Yankee bus at teenage girls; but in print he was the cuddly Yogi, full of quips."[56]

Sportswriters were in the business not only of reporting and opining but of selling characters and heroes, and Berra's public persona made it easier to sell him as the star of the Yankees. Bill DeWitt understood the importance of marketing the team's players to the public. The MVP, he told Mantle, could not "brush off every newspaperman who approaches him, or just clam up." If Mickey was ever to become a fan favorite, he would have to embrace the spotlight. "Mickey," DeWitt advised, "I think you're going to be the greatest star there ever was . . . but you've got to realize that a star has some obligations, too. If you make an effort and keep out of jams, there'll be no stopping you. But you've got to do your part. You've got to come out of that shell."[57]

Mantle took DeWitt's advice. He was determined to rehabilitate his image. During spring training in 1956, he greeted reporters with a modest grin and a welcoming handshake. The beat writers, accustomed to his curt replies, were stunned to find that an affable storyteller had replaced the introvert. After he pulled a writer aside and showed him his approach at the plate, the reporter gushed to his fellow scribes about the new Mickey Mantle. "Imagine," he exclaimed, "*Mantle* trying to explain something to me."[58]

THE SIGHTS AND SOUNDS of spring baseball created a great deal of excitement in St. Petersburg. In the mornings, shortly after sunrise, when the grass was still covered with dew, the Yankees lumbered onto Miller Huggins Field. Rows of players stretched rusty arms and tightly wound leg muscles, complaining about their winter aches. But the warm sunshine on their faces made them feel young again. They came alive, tossing the ball, swinging the bat, and playing pepper, bantering and laughing between drills. The hard, popping sound of the ball pounding into the catcher's mitt, the crack of the bat colliding with the baseball, the clatter of cleats crossing the cement dugout just before the players took the field—all signaled a new season, a fresh start, and renewed hope for glory.

"Spring baseball," Roger Angell once wrote, "is all surmise." Throughout spring training, fans, writers, managers, and players offered optimistic predictions for the coming season. The consensus among writers was that they envisioned a World Series rematch between the Yankees and Dodgers. No one—especially not Mickey Mantle—could forget the drama of October, a seven-game series that ended with the Yankees' slugger nursing a hamstring injury while he glumly watched the Dodgers celebrate their first championship.[59]

The Dodgers brought back essentially the same team that had won the championship a year earlier. The only major difference, excluding the absence of starting pitcher Johnny Podres, who was drafted into the military, was that the players were a year older. The core group, an all-star cast—Jackie Robinson, Duke Snider, Pee Wee Reese, Gil Hodges, Roy Campanella, Carl Erskine, Carl Furillo, and Don Newcombe—formed the backbone of a squad that had won four pennants and one World Series in the past seven years. Writers, however, wondered if this team was finally past its prime. Robinson and Reese were both thirty-seven. In fact, not a single player in the National League was active when Reese made his debut in 1940. Right fielder Furillo was thirty-four; first baseman Hodges was thirty-two. And Campanella, the thirty-four-year-old catcher, looked worn out from years of squatting behind home plate, his left hand battered and bruised from catching too many fastballs. His surgically repaired hands hurt so much that he could hardly grip a bat.[60]

Jackie Robinson arrived in Vero Beach feeling the effects of time too. The frost sprinkling his hair made him appear older than his actual age. He was heavier and slower than before, troubled by aching ankles and sore feet. The previous season, he hit .255, forty points under his prior low, with only thirty-six RBIs; in fact, for the first time in seven seasons, he had failed to hit above .300. Fastballs whizzed across the plate before he could get the barrel around. The bat looked heavy in his hands, as if he were swinging a sixteen-pound sledgehammer. His diminished performance sparked rumors in the off-season that the Dodgers might trade him. Instead, the front office acquired his future replacement: Chicago Cubs All-Star third baseman Ransom "Randy" Jackson. The trade rumors, his reduced playing time, and the arrival of a younger, talented player wounded Robinson's pride, but he remained deeply competitive. He was determined to prove that he wasn't done yet.[61]

If the Dodgers were favored to win the National League pennant, the Yankees, built on pitching and power hitting, seemed poised to meet them again in October—and win this time. "How are you going to beat them?" *Sports Illustrated* asked in its season preview: "Berra is the best catcher in the league. Mantle is so good they say he has a disappointing season if he doesn't hit .400." Right fielder Hank Bauer and first baseman Moose Skowron added power to the lineup too. Billy Martin, one of the best defense infielders in baseball, sparked the team with his aggressiveness. And the Yankees' pitching staff, led by Whitey Ford, "a left-hander with all the pitches," was a polished group that had led the American League in earned run average the previous season. So, *Sports Illustrated* asked again, "How are you going to beat them?"[62]

The Yankees' chances of winning the World Series hinged on Mantle. He devoted spring training to improving his hitting, adjusting his stance, and standing farther away from the plate and deeper in the batter's box. That change helped him better recognize the pitches coming toward him as the ball flew out of the pitcher's hand. In the past, pitchers jammed him with inside fastballs. In the spring of 1956, though, he developed a better sense of the strike zone, waiting patiently for balls that entered his "happy zone"—pitches about chest high that he could pull. Training his eyes to look for the right pitch to hit was essential. So too was realizing that he didn't need to swing from his shoestrings to drive the ball. With his natural strength, a smoother, more efficient swing would produce enough power to propel the ball over any fence. He may have been dubbed "the Natural," but now he finally realized that "good hitters are not born: they are made."[63]

Mantle appeared rejuvenated at the plate, ripping liners into the outfield alleys and driving majestic home runs into the clear blue sky. "The Switcher" crushed ball after ball. From the press box, his bat looked "nine feet long and a yard wide." There wasn't a ball he couldn't hit. "The box score doesn't give a true picture of Mickey Mantle's power," Joe Trimble wrote in the *New York Daily News*. "Mileage charts are needed."[64]

Shirley Povich, covering the Yankees' spring training games, had not seen a player captivate crowds like Mickey since Babe Ruth. "The Mickey Mantle home run has been the season's best show in Florida." Studying him, Povich sensed that he was on the verge of greatness. Remarkably, Mickey struck out only once all spring, and fifteen of his twenty-four hits went for extra bases. Everywhere Povich went, Mickey Mantle was all anybody wanted to talk about. "This, you hear on all sides and are willing to believe, is Mickey Mantle's year. This is the one when he'll burst into full magnificence."[65]

But any veteran observer of spring training had heard that kind of prediction before.

CHAPTER 4

The Great American Game

"Why . . . can't the Oklahoma Kid land the Triple Crown?
This should be his year of decision."

—DAN DANIEL,
The Sporting News, April 25, 1956

At precisely 1:05 p.m. on April 17, 1956, the leader of the free
world and a small retinue of followers slipped silently out of the
White House into waiting limousines at ONION. The motorcade
sped north-northeast past BLACK and LIME, continued until CAR-
ROT, and then headed compass north to APPLE, a massive steel and
concrete structure built hurriedly in 1911. Every step had been carefully scouted and studied, every movement planned and coordinated.
Each intersection along the way had a code name and an ETA. The
entire trip took ten minutes. The man sitting in the bulletproof limo
had time to briefly consider the most pressing problems of the day.
President Dwight David Eisenhower had an election looming and an
important decision to make about whether to keep or dump his running mate. He had upcoming meetings with foreign heads of state,
crucial economic legislation pending, and a brewing crisis in the Middle East.[1]

But all that could wait. Now it was time for the Great American Game of baseball.

On opening day Americans celebrated their country as much as they did the sport. After all, baseball was the national pastime. In 1907 the much-publicized Mills Commission—appointed by Albert Spalding to research the origins of the sport—determined that Major General Abner Doubleday had "invented" baseball in 1839, a conclusion that significantly strengthened the linkages between the sport and the national ethos. Cooperstown, home of author James Fenimore Cooper, was associated with the great American myth of the West, Natty Bumppo's Leatherstocking tales, and the irresistible spread of Anglo civilization toward the Pacific Ocean. And Doubleday, the man who had fired the first shot in defense of Fort Sumter and bravely commanded a corps in the opening engagements at Gettysburg, connected baseball to the struggle for the Union and the abolition of slavery. It hardly mattered that the Mills Commission got the story all wrong, that its evidence amounted to a single, uninvestigated letter written by a man with an addled memory. Then as now, Americans craved a mythical and glorious American past, and authenticity was not terribly important. The trinity of Cooperstown, Doubleday, and baseball became central to our national history.

Even before the Mills Commission's report, presidents had taken note of baseball's distinctive qualities. In the summer of 1862, sometime before the Second Battle of Bull Run, Abraham Lincoln abandoned the White House for an afternoon and took his youngest son, Tad, to a game. According to a story passed down over the years, Lincoln sat along the first-base line, Tad positioned between his father's long legs, and for a few hours forgot about the war and enjoyed the spectacle and the warm sun. Already the mythology of "the national game" was taking shape—its rural imagery, suspension of time, and innocent appeal. That summer men and boys were playing some variety of baseball in Union and Confederate camps, on village greens in New York and Boston, and in open fields in New Orleans and

Charleston. The North and South may have been at war, but even in prisoner camps, Yanks and Rebs could still meet on friendly terms on a baseball diamond.[2]

A formal presidential imprimatur arrived in 1911, on a cold opening day. President William Howard Taft, at one time a fairly good second baseman and power hitter, accepted Clark Griffith's invitation to throw out the first ball at the Washington Senators' first game of the season. A local record of more than 12,000 spectators attended the contest, thrilled to watch Taft lob a ball from his box seat to Walter Johnson, who promptly fired a one-hitter. And Taft liked the action. He stomped his feet to keep warm, tossed peanuts in the air after Herman A. "Germany" Schaefer belted a home run for the Senators, and exhibited the homespun characteristics of the common fan. Commenting on the sport, he later said, "The game of baseball is a clean, straight game, and it summons to its presence everybody who enjoys clean, straight athletics."[3]

So began the springtime ritual celebrating one nation under baseball. Griffith considered the event a promotional stunt, but over the years it helped glue game and nation together. Woodrow Wilson, a genuine baseball enthusiast, frequently attended contests and encouraged the owners to play regular schedules during the Great War. Though he preferred golf and poker, Warren Harding went to games to demonstrate his democratic inclinations. And dour Calvin Coolidge, while seldom ever showing emotions at the ballpark, attended three Senators games, including a scorching-hot June doubleheader during the 1924 season. He expounded on the role of baseball in American life. "There is a place, both past and future, in America for true, clean sport. We do not rank it above business, the occupations of our lives, and we do not look with approval upon those who, not being concerned in its performance, spend all their thought, energy and time upon its observance. We recognize, however, that there is something more in life than the grinding routine of daily toil, that we can develop better manhood and womanhood, a more attractive youth and wiser maturity by rounding out our existence with a wholesome interest in sport."[4]

Franklin D. Roosevelt democratized the opening-day ceremony. Prior to his assumption of the presidency, the ritual of throwing out the first ball was a dignified exchange between the chief executive and the Senators' starting pitcher. The process was entirely too formal for FDR, lacking the hurly-burly quality he loved. So rather than lobbing the ball to the pitcher, he tossed it willy-nilly to a mob of players who scrambled wildly for the souvenir. The president rewarded the winner with a smile, handshake, and autograph.[5]

Baseball, Roosevelt thought, served a political purpose. It was all about having fun. With the gloom of the Depression hovering above Griffith Stadium, he wanted the fans to forget their worries. FDR even laughed at himself. On opening day in 1937, during the president's squabble with the Supreme Court, a plane flew over the stadium pulling a banner reading, "Play the game, don't pack the court." Chomping peanuts, Roosevelt beamed as brightly as anyone in the ballpark.[6]

And in the dark days after Pearl Harbor, when Japan swept American defenders off Guam and Wake Island and US soldiers had retreated to the Bataan Peninsula, with few rations and even fewer hopes of rescue, Roosevelt decided that, no matter what happened, professional baseball would not be a casualty of war. In response to Commissioner Kenesaw Mountain Landis's inquiry about the status of professional baseball, FDR gave his unequivocal support. "I honestly feel that it would be best for the country to keep baseball going," he wrote. "If 300 teams use 5,000 or 6,000 players, these players are a definite recreational asset to at least 20,000,000 of their fellow citizens—and that in my judgment is thoroughly worthwhile." And though the quality of play dipped and the uniforms became a bit threadbare, the game endured through the war.[7]

By the time Ike arrived at Griffith Stadium in 1956, opening day was as much a part of the political calendar as the State of the Union address. He claimed to be a diehard Senators fan—he promised enigmatically to "be for the Senators from the beginning, and I will be there on the last day of the game"—but in 1953 he missed the first game of the season, choosing instead to tee off at Bobby Jones's Augusta National Golf Club. The storm of criticism may have been responsible for what was officially called a rainout in Washington, and Ike hurried back to attend the rescheduled game. It was a lesson in the priorities of his constituents. The democratic diamond trumped the elitist fairways.[8]

In 1956 he performed his patriotic duty. After warming up his pitching arm, Ike removed his tan gabardine topcoat and heaved a short, high pitch toward a covey of players assembled in front of him. "Oddly, all these well paid guys became a group of butter-finger bushers," noted one reporter. When the scramble ended, a Yankee infielder emerged with the ball. Holding it high, he rushed toward Eisenhower, seeking his autograph.[9]

Ike asked his name, and while Casey Stengel listed the infielder's credentials, the Yankee answered, "Gil McDougald." The president smiled, looked briefly at Stengel, and proceeded to write "Joe McDougald" on the ball.

McDougald had a forgiving nature. "With all that yelling and confusion around there at the time," he said, "I can't say as I blame him for blowing the name. It's a wonder he got any part of it right."

On that bathetic note, the 1956 season began. The mood, however, would soon shift radically.

THE FIELD PRESIDENT EISENHOWER looked out upon was oddly disconcerting. To the seasoned baseball fan's eye, it appeared ill designed. Center field was east-southeast of home plate, an orientation that forced center fielders to look directly into the afternoon sun. Furthermore, the fences were irregular, a common feature of early-twentieth-century ballparks. Griffith was a relic of the dead ball era, an age of slashing hitters who aimed at the gaps, not home run sluggers who swung for the fences. Before the 1956 season, however, the Senators' management had given the old stadium a minor facelift. To accommodate a new section of seats, they shortened the distance to the left-field fence from 386 to 350 feet down the foul line and from 400 to 380 feet in left center. The alterations pleased right-handed batters. But the fences in the rest of the ballpark remained distant. It was 408 feet to center and 373 feet to right center, and the modest 320-foot right-field fence was protected by a 30-foot wall. Altogether, the stadium aroused no joy in the hearts of left-handed hitters.[10]

Unfortunately for Mantle, Cuban right-hander Camilo Pascual started the game for the Senators. Young and often wild, the six-foot, four-inch, 220-pound pitcher was coming off an unimpressive 2–12 season. Although only in his third season in the majors, he possessed two devastating, though not always dependable, pitches: a fastball and a sharp curve that broke straight down. When he was on his game, he had All-Star stuff; when he wasn't, he was dangerous to any batter who dug in at the plate.[11]

The Yankees opened the 1956 season auspiciously. Pascual got veteran Hank Bauer to foul out to the catcher and struck out rookie Jerry Lumpe. Then he faced Mantle. Batting left-handed, Mickey took two balls and then settled in, looking for a fastball over the plate. He got his pitch, and the crack of the bat reminded *Washington Post* columnist Bob Addie of the sound of artillery. The ball seemed to gain height as it charged the thirty-one-foot fence just left of center field. It sailed over the wall, out of the stadium, across Fifth Street and bounced off the roof of the home of one Carl T. Coleman. Following in the footsteps of Red Patterson, reporters estimated the ball had traveled about five hundred feet in the air, a distance unimaginable for any other player in the game. Mickey's power, Addie observed, made the cavernous Griffith Stadium seem like "a miniature golf course"; he added that "Mr. Wonderful" made the faraway fences "shrink like a $10 suit caught in the rain."[12]

Had Mantle left the game at that point, he still would have made all the headlines. But he wasn't through. In the sixth inning, with the Yankees comfortably up 5–2, Mantle came to the plate with two runners aboard. Once again Pascual fired a fastball, and again the impact of bat to ball resounded like an artillery crack. Mickey's line drive left the stadium just to the right of left-center field and "was on its way out of town when it struck the branch of a tree" and landed some 438 feet from home plate. From the press box reporters watched the entire flight of the ball, marveling at Mantle's power.[13]

None of the veteran scribes could recall any other player, not even Babe Ruth, hitting two homers in one game over the distant center-field fence at Griffith. After the game sportswriters quizzed Yankees coach Bill Dickey about Mantle's feat. Considering that Mickey had hit almost 1,000 feet of home runs, Dickey judged that "they just don't come any better." In all his years of coming to Griffith Stadium, he had only seen one player hit the tree in center field: Ruth. "I remember that very clearly," he said. "It made that much of an impression on me." Casey Stengel agreed with Dickey's assessment. He rated Mickey's drives above those of Ruth, Jimmie Foxx, Lou Gehrig, Ted Williams, Hank Greenberg, and Joe Jackson. And he even suggested, after this first game of the year, that if Mickey could cut down on his strikeouts, he could top Ruth's single-season record of sixty homers.[14]

Journalists were still buzzing about Mantle's opening-day heroics two days later, comparing his power to Babe Ruth's and his swing to Joe DiMaggio's. It took the marriage between Grace Kelly and Prince Rainier of Monaco to push Mickey off the front page of the New York dailies. And that was fine with him. Uncomfortable with the praise and reluctant to talk about his performance, he dismissed the "crazy comparisons." Reporters tried to get him to explain how he hit the ball so hard and how he rated himself against the best to play the game, and he didn't have the words or inclination to answer them. He just wished Stengel would stop talking so much about him. "I'm no Ruth, Gehrig, Foxx, Williams or whoever they say. I'll just be satisfied with having a good year and that's about it." And the best he could say about his power was, "Those two hits off of Pascual were going to leave the park. They just felt good and I figured they would take a pretty good ride." But it wasn't for him to say how many more he would hit, and it was "right silly" for him to talk about Ruth's record. It was time, he thought, to stop all the chatter about Mickey Mantle.[15]

IN TRUTH, HOWEVER, BASEBALL desperately needed Mantle to be great. The sport was mired in a slump, and nothing the lords of the game did ended the dry spell. And like players struggling at the plate, the owners began to fear that their slump, the sport's slump, might be permanent.

The numbers told part of the story. In the half decade after World War II, baseball dominated the American sports landscape just as the United States dominated the world. These were the boom years. Consider the average attendance at major-league games. During the prosperous 1920s, the figure was 7,531; during the hard 1930s, it slipped to 6,578; and during the first half of the 1940s, when the nation was at war, it rose to 7,438. But with peace and postwar prosperity, attendance soared. Between 1946 and 1949 it more than doubled, climbing to 16,027.

Between 1947 and 1949 total yearly attendance reached about 20 million. Then it tumbled—to 16 million in 1951 and then 14.3 million in 1953. The 30 percent decline in four years was ominous and hard to explain. The owners entertained various theories unsupported by any real evidence. How could they end the freefall? They had no idea.[16]

Only in retrospect would the trend make sense. In 1956 the owners focused on the attendance decline, but their failure to understand the sport's sudden prosperity made it impossible to grasp the reversal. A century of data from 1900 to 2000 demonstrates a fairly steady ascent in attendance marked by occasional swings. The 1946–1955 decade was one of the more volatile periods. The first half was like DiMaggio's fifty-six-game hitting streak—seemingly everything went right. The second was like the Chicago Cubs quest for a World Series ring. Some things simply defied the odds.[17]

The shift had underlying causes. From 1950 to 1955, America was undergoing dizzying demographic changes. The nation was on the move, nowhere more so than in the cities east of the Mississippi River that boasted major-league teams. The race was toward the suburbs. Between 1950 and 1960 all ten of the cities with major-league teams declined in population. Fleeing high real estate costs, taxes, and social problems of the inner cities, citizens relocated to the ring of towns around them, leaving behind their baseball stadiums rooted in deteriorating neighborhoods and serviced by collapsing infrastructure. Attendance at ballparks, including Ebbets Field and the Polo Grounds, mushroomed in the heyday of streetcars and plummeted in the rising age of the automobile.[18]

Postwar suburbanites, furthermore, enjoyed a wide range of entertainment options. "Why should a guy with a boat in the driveway, golf clubs in the car, bowling ball and tennis racket in the closet, a trunkful of camping equipment, two boys in Little League and a body full of energy left over from shorter working hours pay to sit and do nothing but watch a mediocre game?" wondered a fan writing to *Sports Illustrated* in 1958. And if residents of Levittown or some other new development wanted to sit and watch something, they could always turn on their television sets—by 1956 three-fourths of American families owned at least one—and follow the exploits of Lucy, thrill to a gunfight on a dusty western street, or, on almost any given night, cheer as two boxers slugged it out. They could also watch their baseball team in the comfort of their own homes, where beers were less expensive and restrooms infinitely cleaner.[19]

Increasingly in the late 1940s and 1950s Americans opted for private over public entertainment. Movie moguls worried as much as the owners of baseball franchises. As box office receipts fell, Hollywood turned to such innovations and gimmicks as Technicolor, Cinerama, 3-D, and even Smell-O-Vision to pry viewers away from their television sets and lure them back to theaters. But the only theaters that boomed during the period were drive-ins, where families and couples cocooned in their automobiles and watched films in a semiprivate environment. Other public forms of entertainment suffered as well. In New York, for example, fewer and fewer people attended Broadway plays, watched fights at St. Nick's Arena or Madison Square Garden, made a bet at the Aqueduct or Jamaica racetracks, or visited Coney Island's Steeplechase Park.[20]

If the baseball magnates knew that other entertainment entrepreneurs shared their misery, they didn't mention it. They appeared blind to their own suffering and deaf to the complaints of their customers. A day at the old ballpark—and, like Griffith Stadium, most were ancient and decrepit—was like time spent in a Soviet gulag. According to *Sports Illustrated*'s Jim Murray, it was not just that money flew out of spectators' pockets, though it did. The fan had to pay off one shark who "steered him to a fender-denting hole outside the left-field wall" and another predator to guard his car while he was in the stadium. Once he maneuvered through the turnstile, he dealt out additional dollars to an usher who marched him to his seat and ceremoniously dusted it off to encourage an even more beneficent tip. And if the seat was not behind a pole or some other obstruction, it was distant from restrooms, where long lines quickly formed to get into a facility just large enough "to take care of a Cub Scout den." And of course there was the game, more often than not played listlessly by "swell-headed performers who won't even sign autograph books."[21]

The game had become almost Hobbesian—nasty and brutish but not short enough. As one insider told Murray, "Baseball men haven't done a damn thing to their parks for decades except paint them. Show me another industry that has stood still like that." At a time of increasing competition for entertainment dollars, baseball was an aging pitcher who had lost his fastball. "Perhaps," Murray added, "baseball men have swallowed too much of that sentimental pap that baseball is such a super-integral part of the American scene that it will be put on [life support] even if no one shows up except the players—subsidized like farmers, say." But he doubted it. More likely, he warned baseball executives, "your customers won't be fans anymore. They'll be ex-fans."[22]

Rather than looking inward for the cause of the attendance decline, team owners gazed outward. Some thought with T. S. Eliot that April was the cruelest month. An editor for *The Sporting News* lamented that every year cold, drizzling rain, chilly, blustering winds, and even snow marred baseball's opening-day celebrations. The weather flattened ticket sales, got the season off to a horrendous start, and was lousy public relations. Since baseball was "not a cold weather game," the editor mused that the best policy would be to begin the season later in the month. In the meantime, the owners could stop the tradition of announcing game attendance over the loudspeaker. It was a blatant admission of failure. "When the Giants play before 2,500 in the mammoth Polo Grounds, when the Indians have to settle for 18,000 for their first Sunday double-header, do outsiders get an attractive picture of the old game's drawing power?"[23]

But for all of baseball's troubles, from nasty weather to the appalling absence of easy parking options, television dominated virtually every discussion. One school of thought argued that TV was a Trojan horse that would soon enough kill attendance at ballparks. As legendary boxing manager Jack "Doc" Kearns noted about the impact of the tube on the fight game, "You can't give it away and sell it at the same time." As early as 1951 the dean of sportswriters, Grantland Rice, fretted about the long-term threat that TV posed for baseball. The central problem was that the medium and the sport were in competition with each other. Television executives might broadcast baseball games, but their ultimate goal was not to produce baseball fans—it was to cultivate TV viewers. They sought to please their sponsors, not baseball men. For them, baseball was merely a means of selling Gillette razors and Ballantine beer.[24]

Yankees general manager George Weiss agreed with Rice. Staunchly traditionalist, committed to the bottom line of gate receipts, he had bellowed against radio broadcasts in the past. And television, he maintained, competed even more directly with live attendance, drawing fans away from Yankee Stadium where they not only paid to see the game but bought hotdogs and beer as well. In the late 1940s he fought a rearguard action against television, but it was a lost cause from the very start. Broadcasters won important battles over the number and placement of cameras at the game. In return, Weiss bumped up the cost of broadcasting rights. But he grumbled all the way to the bank.[25]

Yet, even as Weiss grudgingly accepted television cameras in Yankee Stadium, veteran New York sportswriter Dan Daniel predicted troubles ahead. Although television sponsors were willing to pay large sums for the rights to televise games, it was becoming increasingly clear that TV was eroding box office receipts and causing many minor-league and semiprofessional teams to close their doors. For Daniel, as for Kearns, the irreducible fact was, "You cannot give away your commodity. . . . [Y]ou cannot be in competition with yourself . . . and either hope or expect to stay in business."[26]

Certainly the owners of major-league franchises recognized the threat of television, but in a vicious cycle, as their live audiences shrank, they became even more dependent on the dollars from broadcasters. And the money was very good. In 1956 major-league TV and radio sponsors paid a record $26.2 million to broadcast games. For the thirteen teams that had television agreements—Milwaukee, Pittsburgh, and Kansas City were the only teams that did not—this amounted to an average of 10.5 percent of each club's income. The percentage was even higher for the New York franchises. The Yankees, Dodgers, and Giants received at least twice as much for television rights as did the other teams. Warren Giles, National League president, admitted that TV revenues offset gate losses. Furthermore, he asserted that watching a baseball game on the tube could never replace going to the ballpark. It was like watching a Sunday church service on one's couch, he said. It was a fine substitute, but "the exhilarating atmosphere is lacking. So are the rewarding emotions one experiences from actual participation."[27]

Giles's rosy optimism was lost on columnist Walter "Red" Smith, who mourned the marriage of baseball and television. The technology was consuming the sport, he thought. "Baseball isn't a game any longer. It is a streamlined, high-pressure medium for peddling beer and cigarettes. The carpetbaggers who operate the game for profit alone have sold out shamelessly, without qualm or apology." The game he learned to love as a boy and the heroes he worshiped as a youth and wrote about as a young reporter had lost their romantic patina. The fans were avoiding the ballpark because salesmen duped them into believing that the game on television was the only game.[28]

WHILE TEAM OWNERS grappled with the implications of television, they also wrestled with another issue. Some blamed declining attendance on the changing demographics of inner cities and the neighborhoods that surrounded major-league stadiums. The exodus of white middle-class fans to the suburbs and the increasing migration of working-class minorities into the inner cities troubled them. In 1958, Bill Furlong, a snooping reporter from the *Chicago Tribune*, eavesdropped on a group of American League owners through a hotel air vent, overhearing Washington Senators owner Clark Griffith explain why he wanted to relocate his team to Minneapolis. "The trend in Washington is getting to be all colored," he complained.[29]

In the South Bronx, the influx of blacks and Puerto Ricans transformed the neighborhoods around Yankee Stadium. In 1950, two-thirds of the residents were white, but by the end of the decade two-thirds were African American or Hispanic. "As more Negroes moved in, followed more recently by Puerto Ricans," the *New York Times* reported in 1955, "more Jews and Irish have moved out." The declining number of entry-level manufacturing jobs increased competition for work and intensified racial tensions between whites and minorities throughout the borough. The construction of subsidized housing projects, inhabited mostly by poor blacks, and the rising number of minorities moving into previously white neighborhoods created friction. "We may *have* to live together," a longtime white resident said, but "most of us don't like it."[30]

In the first half of the 1950s, as the South Bronx became more racially diverse, the New York Yankees remained lily-white. Some critics suggested that the club shaped the team's roster to appeal to affluent white fans in Westchester County. Robert Creamer, one of the original editors at *Sports Illustrated*, wrote years later that the Yankees' segregation "stemmed as much from economic racism, the fear that black players in the Yankee lineup would hurt the sales of tickets to their supposedly upscale audience, as it did from blatant bigotry." The *New York Post's* Leonard Koppett, a Bronx native who grew up a block away from Yankee Stadium, agreed. He believed that George Weiss did not want to offend "his white customers, the upper-middle-class gentry from the suburbs." Weiss believed that white fans would not "sit with black fans, and he did not think his white players wanted to play with blacks"; "worst of all," he was convinced that black players were inferior to white ones.[31]

Koppett was not alone in suspecting Weiss of racism. On November 30, 1952, Jackie Robinson appeared on a television show, *Youth Wants to Know*. When a teenager asked him if the Yankees were "prejudiced against Negro players," Robinson didn't hesitate. "Yes," he answered. "I think the Yankees management is prejudiced. There isn't a single Negro on the team now and very few in the entire Yankee farm system."[32]

The Yankees were not the only segregated franchise. In 1953, six years after Robinson broke the color line in the sport, only six of the sixteen major-league clubs fielded black players. The absence of a single black player on the Yankees inspired protests outside Yankee Stadium. That season the Bronx County Labor Youth League disseminated flyers that read, "How Can We Get Greater Democracy on the Yankees?"[33]

Years later Mantle recalled seeing protestors outside the stadium, carrying placards and chanting, "Don't go past the gate! Don't go past the gate! The Yanks dis-crim-i-nate!" At the time he said nothing publicly about the demonstrations or the Yankees' segregated roster. And reporters didn't ask him about race. On virtually every social and political issue he remained mute. Growing up in Oklahoma, Mantle had no black teammates. His world had been virtually all white. "There were never any black people in our area," his friend Nick Ferguson recalled. That wasn't merely happenstance. Mickey's home county was "closed" to blacks until the early 1950s, and during his childhood signs warned them to leave town. As a major leaguer, he didn't view himself as anything more than a ballplayer. Segregation was an accepted fact of American society that Mantle and his teammates never challenged.[34]

Facing protests, Weiss maintained that neither he nor the Yankees' ownership harbored racist policies. "The Yankees never have been averse to having a Negro player," he insisted. But rumors among the press corps suggested a different story. *New York Herald-Tribune* reporter Roger Kahn recalled that in the early 1950s a high-ranking club official admitted after a few drinks that a black player would never wear Yankee pinstripes. "We don't want that sort of crowd," he said. "It would offend boxholders from Westchester to have to sit with niggers."[35]

By the end of the 1953 season, it appeared that Vic Power, a talented young first baseman who led the AAA American Association with a .349 batting average, might break the Yankees' color line. Power, a black Puerto Rican, showed great ability at the plate and was a superb defensive player, but Yankees management worried about his allegedly flamboyant style of play. They said he lacked discipline and intelligence, ugly code words long deployed against black players as pretexts for keeping them off the team. Sportswriters reported that he didn't hustle and was obstinate. Even more damaging were rumors that he dated white women. That was enough for the Yankees to ship him to the Philadelphia Athletics. If the team was going to sign a black player, *New York Times* columnist Arthur Daley noted, he had to fit "the Yankee type," which Vic Power clearly didn't.[36]

But "the Yankee type" was a myth. If team management disapproved of Power's defiance and his unwillingness to stand down when opposing players challenged him to fight, club officials mostly turned a blind eye to Mantle's, Billy Martin's, and Whitey Ford's flaunting of club rules. Weiss really wanted a nonthreatening "Negro," polite and passive on civil rights. In Elston Howard, he found his man.

By all accounts, the Yankees promoted Howard in 1955 because he had not only the skills but the temperament management required. Reporters described him as "clean-cut," "religious," and "a nice quiet lad" with a "gentlemanly demeanor." There is no question Howard was chosen as the first black player to suit up for the Yankees because of his deferential attitude "on race questions." He was the antithesis of the outspoken Jackie Robinson. "I like that young man," Yankees head scout Paul Krichell said. "Even though he's black, he has manners. Both as a man and as a ballplayer this boy Howard looks every inch a Yankee."[37]

Yet the face of the Yankees—Mickey Mantle's—was white. And by 1956, when Howard remained the lone black player on the team, Mantle's value as a marketable commodity was tied to his whiteness. His emergence as the biggest star in baseball occurred at the same time that the first wave of great black and Latino players broke the color line. For some whites, it appeared that dark-skinned players were gradually taking over the game. By 1956, there were approximately forty black players out of four hundred players in the major leagues. And there was widespread fear among white players and fans that more blacks were coming soon. "They can run faster," an anonymous Dodger told a reporter. "They'll run us white guys right out of the game."[38]

As minorities continued to displace white players, some reporters—black and white—wondered if the owners had established a quota system. In 1954, a writer for *Our World*, a popular black magazine, asked, "Is the color line being drawn on Negroes in baseball? Has the 'saturation point' of hiring Negro players been reached?" Two years later, *Newsweek*'s John Lardner suggested that the owners had secretly agreed to limit the number of black starters. But it was not just the owners who refused to select more black players. In 1956, baseball fans voted for only one black starter on the All-Star teams—Cincinnati's Frank Robinson. And on the American League, squad manager Casey Stengel selected only one black substitute—Kansas City's Vic Power.[39]

That season Mickey Mantle effectively made the case that a white player was once again the best in the game, challenging the title held by former National League MVP and home run king Willie Mays, who was part of a group of exceptional black players that also included Hank Aaron, Ernie Banks, and Roy Campanella. In boxing, heavyweight champion Rocky Marciano had recently retired, and there were no other serious white contenders; many fans feared a similar situation in baseball. Yet Mantle's success on the field reminded white fans that their place in the game was secure. His former teammate, Tony Kubek, maintained that Mantle earned his acclaim. "But," he added, "I really think it was like in boxing, that maybe Mickey was a great white hope."[40]

"NOBODY GOES TO the Bronx," announced Jerome Weidman in an October 1955 article in *Holiday* magazine. The borough had slid downhill since Weidman's youth, a victim of changing demographics, rising crime rates, and Robert Moses's Manhattan-centric vision for New York City. The Cross Bronx Expressway, whose construction had begun in 1948 and dragged on for more than two decades, scarred the South Bronx physically and psychologically. Yet, for all of the borough's woes, New Yorkers from Manhattan and Queens, and even some from Staten Island and Brooklyn, continued to board subways destined for 161st Street and River Avenue. There they were joined by Yankees fans from Westchester and Fairfield counties, who drove into the Bronx to visit America's greatest sporting shrine.[41]

The original Yankee Stadium was much more than a venue for playing baseball. Opened on April 18, 1923, it signaled, in retrospect, the start of the Yankees dynasty and the birth of modern American sports. Before the stadium was built, professional baseball was played in places like Ebbets Field, Shibe Park, or the Polo Grounds, all of which suggested a calm, bucolic past. In contrast, Yankee Stadium connoted an urban reality, the cacophony of blaring horns, screeching tires, pounding jackhammers, and a thousand languages. At a time when the national census noted that more people lived in cities than in the countryside, Yankee Stadium underscored the new America of factories and immigrants, technology and commerce.[42]

It was both a product and an emblem of New York, as much a shrine to the city as the Brooklyn Bridge and the Empire State Building. "Yankee Stadium is the Babe Ruth of ballparks, the unforgettable, oversized, off-the-scale standard that changed everything," noted baseball historian Glenn Stout. The concrete-and-steel structure was nearly twice as big as any other park, built roughly along the lines of the Roman Coliseum to signal its importance as the center of the baseball universe. Like Babe Ruth, like New York City, Yankee Stadium was a draw in and of itself, a monument to the outrageously audacious dreams that made America great.[43]

Built in only 284 days, it was properly christened on the day it opened to the fans. More than 67,000 enthusiasts, the largest crowd ever to see a ball game, filed joyously through the turnstiles. In the celebrity box on opening day, wedged close to team owner Colonel

Jacob Ruppert, sat baseball commissioner Kenesaw Mountain Landis, New York governor Al Smith, and New York City mayor John Hylan. John Philip Sousa directed as his band played "The Star-Spangled Banner." Smith threw out the first ball. Then, almost on cue, Ruth stole the show. Before the game he told reporters, "I'd give a year of my life if I can hit a home run in the first game in this new park." In the fourth inning he responded to the three tiers of imploring fans by clubbing the ball toward the right-field stands. It was "a savage home run," commented a *New York Times* sportswriter, "that was the real baptism of Yankee Stadium." "It would have been a home run in the Sahara Desert," added Heywood Broun. As the ball arced toward the fence, spectators exulted. And when it landed, said a *New York Daily News* scribe, "The revelry became riot [as] people tore up programs, smashed canes, and launched all manner of foodstuffs" into the air. Years later, after the Bambino had retired, he said it was his favorite home run.[44]

The Yankees won their first World Series that year, and as other championships followed with metronomic regularity, Yankee Stadium became synonymous with Hall of Fame players and winning. Ruth, Gehrig, and DiMaggio, Murderers' Row, the Pride of the Yankees, and the Subway Series—the lore of the Yankees and Yankee Stadium were the central characters in the tale of baseball. It was in Yankee Stadium that Ruth crushed his record-breaking sixtieth home run in 1927, that Gehrig delivered his iconic "Luckiest Man on Earth" speech in 1939, and that DiMaggio kicked off his fifty-six-game hitting streak with a single off White Sox pitcher Eddie Smith in 1941.

Yankee Stadium's reach even went beyond the Great American Game. In autumn, when the leaves along the Hudson turned red and gold, Yankee Stadium hosted football games. It was the site of Notre Dame's 1928 12–6 victory over Army, the contest in which Knute Rockne gave his "Win One for the Gipper" halftime exhortation. And in 1946 the cadets from West Point, the Notre Dame subway alumni, and other fans filled the stadium to watch the Irish and Army battle to a 0–0 tie in the "Game of the Century," a contest that gave rise to the newspaper headline "Much Ado About Nothing-Nothing."

Boxing also played an important role in Yankee Stadium's sporting calendar. In 1927 Jack Dempsey knocked out Jack Sharkey there to win a title rematch with Gene Tunney. Joe Louis fought a dozen matches under the stadium's lights, including the most famous and important fight in the history of the sport. On June 22, 1938, he squared off with Germany's Max Schmeling, who had defeated him two years earlier, also in Yankee Stadium. With Europe heading again toward war, the fight assumed enormous cultural and political significance. Right or wrong, Schmeling symbolized Adolf Hitler's jack-booted, racist, war-mongering thugs. Ironically, Louis, a black man from the Jim Crow South, took on the mantle of freedom, the rule of law, respect for all peoples, and the love of democracy. "One didn't need to be an anthropologist to know there had never been anything like it, or a soothsayer to know there would never be anything like it again," wrote David Margolick of the contest. When Louis knocked out Schmeling in the first round, the celebrations stretched south from Yankee Stadium through Harlem all the way down to Battery Park.[45]

Joe Louis fought so often in Yankee Stadium that he had an impact on the baseball team. In the years before World War II, *New York World-Telegram* writer Dan Daniel transformed Louis's most publicized moniker, "the Brown Bomber," into the Yankees' "Bronx Bombers." It was a confluence of greatness, the golden triangle of sports—Joe Louis, the New York Yankees, and Yankee Stadium linked together in one nickname.

Yet, for all the punches thrown and touchdowns scored, "the house that Ruth built" was primarily a ballpark—though it was not always to the Babe's liking. Its dimensions favored controlled hitters who pulled the ball, not free swingers like Ruth and Mantle. Welcoming porches with four-foot fences beckoned balls hit down the lines—301 feet in left and 295 feet in right. But then the fence became more forbidding. It seemed to grow like a giant and stretch toward the horizon. Center field—"Death Valley," close to where the monuments to Miller Huggins, Ed Barrow, Babe Ruth, and Lou Gehrig were erected—was where home runs went to die. Dead center was a daunting 461 feet from home plate, and left center was even a few feet further. In addition to pull hitters, the park seemed made for players like Joe DiMaggio and Ted Williams who slashed at the ball, sending line drives into the wide gaps and turning what would have been singles in smaller parks into doubles or even triples.

Fog and a chilly, light drizzle delayed the first game at Yankee Stadium in 1956. "Football Weather at Stadium," headlined the *New York Herald-Tribune* the next day. The hundreds of fat pigeons that dined on popcorn and peanuts and lounged in the rafters and beams during the summer were scrawny and cold on opening day. But even in the inclement conditions the stadium had a festive air. Before the game the Yankees assembled at home plate to receive rings for winning the 1955 American League pennant. One by one, as Mel Allen called them to the plate, they stepped forward, took a ring, and then shook hands with Commissioner Ford Frick, American League president Will Harridge, and Mayor Robert Wagner.[46]

Veteran sports columnist Frank Graham, watching the ceremony from the press box in his fedora and coat and tie, thought about how young the players looked. "They reminded me of high school kids getting their diplomas," he wrote. "I wish I were close enough to them to see them blush and to hear them stammer in the presence of the three celebrities." Of course, on that day and in that place, the Yankees were the celebrities. Although Mickey had already started his season in spectacular fashion, the 1955 MVP Yogi Berra and revered Phil Rizzuto received the loudest cheers. Yogi was supposed to say a few words over the public address system but at the last second chose to remain silent.[47]

If Yogi and "the Scooter" won most of the pregame applause, the fans cheered for Whitey Ford and Mickey once the action against the

Boston Red Sox began. Ford showed why Stengel had saved him for the home opener, scattering five hits over nine full innings and allowing only one run. And Mantle provided all the offense the Yankees needed. In the fifth he drove in a run with an unexpected and perfectly executed drag bunt and in the seventh added three more RBIs when he homered into the lower right-field seats.[48]

In seven innings Mantle demonstrated his potential for greatness and tendency for self-destruction. He drove in runs with a short ball and long ball, roamed center field like a gazelle, and captivated everyone at the ballpark. Even the Red Sox's Ted Williams, sitting out of the game because of a foot injury, could not take his eyes off Mickey. A slugger who can beat out bunts, a switch hitter who had mastered the strike zone—that was a player to be reckoned with, Williams thought. "He's reaching his peak," Ted told reporters after the game. "There's no reason why he shouldn't hit .340. He's the only guy who has a chance to break Babe Ruth's homer record."[49]

Mantle's body seemed his only obstacle. Sprinting toward first after his fifth inning bunt, he felt a twinge in the hamstring behind his right knee, a problem that had plagued him for years. In an age when warming up before a game entailed nothing more than a slow jog to the batting cage and a few on-deck swings, stretching was something to avoid rather than make a habit of. When he felt the pain in his leg, Mickey began to worry. By the seventh he was visibly limping, and Stengel sent him to the training room after his home run. Trainer Gus Mauch gave the time-honored prognosis: "Mantle's condition is a day-to-day proposition and I can't predict how long he will be out." After a hot shower, however, Mickey said his leg felt better, "but I'm afraid it might be worse tomorrow."[50]

His hamstring was stiff and heavily bandaged when he took the field the next day. He moved cautiously, like a man trying to run on ice without falling. But the injury didn't appear to affect his swing. Batting left-handed in the second inning he smashed a home run 415 feet into the far corner of the upper right-field deck. In a twenty-seven-hit game against the Red Sox that ended in a 14–10 Yankee victory, "Limping Mantle" garnered the headlines. A Willard Mullin illustration pictured Mickey in a left-handed batting pose, wrapped in a tape measure and looking toward immortality. "Granted it's a long, long way from May to September," read the caption, "but as long as they are putting the tape measure to everything Mickey Mantle hits— if he holds his present pace just throw the record book away." As of April 24, in 22 at bats, he had 10 hits, 4 homers, and 13 RBIs, on pace for a .454 batting average, 102 home runs, and 333 RBIs.[51]

Suddenly Casey Stengel, the master of malapropism and hyperbole, counseled restraint. The Yankees had won five of their first six games, Ford had looked great in his first start, and the team was hitting like an all-new Murderers' Row. New York sportswriters jested that Congress might move to break up the Yankees for antitrust violations. But Casey warned that the team could not be that good—no team could be. The same could be said about Mickey Mantle. "There he is, 24 and limping, the greatness disfigured," wrote Jimmy Cannon. How long could he continue to play hurt? Cannon wondered whether Mantle would be another Pete Reiser, a talented Dodgers player whose career was cruelly cut short by injury, including concussions resulting from running into fences. In a bitter article about "the losers" in sports, "the fools who don't know enough to chalk their cues," Cannon advanced Mantle as exhibit number one.[52]

CANNON'S DYSPEPTIC COMMENT indicated his growing bitterness toward sports, which he had once watched with "the glad astonishment of a boy following his first parade." As Joe DiMaggio, Joe Louis, and his heroes of the 1930s retired or fell on hard times, Cannon's writing turned edgier, and he took a cynical approach to the younger class of sports idols. But his colleagues covering the New York sporting scene did not share his attitude. More often than not, they saw their job as creating, not tearing down, sports heroes.

In the 1950s such writers as Grantland Rice, Red Smith, Frank Graham, and Dan Daniel were the last of a dying breed. They had worked alongside—attending games and fights and often drinking long into the night with—Ring Lardner, Damon Runyon, Westbrook Pegler, Paul Gallico, Heywood Broun, and other giants. If they didn't launch the golden age of sports in the 1920s and 1930s, they promoted the hell out of it, nurturing the legends of the Great Bambino, the Manassa Mauler, the Galloping Ghost, the Iron Horse, "Big Bill" Tilden, the Brown Bomber, and Joltin' Joe. They formed the "Gee Whiz" school, using every ounce of their considerable talent to glorify the accomplishments of athletes. On long train trips across the country, they traveled with the players, drank and played cards with them, and knew their strengths and flaws. Yet, when they wrote about them, they underscored their achievements and erased their blemishes. Theirs was a god-creating business. "The Golden Age sportswriters," observed Robert Lipsyte, "hyped the country's post–World War I sports boom, rode the gravy train and then, for the good of the game, maintained the myths and legends as the country slid into a bust."[53]

In the 1960s, television would radically change journalists' approach to sports, but in 1956 the old school still ruled. Red Smith, arguably the best writer of the group, perfectly exemplified the process. In 1945, when he arrived at the *New York Herald-Tribune*, he was already a seasoned journalist. The paper boasted some of the finest newspapermen in New York and an editor, Stanley Woodward, second to none. Woodward didn't want Smith to write about games as much as to evoke the mise-en-scène of sports. He once had Smith and a few other sportswriters cover a World Series. Woodward gave everyone but Smith a specific assignment. Confused, Red asked, "What do you want me to write about?" "Write about the smell of cabbage in the hallway," the editor replied. Smith never forgot the advice and labored in his columns to record the irreducible essence of sports. Woodward also counseled Smith to avoid "Godding up those ball players."[54]

Smith proved less successful in following Woodward's second recommendation. He admitted that on occasion he transformed athletes into heroes. And why not? he thought. "When you go through Westminster Abbey you'll find that except for that little Poets' Corner almost all of the statues and memorials are to killers. To generals and admirals who won battles, whose specialty was human slaughter. I don't think they're such glorious heroes."[55]

In the mid-1950s, faced with plummeting attendance caused by demographic change and the rise of competing entertainment opportunities, baseball needed a little "Godding up" to bring spectators back to the ball parks. With DiMaggio retired, Ted Williams claiming he was washed up, and Jackie Robinson graying and overweight, the game sorely needed a young hero, a downy-cheeked, blue-eyed Lancelot. It needed someone who looked and hit like Mickey Mantle. And in April 1956, when Mantle started slugging homers from the first day of the season, the god-makers in the press box sharpened their pencils.

CHAPTER 5

"Match That!"

"Home run hitters drive Cadillacs!"
—CASEY STENGEL

For all the pennants and the World Series championships, the history of the Yankees—in fact, all of baseball in the 1950s—could be reduced to three numbers: 2,130, 56, and 60. Together they conjured the legacy of the franchise, its iconic personalities, and its glorious past, and many baseball experts believed they would stand as long as the game was played. The first, 2,130, belonged to Lou Gehrig, the Iron Horse, whose consecutive game streak matched, for sheer longevity, Franklin Roosevelt's four straight presidential victories. The streak was a pure expression of Gehrig's essence—constant, consistent, dedicated, quietly taking the field day after day and year after year.

Fifty-six belonged to Joe DiMaggio, who exploded onto the game like a supernova, arriving in New York and immediately becoming the centerpiece of the Yankees dynasty. Hitting in twenty consecutive games is an accomplishment worthy of celebration; a fifty-six-game streak boggles the imagination. By all the mathematics of hitting a baseball, where failure is almost a dead certainty at least seven out of ten times, it is a virtually impossible feat. Before the summer of 1941, it had never been done; since then it has never been repeated. Only a player like DiMaggio—steady, magnificent, brilliant—could have pulled off such an accomplishment. At the height of the game's popularity, he was simply and unarguably the best.

Even alongside these numbers, however, sixty was special. It stood at the summit of baseball statistics and was held by the most celebrated player in the sport's history. Babe Ruth single-handedly transformed baseball into a power game, and the 1927 season when he clobbered sixty home runs was his pièce de résistance. During that memorable year Charles Lindbergh flew the *Spirit of St. Louis* across the Atlantic, Jack Dempsey fought Gene Tunney in the famous "Long Count" match, and "the Babe" consumed cigars, beers, and women and clouted more and longer home runs than other ball players ever thought possible. And he did it in a way that left even the most casual observer breathless.

Before the 1920s the notion that any player would blast sixty home runs in a season bordered on lunacy. In December 1919, when Boston Red Sox owner Harrison Herbert "Harry" Frazee sold the rights to Ruth to the hapless New York Yankees, the most home runs hit by any player in a single season was twenty-nine—which Babe Ruth had done the previous season. That was almost double the previous American League standard of sixteen launched by Ralph "Socks" Seybold in 1902. Home runs were mostly magnificent accidents, often the results of poor outfield play or a lucky swing connecting with a fresh ball.[1]

Then Ruth arrived in New York and changed everything. His home runs were not accidents but the intended results of a lethal swing. He gripped the bat low, his right hand down to the knob, giving his swing a whiplike motion and generating 8,000 pounds of force, enough to convert an incoming 90-mile-an-hour fastball into an outgoing 110-mile-an-hour ball. And given that Ruth swung a heavy bat—forty ounces or so—and possessed extraordinary timing, when he connected, he hit high, deep shots, long enough to sail over any fence in the major leagues.[2]

Ruth's stunning home runs caused Americans to reimagine the game. Baseball historian Lee Allen understood Babe's importance: "Ruth filled the parks by developing the home run into a hit of exciting elegance. For almost two decades he battered fences with such regularity that baseball's basic structure was eventually pounded into a different shape." He challenged Ty Cobb's small-ball notions of scientific baseball, a strategy that emphasized getting on base, sacrificing the runner to second, executing hit-and-run plays, and protecting a one- or two-run lead. But his impact transcended the sport. Ruth's approach dovetailed with the instant gratification peddled by the nascent advertising industry. Swing for the fences, buy now and pay later, the world is at your fingertips—it all became part of the same consumer-driven culture. In Yankee pinstripes he was more than just a baseball player; he was a prophet whose mighty swings made spectators gasp in wonder at the potentialities of man. He was the Great Gatsby of baseball. It seemed as if nothing was beyond his reach.[3]

In 1920 he led the American League with fifty-four homers, miles ahead of Cy Williams's National League best of fifteen. In 1921 Babe won the AL home run crown with fifty-nine, the same year that George "High Pockets" Kelly took the National League title with twenty-three. He was in a class by himself and seemed likely to set a new record each year. But he didn't. And after he had hit so many home runs in his first two seasons with the Yankees, any smaller number seemed anticlimactic. In 1922 he hit only thirty-five, losing his home run crown to St. Louis Browns' outfielder Ken Williams. He seemed almost mortal during the next four seasons, smacking forty-one, forty-six, twenty-five, and forty-seven. Success, some reporters and fans muttered, had gone to his head and was singularly visible around his waist. Where he had once dazzled spectators, now he just impressed, and occasionally disappointed, them.

Something of the swagger of the younger Babe returned in 1927. Ruth batted third in the lineup, with Lou Gehrig hitting cleanup behind him, which meant pitchers were forced to pitch to Babe. Putting Ruth on base with a walk and bringing Gehrig to the plate was a dangerous strategy in its own right. Better to "pitch and pray" that the Babe of 1927 was not the Babe of 1921. Suddenly it appeared that Ruth had discovered a fountain of youth at the same time that Gehrig emerged in full force. From April to mid-August the two dueled for the home run title, almost daily matching each other in four-baggers. By August 15 the younger man had taken the home run lead: thirty-eight to thirty-six. Gehrig was the first player to challenge Ruth's home run supremacy. (When Ruth lost the title in 1922 and 1925, he had missed long stretches of the season.)[4]

The Bambino responded by hitting two blasts in Chicago to pull alongside Gehrig. The race was still on. By the end of August Babe had hit forty-three home runs, and Gehrig was close behind at forty-one. With a month remaining in the season, the teammates accounted for eighty-four homers, more than any team other than the Yankees had ever hit in a single season. But for all that, Babe was nowhere near his record of fifty-nine. With no one close to the Yankees in the standings, Ruth and Gehrig had no incentive to deliver wins.

By the second week of September, Gehrig had reached forty-five, but at that point he dropped out of the race. He hit only two more home runs the rest of the regular season. Then, with the pennant won and the season grinding toward the World Series, Ruth sprinted toward immortality. In September 1927 he cemented his legacy. By September 26 he had hit a staggering thirteen home runs that month. And with four games remaining in the season he had raised his home run total to fifty-six, only three behind his single-season record.

On September 27 he launched fifty-seven, a magnificent grand slam off the Philadelphia Athletics' future Hall of Famer Robert "Lefty" Grove. The Yankees finished the season in New York with a three-game stand against the Washington Senators. In the first inning of the first game, Ruth hit fifty-eight. Then in the fifth inning he came to the plate with the bases loaded and two out. On a 3–2 count, right-hander Paul Hopkins threw Babe a slow, snakelike curve. "A beautiful curve," the pitcher reminisced seven decades later. "It was so slow that Ruth started to swing and then hesitated, hitched on it and brought the bat back. And then he swung, breaking his wrists as he came through it. What a great eye he had! He hit it at the right second. Put everything behind it. I can still hear the crack of the bat. I can see the swing."[5]

As Hopkins watched admiringly, fifty-nine sailed over the right-field fence. Improbably, Babe had tied his record, and two games remained in the season.

Ruth didn't need both to reach sixty. On a muggy September 30, the Yankees and Senators played a game that was meaningless in the standings, yet all-important for Ruth and the millions of Americans enthralled with his pursuit of the record. With the score tied 2–2 in the eighth inning, he came to the plate. Pitcher Tom Zachary recalled, "Everyone knew he was out for the record, so he wasn't going to get anything good from me." On a 1–1 count, Zachary threw a screwball, down and in, ankle high, "as good as I had," he remembered. Babe swung like a golfer taking a tee shot. As everyone in Yankee Stadium seemed to hold their breath, the ball tracked in a high arch toward the right-field foul pole and then dropped, dropped, dropped—into the bleachers, inches inside the pole. Zachary threw down his glove, yelling, "Foul ball! Foul ball!" and argued with the umpire. But it was already in the books. Sixty! Ruth didn't even need the final game.[6]

Babe celebrated in the clubhouse. "Sixty, count 'em, sixty!" he shouted. "Let's see some other son of a bitch match that!"[7]

NO ONE IN THE NEXT generation of hitters could match the feat. A few hit over fifty home runs, and Jimmie Foxx and Hank Greenberg

reached fifty-eight, but well more than half of the home run champions in the major leagues won their crowns with fewer than forty.
Ruth's 60 home runs in a season, as well as his lifetime total of 714,
set him apart from all other hitters. Babe Ruth, most baseball experts
agreed, was an outlier, a phenomenon, an exception that proved the
rule. "Who do you think you are, Babe Ruth?" was an instant rebuke
to any player from the Little Leagues to the majors who was a bit too
full of himself. There was only one Babe Ruth, and consensus had it
that there would never be another. As great as he was, even Joe
DiMaggio could not match Babe's batting average, let alone his home
run records.

Yet, a month into the 1956 season, veteran sportswriters were using
the yardstick of Babe Ruth to measure the accomplishments of Mickey
Mantle. At the beginning of May, when the Yankees returned to New
York for a fourteen-game home stand, low attendance plagued their
weekday afternoon games, a continued cause of concern throughout
professional baseball. Bill Corum of the *New York Journal-American*
blamed the nasty spring weather and counseled fellow scribes to stop
writing about sagging attendance figures. Focusing on the issue, an editor from *The Sporting News* insisted, only compounded the problem.[8]

Mantle was the solution. On May 1 he homered in the first inning
against the Detroit Tigers, threw a runner out at home plate from
center field, and led the Yankees to a 9–2 victory. So what if only
6,771 spectators attended the contest? They saw Mickey and Whitey
Ford at their best. The next day was cold and overcast, with rain and
darkness forcing the Yankees to turn on the lights in the seventh inning. New York's play matched the weather. Ford was not on the
mound, and the Tigers clocked Johnny Kucks for eight runs in less
than three innings. But Mantle was unaffected by the conditions or
the score. In the last inning he prevented a shutout by pounding a
home run deep into the right-field stands.[9]

The chilly rain in the fifth inning chased away many of the 5,318
spectators, including recently retired heavyweight title holder Rocky

Marciano, who watched Mickey's home run on television in the toasty Stadium Club. Marciano and Mantle were friends and, when both were in New York, often enjoyed dinner and a night on the town to-gether—along with a dozen or more associates and hangers-on. Since Rocky made a practice of never paying for anybody, someone was al-ways with him to pick up the check. Frequently Marciano would ap-pear at an event without a coat and tie, insisting that someone buy one for him. Then at elegant clubs he would overeat, grabbing oily plum tomatoes with his hands, and wiping his fingers on his coat sleeves. And Mickey, along with everyone else, would laugh with the champ as if he had uttered a memorable bon mot.[10]

That, Mantle observed, was celebrity style. Men gladly paid to bask in the radiance of a star athlete. They bought drinks, paid hotels bills, purchased clothes; they provided what was necessary to be part of the scene. At the top of the celebrity pyramid stood the heavyweight champion of the world and the best hitter of the New York Yankees— Jack Dempsey and Babe Ruth in the 1920s, Joe Louis and Joe DiMag-gio in the 1930s and 1940s, and Rocky and Mickey in the 1950s. Marciano's boorishness and Mantle's sullen indifference were a prod-uct of the same irreducible fact: It just didn't matter. As long as they knocked out opponents and belted out home runs, they could do or say almost anything. They got a pass, a get-out-of-jail-free card.

In 1956, as Marciano's star faded, Mantle's brightened. The wind of celebrity was at his back—the Yankees were winning, and he was seeing the ball as if it were the size of a grapefruit. The Kansas City Athletics came to town for a three-game series, and the Yanks won two. Mickey went 2–4 with a home run in an 8–7 loss in the first game, then 2–3 in the second, and in the final contest of the series pounded two more homers. The first blast landed in the right-field upper deck; the second kicked off the facade of the upper deck and bounded back onto the field. When the Saturday Ladies' Day game ended, Mantle had raised his season home run total to nine and his batting average to .433.[11]

Nine homers in sixteen games was nothing less than Ruthian. After the Kansas City series the ghost of the Bambino haunted virtually every newspaper's sports section. "The time has come, perhaps, to acknowledge that Babe Ruth's record of 60 home runs in a single season is in greater jeopardy than ever before," wrote Shirley Povich. "Another fellow with Yankee lettering across his chest, Mickey Mantle, is taking such dead aim at the record that his challenge must be honored even with the season only three weeks old."[12]

Povich admitted that some fans would be saddened to see Ruth's 1927 total surpassed—"The Babe's record comes closer to being sanctified than any other in baseball." And he confessed that other experts might think he was ludicrously premature to talk about records while spring was still in the air. "But Mantle is a very special challenger. He hits the ball farther than anybody since Ruth, and some of his blows in Yankee Stadium have reached sectors that not even the Babe's wallops attained." No doubt about it, Povich concluded, Mantle had the talent to break the record. His power from both sides of the plate, increased patience in the batter's box, and advantage of hitting in front of Yogi Berra were auspicious signs. Joseph M. Sheehan of the *New York Times* agreed, emphasizing that in 1927 Ruth didn't hit his ninth home run until his twenty-ninth game.[13]

MANTLE'S TORRID PACE piqued the interest of fans as well as sportswriters. On May 6, 49,016 spectators paid to watch him in a doubleheader against the Chicago White Sox. He collected two hits, drew two walks, and scored twice as New York swept Chicago, an unspectacular performance by his standards. But his presence dominated the day. He was all that the players and coaches wanted to discuss. White Sox manager Marty Marion had predicted his team stood a good chance of winning the pennant, but after watching Mantle he changed his mind. "All I talked about [during the pregame meeting] was how to pitch to Mantle," he told reporters. "A fellow's got to

In 1956 the Babe's monument in center field of Yankee Stadium cast a long shadow over Mickey Mantle as he chased Ruth's single-season home run record. His pursuit of Ruth's feat made him the story of the season. Both Yankee sluggers fulfilled American desires for heroes who demonstrated awesome power. *Courtesy of Getty Images.*

throw very hard and in a spot to get Mantle out," he explained. "And there aren't many in the league who can throw that hard. . . . He's really great. Looks wonderful."[14]

And he did look wonderful. But, as always with Mickey, looks were deceiving. Despite appearing virtually indestructible, his body was sometimes as fragile as a Fabergé egg. Sportswriters knew his injury history and watched him on the field as closely as a thoroughbred trainer scrutinized a Kentucky Derby winner, looking for some hitch in his gait or grimace of pain. An end to Mickey's brilliance was only a misstep away.

In the second game against Chicago, he slightly pulled a muscle in his left groin. He pronounced himself fine, and two days later prepared to play in an afternoon contest against the Cleveland Indians. But on his first swing in batting practice, he fouled the ball onto his foot. Wincing, he limped out of the batter's box. He had injured his right big toe and, after a few painful steps, headed toward the club-house, where the trainer iced his foot. He returned to the dugout a few minutes before the start of the game. A hole was cut in his shoe to take pressure off the swollen toe. Casey Stengel looked at the foot and asked, "Do you want to play?" It was Mickey's call.[15]

"You bet your life I want to play," Mantle snapped. He knew Stengel's question was a gambit in a psychological game.

"Okay, you're in," Casey said.

Mickey hit a home run and a single off future Hall of Famer Early Wynn to pace the Yankees for a 4–3 victory. It was his tenth homer of the season, but his injury was the story in the next day's papers. Stengel thought it proved he could hit against the best pitchers in the league—even when he was hurt. Sportswriters reported it as another indication of how brittle the slugger's body was. Although he had looked great at the plate, he had played the outfield cautiously, like an older player limping toward the end of his career.

Mantle moved better the next day and, the day after that, swat-ted his eleventh home run of the season. During the same contest, a loss to the Indians, Yogi Berra hit his tenth homer. Stengel's strat-egy was working perfectly. As long as Yogi remained hot, opposing pitchers did not have the luxury of playing coy with Mickey. They had to give him something in the strike zone, and he responded by ripping the ball. Not only was he far ahead of Ruth's 1927 pace, but his batting average was inching close to .450. These were statistics worthy of celebration.

Not that Mantle needed much of an excuse. After two years in the army, Billy Martin was back playing full-time with the Yankees. The army had granted him a temporary leave late in the 1955 season for the stretch run and the World Series, but after the Yankees lost to the Dodgers, he had returned to Fort Carson, Colorado. By the beginning of the 1956 season Casey Stengel's favorite troublemaker had received his discharge papers as well as a divorce decree from a Berkeley court.

With money in his pocket—something he had seldom had on his military pay—he was ready to play ball and resume his nighttime sprees with Hank Bauer, Whitey Ford, and especially Mickey.[16]

FOR YOUNG, FAMOUS BALLPLAYERS in the 1950s, the lights of Manhattan beckoned like a wonderland. It was an eastern version of a Wild West cattle town. The saloons were open all night, beautiful women were only a nod away, and sports reporters stuffed away their note pads. Although a gossip columnist might write an innocuous line or two, generally what transpired after the moon came out was off-limits. What happened at night outside Yankee Stadium died with the morning's first light.

With his wife still in Oklahoma, Mickey operated out of a tiny suite at the St. Moritz Hotel at 50 Central Park South, on the east side of Sixth Avenue. A historian of the city described the thirty-eight-story building as "a picturesque cliff, amidst towering trees to the north and other soaring skyscrapers to the south." Completely redecorated in 1950, the hotel featured redesigned rooms, the side-walk restaurant Café de la Paix, and Rumpelmayer's tea and pastry shop. Mantle wasn't much of a tea drinker or, for that matter, a sidewalk-café sitter, but the St. Moritz was perfectly located for sampling less refined haunts that served stronger drinks.[17]

Mantle, Martin, Ford, and other Yankees regularly ate at Danny's Hideaway on Steak Row along East 45th Street. It was Martin's favorite restaurant. Opened in the mid-1940s as a small bistro with Danny Stradella taking orders and tending the bar and Mamma Rosa cooking the meals, it became popular and expanded, eventually becoming the largest establishment along Steak Row. It attracted celebrity actors and writers. In 1956 Mantle and Martin met Elizabeth Taylor, Mike Todd, and Rock Hudson in Danny's. The actors had just finished filming *Giant*, and Danny wanted a photograph of the entire group. Of course, the ballplayers agreed. After all, Stradella loved the

Yankees, and Mickey never saw a tab on one of his tables. It was one of the smaller benefits of his status.[18]

Some celebrities, to be sure, were renowned for their generosity—none more than Frank Sinatra, generally recognized as the biggest tipper in show business. When he was in New York every door opened. Once, during a slow day at the restaurant Toots Shor's, Joey Rivera, one of the waiters, approached Toots himself and whispered something in his ear. "Okay, set up the table," he replied.

Less than an hour later Sinatra arrived with about twenty people. They had come from the cemetery where they had put Frank's father to rest. Sportswriter Jack Lang recalled, "They sat down, with Sinatra at the head of the table, had one round of drinks, got up, and left." The next day the singer tipped every waiter and every captain $100. "When Frank comes in, he pays the rent," said Rivera.[19]

Mantle had learned the rules of the celebrity game watching Joe DiMaggio and Rocky Marciano—not Frank Sinatra—and neither paid any restaurateur's rent. Both were cheap on a heroic scale, but in a head-to-head contest the ballplayer would probably have edged out the boxer. Throughout his illustrious career DiMaggio dined regularly at Rao's, an exclusive southern Italian restaurant on East 114th Street. For years, while the tiny place was run by Vincent and Anna Rao, there was always a table for DiMaggio and never a bill at the end of the dinner. After they died, their relatives Ron Straci and Frank Pellegrino followed the same policy. Even in old age, DiMaggio always ate on the house. That is, until the day Pellegrino requested a small favor. He waited until Joe had finished his coffee and then asked him for an autograph for a young boy at another table.[20]

"You know, Frankie, I get paid for signing autographs," DiMaggio said.

As he left the restaurant Pellegrino told him, "Joe, you are not welcome here anymore."

It was a sentence he never heard at Toots Shor's. Newspapermen, writers, movie and stage stars, and athletes went to Toot's primarily to drink, though the food served there was more than acceptable. Located at 51 West 51st Street, close to the St. Moritz, Toots Shor's was designed for people to see each other and be seen. Walking past the American colonial facade, a visitor entered the lobby and immediately noticed a large circular bar, fifty-four feet in circumference, which after a ballgame in Yankee Stadium or a fight in Madison Square Garden was normally packed, often three or four deep. "That's my roulette wheel," Toots explained. Journalist John Bainbridge said that the place was "as devoid of subtlety and fussy trimming as a boxing ring." Unlike the Stork or the 21 Club, it oozed a masculine comfort—plank oak floors, redbrick and knotty-pine walls, red-leather upholstered bar stools. The main dining room was open and well lit with a high vaulted ceiling and an enormous brick fireplace. Beyond the showcase territory, there were other rooms and bars where the noncelebrities were seated and served.[21]

Toots, a big, loud, backslapping man, seemed to live in his establishment. The restaurant opened at noon every day but Sunday, when the doors were unlocked at four. It closed at four in the morning, except on Saturday, when it closed at three. When it was open, Toots worked the main rooms, a drink in one of his large fists, a wisecrack or an insult on his lips, and an eye always out for a more famous celebrity. He judged celebrities like a jockey appraises horseflesh; he had an unerring sense of who was up and who was down, who was hot and who was at the absolute top. He entertained fixtures of the stage and screen, sportswriters and columnists, and television actors and literary figures, but he favored athletes above anyone else. They were the gods of Toots Shor's. And the saloon was the recognized center of New York sports.

Gay Talese called Toots Shor's "the first sport's restaurant." It was where the ballplayers and boxers went to celebrate a victory or forget a defeat. Its bar was often so crowded with athletes and sportswriters—and visitors gawking at the stars—that it was difficult for a newcomer to get a drink. Yogi Berra reportedly once observed, "Toots Shor's is

so crowded, nobody goes there anymore." Yogi's opinion notwith-
standing, for the sports crowd it was the place to be. "What you have
to understand is that Toots was *the* pivotal character in New York.
Everything revolved around him," said Talese. "His place was *the* celebrity hangout, like Sardi's is for the theater crowd and Elaine's is for
the writers." And although it was a public place where athletes and
sportswriters mixed, the next day's papers did not report what athletes
said and did in Toots Shor's.[22]

As far as Toots was concerned, sport was America's civic religion,
and the most celebrated athletes were the nation's high priests. One
observer commented, "Shor believes that sports are the backbone of
American life and that good citizenship demands a close interest in
them." Athletes' youth and virility, grace under pressure, and competitive drive underscored the strengths of the country, then locked in the
Cold War with the Soviet Union. How could anything be wrong with
America, he reasoned, when the Yankees ruled baseball and Rocky
Marciano dominated the heavyweight division?[23]

DiMaggio proved his case. Even after he retired, Joe was the un-
official king of Toots Shor's. Years after the Yankee Clipper left the
game, Toots ranked him as one of the ten most important living men,
right up there with Dwight Eisenhower and Winston Churchill.
"DiMaggio always got a premier table at Toots Shor's," noted Jack
Lang, "right in the front." When Joe showed up with Marilyn Monroe
it was the equivalent of a royal appearance. Of course, their presence
also made clear that there was no saloon in the city like Toots Shor's.
No place in America—or the world, for that matter—more consistently attracted celebrities. Shor could be excused for beaming at the
constellation of stars that nightly appeared at 51 West 51st Street. For
that reason he never bothered to advertise his establishment. He knew
that the columnists and celebrity photographers would give him all
the free publicity he desired.[24]

A celebrity's standing often determined his opinion of Toots. For
those at the summit of their profession, he was "as kind as Saint Fran-

cis of Assisi, as generous as Santa Claus, as worldly as [financier] Bernard Baruch, and as understanding as [famed advice columnist] Dorothy Dix." For them he was the gruff but genial host, his rough exterior covering his soft heart. But his detractors were as harsh as his supporters were generous. "He's a slob with delusions of grandeur," commented one. "When his friends are batting three-fifty, Toots can't do enough for them. Then they're real, solid-gold crumb bums. But when they start hitting two hundred, something happens to Toots's eyesight—he can't see the old pals so good anymore."[25]

His eyesight was twenty-twenty when it came to the 1950s Yankees, especially Mantle. Shor admired and respected DiMaggio, but usually at a safe distance. Their affection was undoubtedly genuine, but like everyone else Toots was careful not to get too familiar with the aloof, often moody Clipper. DiMaggio was always uncomfortable with his public. Like a marble statue, he commanded respect but was apt to be cold. In contrast, Mickey was a lovable kid, a big, smiling puppy of a man. When he came into the bar, Toots always hurried over and hugged him, sometimes spilling a little of his brandy and soda on Mantle's jacket, which only made Mickey laugh more. "God, Toots loved Mickey. And vice versa," Whitey Ford remembered. "He was closest to Mickey. He would hug Mick. He couldn't hug Joe."[26]

The Yankees received the best of everything—Shor's biggest smile, his finest tables, his best liquor. Mantle, Martin, Ford, Bauer, Berra, and other Yankees Dead End Kids were regulars. They dropped by during off days and following afternoon games and even showed up for nightcaps after playing under the lights. Baseball lore is rife with stories about heavy-drinking major leaguers—from Babe Ruth's frequent bellyaches to hungover Hack Wilson losing a ground ball in the sun—but, as one authority on the subject wrote, "this hard-drinking world reached it apotheosis in New York . . . during the 1950s when Mickey Mantle, young and vibrant, was the biggest star in the brightest constellation in the baseball firmament."[27]

For Mantle, professional baseball players, and millions of other Americans, booze was the drug of choice in the 1950s. At the time, a "problem drinker" was not a man who drank too much but one who couldn't hold his liquor. When Mickey and "the boys"—the very designation is telling—ventured out for a night of fun at Toots Shor's they intended to drink heavily. They followed Toot's personal philosophy: "Drink, certainly, and drink a lot, but *hold* it." The argot of Toots Shor's was part of a national idiom. A person who was drunk but holding it was "loaded" or had "a load on." But a patron could also be "half loaded," "three-quarter loaded," "winged," or "bouncing." None of that mattered, except if the drinker slid past "loaded" to "sloppy." A sloppy drunk—mawkish or aggressively belligerent—was an embarrassment and unwelcome at Toots's.[28]

This culture of drink transcended Toots Shor's and baseball. In the publishing industry it was the decade of the three-martini lunch, a time when the most important business was completed early in the day. In white-collar professions it was common to take a prospective employee out to lunch. If he didn't drink, he didn't get the job. If he drank too much and became "sloppy," he didn't get the job. If he got "half-loaded" but showed no signs of wear, he had a good shot at whatever position he was up for—that is, if anyone could remember after the midday binge. The main difference between white- and blue-collar drinking was not the quantity but the brand of booze. On Wall Street and Madison Avenue they drank Scotch, bourbon, vodka, and gin. In Astoria and Brooklyn, beer was the beverage of choice.

In the world of professional baseball, drinking was part of the daily rhythm of life. Big-league players spent most of their days waiting for a game to begin and dealing with long stretches of boredom. So they turned to the bottle. They drank on the road, in the bar cars during lengthy train rides, during low-stakes poker games, and at late-night bull sessions. They drank in bars while they trolled for one-night stands or just engaged in some "innocent" flirting. They drank beers in the clubhouse after games. Normally Pete Previte, the clubhouse assistant who, when he was younger, had brought hot dogs to Babe Ruth and coffee to Joe DiMaggio, made sure that there were cold beers for Mickey and the Yankees to sip as they unwound after a contest. Often after victories Casey Stengel paid for the beer. Drinking made them feel like winners.[29]

It was like the old joke: "If you avoid the bottle, don't overeat, save your money, go to bed and arise early, you will live longer—or at least it will seem a hell of a lot longer." Mickey, Billy, and the rest did not aspire to long lives of asceticism. At the plate Mickey swung for the fences. Away from Yankee Stadium he lived the same way—drinking hard, ignoring curfews, and behaving as if he were a bachelor.

If some players drank to escape boredom, others drank out of fear. Theirs was a precarious profession. Most knew that they would be forced out of the game in their thirties, if not earlier. And it could all end in the blink of an eye. A pitcher might tear a rotator cuff on one fastball. A fielder might stumble and "blow out" a knee beyond the limited skills and knowledge of surgeons at the time. A slightly below-average batter might go into a slump and simply be replaced by a promising minor leaguer. In the mid-1950s the Yankees had second baseman Bobby Richardson and shortstop Tony Kubek in their farm system. Young, talented, and fresh faced, they were waiting for the opportunity to replace Billy Martin and Gil McDougald, respectively. It could and would happen. Every Yankee knew the popular legend of Wally Pipp—the outstanding first baseman who sat out one game with a headache and was replaced by some kid named Lou Gehrig. Pipp never got his job back. Maybe the details of the story were apocryphal. Perhaps manager Miller Huggins was punishing him for gambling or had lost confidence in his hitting against left-handed pitchers. It hardly mattered. The essential story line was correct: here one day, gone the next. None of Mantle's teammates wanted to be the next Wally Pipp.

Added to all this was the code in the big leagues: "Drink hard, play hard." Drinking and playing baseball defined a major-league man. Mickey Mantle epitomized this ideal of red-blooded masculinity. The stories of Mantle showing up at the ballpark bleary-eyed with a hangover—or still half loaded—and blasting a home run are staples in the folklore of the game. "Shit," Mickey would say, "the home runs weren't nothin'. Now, runnin' them damn bases was a killer." That was big league, Babe Ruth stuff. Legend material. Ryne Duren, a former Yankee whose career was cut short by alcoholism, understood the deeper ties between baseball and the bottle: "Alcohol is tied to masculinity—the more you drink, the better man you are."[30]

In 1956, as his incredible start to the season suggested he might break Ruth's single-season home run record, Mickey Mantle was simply the best. Digging in at the plate, swaggering into Toots Shor's, or ducking into a woman's hotel room, he was the heir apparent to Babe. "If you could drink all night, get the girl, get up the next day, and hit a home run, you passed the test," he recalled. "Temptations were everywhere. Fans would buy us drinks [and] girls would hang around to meet us." Unfortunately, Mickey was better at passing the test than resisting temptations. Not that he tried very hard. He had a code to uphold. "In those days, how well you could hold your liquor was, for many of us, a measure of being a man. At the ballpark, you belted them out. At the bar, you belted them down." That was the way he played—and the way he lived.[31]

THE YANKEES NEEDED Mantle to be at the top of his game. At home they dropped two of three to Cleveland and split four against Baltimore. Though they were still in first place on May 13, their lead had shrunk to a single game. Casey Stengel admitted that he didn't know what to do with the infield. Billy Martin was hitting under .200, Andy Carey and Gil McDougald weren't much better, and they were committing too many errors. "I can't understand it. They're out there practicin'," Stengel told reporters. "Yet they're makin' bad plays and I

In the 1950s, the most famous athletes went to Toots Shor's to drink and socialize when in New York. The saloonkeeper welcomed them with open arms and treated them like family. Pictured from left to right: golfer Jimmy Demeret, Mantle, Shor, fellow restaurateur Ed Wynn, and boxer Rocky Graziano. *Courtesy of Getty Images.*

don't know what it is but I'll tell you it better get better." To instill some fear into the miscreants, he inserted twenty-year-old Bobby Richardson in the lineup for Martin at second. It was his Wally Pipp–Lou Gehrig moment, but Richardson failed to deliver and was promptly shipped off to the Yank's Denver farm team.[32]

As the team prepared for a twelve-game road swing through the West, it was an open question whether they could continue to count on the bats of Mantle and Berra. Yogi was tough and dependable, but he was outperforming his career statistics by a long way. If he reverted to form, his batting average would fall slightly below .300 and his home run pace would falter. Although he already had ten homers, he had never hit more than thirty in a season. Mickey was more mercurial. He was capable of reaching unimagined heights, or he might stub a toe or wreck a knee. The uncertainty unsettled Stengel and George Weiss, leading them to question what they had and to look to make changes.[33]

New York Post writer Jerry Mitchell judged that the team's "dreams of quick conquest [had] broken into small pieces." Stengel had loaded his squad with right-handed hitters to match up with teams like the Indians that had talented southpaw pitchers. But the Yankee right-handers were popping up, hitting into double plays, and striking out. "Pitiful," their manager remarked. The thought of an extended road trip with a squad of light hitters sat poorly with Professor Stengel.[34]

On May 14 Cleveland's Bob Lemon tossed a three-hit victory against the Yankees, despite Mantle's fourth-inning home run. The win gave the Indians a small lead in the pennant race. Two days later, on a cold, windy Wednesday, fewer than 7,000 spectators watched as New York regained its one game margin. It was Billy Martin's birthday, and fittingly enough he broke out of a slump. Leading off in the first inning, he drove the ball over the left-field fence for his first home run of the season. Mickey hit a home run in the seventh. It was his thirteenth of the year.[35]

The Yankees' win and Martin's birthday home run were cause for a mild celebration. Had they been in New York, Martin, Ford, and Mantle would have closed down Toots Shor's, but they weren't in Manhattan. And, Mantle later noted, "how are you going to have a real celebration in Cleveland?" They settled for dinner and a few drinks to toast Billy. Their activities were as uneventful as the following year's birthday bash would prove life changing.[36]

The win also brought an end to the Yankees' early-season doldrums. As if by some magic, Martin started to hit, draw walks, and score runs. His swagger returned, and with it, his team's imperial dominance. They scored twenty-four runs during a three-game sweep in Chicago and knocked in twelve more in two wins against Kansas City. Then, after losing a one-run game to Detroit, they took the next two in the series 13–5 and 11–4. The Yanks finished the road trip splitting two games with Baltimore, having won nine of twelve. Once again, they owned the American League.

The team was as arrogant as it was dominant. In the eighth inning in a game in Kansas City, the Royals' manager, Lou Boudreau, sent in relief pitcher Tommy Lasorda. Lasorda proceeded to throw high and tight. He "shaved" Hank Bauer in the eighth and then struck him out looking. He used the same tactic against Martin in the ninth. Hitless for the day, Billy retuned to the dugout hot. "I'm going to get you later," he screamed at Lasorda.[37]

The stocky pitcher took a step toward New York's dugout, challenging him: "You don't have to wait, banana nose, come out now."

Martin didn't need a second invitation. He led as Bauer and several other Yankees charged toward the mound. A reporter suggested that "a general riot threatened," but in truth the umpires quickly restored order, and the game finished without further incident. But to be on the safe side, Casey Stengel left the field carrying a bat. It was a clear indication that he approved of Martin's behavior. Fighting showed Stengel that a player was taking an interest in the game. Winners battled, and Martin, no matter how disliked by George Weiss, was a winner. As was often the case, he ignited the entire team.

During the road swing, Mickey used his bat at the plate, not like Stengel to get off the field. He hit his fourteenth and fifteenth homers in an afternoon game against the White Sox, the first right-handed and the second left-handed. Few batters had ever accomplished the feat; Mantle had now done it twice. Both shots traveled over four hundred feet into the upper decks of Comiskey Park. And he hit the second homer in the ninth inning with his team down by one. The Yankees won the game in the tenth.[38]

Beat writer Harold Rosenthal commented that the performance raised Mickey's batting average to "a giddy .409." It was Homeric—Mighty Casey, Roy Hobbs, the Great Bambino heroics. The Yankees, hated in every American League city, were not America's team, but twenty-four-year-old Mickey Mantle was fast becoming America's baseball player. Fans around the circuit applauded his feats. In Chicago and Detroit they booed their own pitchers for walking the slugger. "There hasn't been such mass indignation over a batter not being given a chance to hit since the days of Babe Ruth," suggested Jerry Mitchell. Spectators in several cities appeared more interested in seeing Mickey hit one out of their park than watching their team win. With Mantle at the plate, a competitive baseball game took on the air of an exhibition.[39]

Even John Franklin "Home Run" Baker, the symbol of hitting power in the era before the Great War, was caught in the Mantle craze. Mickey, he said, "finally has found himself." He was a transcendent slugger. Baker predicted that Mantle would break Ruth's record and "put the home run mark clear out of sight," adding, "There's no limit to what that young man just might do."[40]

The opinions about Mantle's future solidified into a consensus. A drawing in the *New York World-Telegram and Sun* pictured Mantle's swing in full extension. Below a large "Ruth's 60 Homers," the artist added two smaller lines: "Homer No. ___ for Mantle" and "Now ___ Games Ahead of Ruth's Pace." As the illustrator explains to the copy boy, "See? You just fill in the right numbers . . . and you can run this on Mondays, Wednesdays and Saturdays." Baseball had long been about "the right numbers," but in May 1956 Americans converted Mantle's glorious performance into a dogged pursuit of the home run record. It wasn't the Yankees versus the other teams of the American League or even Mantle against American League pitchers. The season was now about Mickey versus the Babe's ghost, a race between the "Wonder Boy" and the peerless legend who had died in 1948.[41]

Even Jimmy Cannon, whose attachment to Joe DiMaggio was so great that he always seemed to be secretly rooting against Mantle in the apparent belief that the young star's success somehow diminished the Yankee Clipper's brilliance, reluctantly joined the stampede. "This appears to be the year when Mickey Mantle will cross the frontier and pass into the country of greatness," he wrote.[42]

One reason for Mantle's newfound success was that he had become as comfortable in Manhattan as he was in Yankee Stadium. Early in Mantle's career, Yankee player and coach Tommy Henrich had explained to Cannon Mickey's only flaw: "He lives in Commerce, Okla., and plays ball in New York." He meant that Mantle was *in* New York but not *of* New York, that Mickey's cultural baseline remained rural Oklahoma. The further from his hometown he traveled, the more uncomfortable he became, and no place in the United States was more spatially, socially, and culturally different from Commerce than New York. There Mickey seemed like a plow horse in the Belmont Stakes.

That, Cannon asserted, had changed. "Now New York is his town as much as Commerce." As a celebrity he now moved through Midtown Manhattan as comfortably as Sinatra or DiMaggio. New Yorkers "knew him on Park Avenue and Madison Avenue," his wife, Merlyn, recalled years later, "and they were singing his name on Broadway. Everywhere we went, his admirers sent over bottles of champagne or whatever he was drinking." He didn't have to make speeches or curry favor. He was Mickey Mantle, and as long as he hit tape-measure homers for the Yankees, he ruled the city.[43]

And in May 1956 he reached new heights of performance and fame. He hit his sixteenth home run for the season against the Athletics and his seventeenth three days later against the Tigers. In the Detroit game he went 5–5, raising his batting average to .421 and his RBIs to thirty-nine. When he was intentionally walked in the seventh inning, a chorus of boos echoed throughout Briggs Stadium. Yet Mickey didn't complain. Now twelve games ahead of Ruth's home run pace, he pleased even his New York critics with his awe-shucks approach to the record. He would let Ted Williams talk about the intricacies of hitting. He merely swung at the ball. "I just hope I can keep it up. I'm just going to keep swinging and hoping. That's all that I can do." Then, stealing a page from baseball's book of clichés, he added, "I'm taking every day one at a time."[44]

Coming from a batter hitting .421 with seventeen homers, banalities read like rare insights. As never before in New York, anything with Mickey's name on it sold. There was a rush to capitalize on him. On May 26, for example, the *New York Journal-American* headlined, "The Mantle Story . . . Begin It Tomorrow!" The theme of the profile was "Can the Oklahoma Kid break Ruth's record?" In it veteran sportswriter Hugh Bradley took on such "hard-hitting" questions as "Is this hitting spree just one of those passing things?" What Bradley wrote hardly mattered any more than what Mickey said. His photograph and name in a headline sold papers.[45]

The Yankees played their thirty-ninth game of the season against Boston. It was not their most impressive performance, with Red Sox knuckler Willard Nixon taking a 7–0 shutout going into the ninth inning. Then, with two outs, Mantle parked a pitch into the right-center bleachers for his eighteenth homer. It put him nine games ahead of Ruth's pace. The Babe's eighteenth homer in 1927 did not come until the Yankees' forty-eighth contest of the year. Increasingly in New York and across the country, such minutia seemed to matter.[46]

By the end of the month, Mickey had hit twenty home runs, sixteen of them in May. No previous player in the history of the game—not even Ruth—had enjoyed such a brilliant May. In 1920 Ruth heralded a new age in the evolution of baseball. Now, in 1956, Mantle seemed poised to do the same. And all the while advertisers, television executives, and media consultants clamored for his attention. With each home run, one could almost hear an echo of the Babe: "Let's see some other son of a bitch match that."

CHAPTER 6

The Boy Has Come of Age

"Baseball is not a game for boys."
—MURRAY KEMPTON,
New York Post, 1956

It was an ideal day for baseball, especially in the eyes of a young boy. On a gloriously sunny Memorial Day afternoon, eight-year-old Billy Crystal tugged on his father's sport jacket as he followed him into Yankee Stadium, which looked to him like a cathedral. A wave of excitement washed over him and his teenage brother. The colorful sights were unlike anything Billy had ever seen on his black-and-white television. Greeted by the aroma of hot dogs, mustard, beer, and cigarettes, crowds of people streamed through the turnstiles while gatekeepers welcomed them. "Tickets, please. Yearbooks here. Programs. Tickets, please."[1]

When the Crystals reached their seats down the third base line, Billy looked in awe at a scene that seemed plucked out of *The Wizard of Oz*—the expansive emerald field, the beautifully manicured diamond, and the bright white bases sitting "like huge marshmallows." Mesmerized, he scanned the field, watching his idols, some running and throwing, while others lounged around the batting cage, laughing and shouting encouragement. For a boy growing up in New York, baseball was everything. It was the game that defined his summers, bonded him with his brother and father, and filled him with dreams of playing in the house that Ruth built.

In the fifth inning, Billy's hero, a rugged, handsome man with a bull's neck, carried a bat to the left side of the plate. Digging his spikes into the dirt, Mickey Mantle firmly planted his back foot like a stake. Bending at the knees into a deep crouch, he cocked the bat, his fingers flexed around the thin handle. He focused his eyes on the pitcher, the Washington Senators' Pedro Ramos, who nodded at the catcher, preparing to deliver a fastball. As Ramos wound up, Mantle clenched the bat, appearing—for only an instant—motionless. Then, as the ball reached the plate, he twisted his muscular torso, swinging in a flawless motion. *Crack!* The baseball took off like a rocket.[2]

Mantle's eyes followed its flight into deep right field, his bat wrapped all the way around his back. The moment the wood collided with the baseball, everyone in the stadium leapt to their feet. As he remembered it, Crystal couldn't see a thing over the tall priest standing in front of him. He only heard that *crack*, prompting him to jump onto his seat, trying to see where the baseball had landed. The ball ascended toward the gray-green facade of the far-right-field upper deck and would have flown over the stadium roof had it not hit the filigree. Stunned, the priest blocking Billy's view shouted in an Irish accent, "Holy fucking shit!"

No one had ever hit a ball that far in Yankee Stadium. No one had even come close. Not Babe Ruth, Lou Gehrig, Joe DiMaggio, Jimmie Foxx, or Hank Greenberg. Using the Reeves Analog Computer, "one of the world's most intricate computing machines," Dr. Louis Bauer and his wife, Dr. Frances Bauer, claimed that had the ball not struck the high right-field facade, it would have traveled 481 feet. For the rest of the season, whenever Yankees fans found their seats, their eyes inevitably wandered to "the Spot." "Arms point and people stare in admiration," *Sports Illustrated*'s Robert Creamer noted. That home run and the nineteen others he had hit since opening day imbued Mantle with more confidence than ever before. Sportswriters and teammates observed that he had matured, becoming more poised on and off the field. "The boy," teammate Jerry Coleman said, "has come of age."[3]

AT THE BEGINNING of June it appeared that Mantle had a legitimate chance of breaking Babe Ruth's home run record and winning the Triple Crown. Leading the majors in six hitting categories, Mantle had a .425 batting average, twenty home runs, and fifty RBIs; he was eleven games ahead of Ruth's record pace. With the Yankees six games in front of the Indians and White Sox, it seemed that nothing could stop them or Mickey, except maybe Lou Boudreau.[4]

When the Yankees faced the Kansas City Athletics on June 5, they hoped to end a three-game losing streak. However, Boudreau, the A's manager, had other plans. In the bottom of the first, when Mantle stepped to the left side of home plate, Boudreau gave his team the signal, calling for a dramatic shift toward right field. Only the A's pitcher, catcher, and first basemen remained in their traditional positions. The second baseman backed into shallow right field, the shortstop shifted over toward the second baseman's usual slot, and the third baseman played shallow center field. The left fielder moved in closer to third base, while the center and right fielders covered the deep gaps.[5]

Puzzled, Mickey saw an empty left side of the infield. He figured that Boudreau was daring him to bunt down the third baseline. He had never seen this defensive alignment, but it was not the first time that Boudreau had employed the shift against a powerful left-handed hitter. As manager of the Indians in 1946, he instructed his team to pack the right side of the field against Ted Williams, but the "Splendid Splinter" refused to take the opportunity given to him by Boudreau's shift. Hitting to the left side of the field would be too easy.

And besides, he thought, he could just drive the ball through the fielders or over them. *Damn the shift.* "If I smack the ball over the fence," he'd said, "they'll have a hard time fielding it."[6]

Facing the Boudreau shift, Williams hadn't asked anyone for advice. By contrast, Mantle looked into the dugout, hoping Casey Stengel could offer help. After reading the signals from his manager, he tried bunting, notching two foul balls before striking out. He struck out again during his second at bat and grounded out to first later on, in the sixth inning. Finally, in the eighth inning, with Hank Bauer on first, Boudreau was forced to call off the shift. Without the distracting defensive alignment, Mantle slammed a two-run home run. Still, the Yankees lost, 4–7.

Yet Mantle had shown that he wasn't afraid to sacrifice his power numbers by bunting for the good of the team. He knew that if patient, he would get a chance to drive the ball. A few days earlier, he admitted that he already sensed that something had changed for him by that point in the season. "I'm certain that I'm a better player than I have been," he said. "I think I have acquired confidence." It was that quiet confidence that made him more dangerous than ever, the kind of confidence that made pitchers nervous at the sight of him.[7]

DAY AFTER DAY, week after week, month after month, Mickey Mantle was great copy. He was the story of the season. And as long as he produced at the plate, generating daily headlines about superhuman deeds, readers demanded more stories about him, and publishers sold more newspapers. There was not a newsstand in New York, or any other major city for that matter, where people could not find a feature story about him. When he finally fulfilled his potential in the summer of 1956, leading columnists began shaping Mantle's heroic image, fashioning a tale about the country boy who made good, a modest, hardworking husband and father who overcame injuries, immaturity, and struggles at the plate to become the embodiment of the American dream.

"One thing is sure," Dan Daniel declared in *The Sporting News*. "Mantle has become a great box office attraction, an established hero." Daniel and other sportswriters noted how Mantle had become more cooperative with the press, making a clear effort to win their favor. If he had come to New York in 1951 "a scared, confused kid," the *New York Times*'s Arthur Daley suggested, he had now become a "reasonably poised man." Mantle was no longer an immature boy bashfully walking through the clubhouse with his cap pulled low. Now, he looked reporters directly in the eye. He embraced the responsibilities that came with being a professional and the game's biggest star. Studying him, Hugh Bradley agreed with Daley. "At last," the *New York Journal-American* columnist observed, "the kid has become a man."[8]

His accomplishments on the field and his improved relationships with writers led them to conceive of Mantle as an ideal man. He was the strong, silent type, modest, resilient, and reliable. He was the perfect athlete for an era when John Wayne was the nation's most popular movie star. Like Wayne and the other Western regulars, Mickey spoke sparingly. He demonstrated his character through action rather than words. In a photo essay, *Life* portrayed him as a maturing young player, "the most valuable man on the team." Boys idolized him, dreaming of being just like Mickey, while grown men marveled at his athletic feats.[9]

Mantle's ascendance occurred at a time when Americans revered traditional masculine vigor and rugged individualism. In postwar America, after GIs returned home from the battlefields of western Europe, Japan, and Korea, many felt lost working in factories and massive corporations. Ordinary men became faceless cogs of corporate America, emasculated by hierarchical organizations. In 1956 *Fortune* editor William H. Whyte argued in *The Organization Man* that a collectivist ethic made American men soft. Other writers saw the threat against traditional masculinity in a variety of sources: affluence, excessive leisure time, women in the workplace, suburbanization, and the decline of rural America—Mickey Mantle country. "For men to become men again," Harvard historian Arthur Schlesinger Jr. wrote, "their first task is to recover a sense of individual spontaneity."[10]

Sports provided men that opportunity, offering the kinds of thrills that no job could. Driving a truck or selling insurance, reporter Dan Wakefield wrote, was "predictably empty of moments of truth, glory, or excitement on the job." But baseball, he claimed, was an unpredictable game of action and risk, a sport that tested men's individual skill and mettle. Fans venerated Mantle and other ballplayers in part because they confronted the threat of injury, jeopardizing their own security and livelihoods.[11]

As the public learned how Mantle's debilitating injuries hampered his capacity to play the game, he became all the more heroic in their eyes. He embodied the tension between promise and failure, strength and fragility. His vulnerability on the field made him a flawed hero, yet more authentic and relatable. Longtime Yankees fan and comic Richard Lewis observed that Mantle appeared to be Superman in pinstripes. "But the truth is," Lewis added, "he was just a regular guy. He had this aura about him that he was just one of us."[12]

Spectators in the stands seemed to identify with Mantle. It was almost as if, writers suggested, they lived vicariously through his performances. Each game, each time he went to bat, offered him—and them—a shot at redemption, the opportunity to demonstrate self-worth and prove that the lone individual still mattered. Sacrificing his body, he displayed his manliness on the field: running hard around the bases on brittle legs, sliding across the dirt into home, crashing into outfield walls. But most of all, men admired him for the way he harnessed his raw power, punishing fastballs and crushing home runs farther than any other man. "That's what made the male regard Mantle that way," Dodgers pitcher Ed Roebuck said. His towering home runs did more than break stadium records. Those tape-measure shots defined him as the quintessential man. A few seasons later, when a reporter asked what made Mantle so special, Yankees publicist Jackie Ferrell answered, "He led the league in manhood every year."[13]

MICKEY'S BRAWN MADE HIM the "most valuable property anywhere in the baseball world." By early June, he had become a commodity, the face of Mickey Mantle Enterprises, Inc. His agent, Frank Scott, a diminutive, fast-talking man, opened an office at 400 Madison Avenue where he bargained with advertisers, television executives, and corporate sponsors. Before the season, Shirley Povich noted, Scott's "efforts to peddle Mantle" generated little enthusiasm. "The Madison Avenue set had put him on a don't call us we'll call you basis." But after Mantle's torrid May, corporate reps "began calling madly."[14]

Capitalizing on Mantle's blossoming popularity, Scott made sure that his handsome face appeared everywhere: television shows, print ads, and "every magazine cover except the *Ladies Home Journal*." In the month of June, he graced *Newsweek* and *Life* as well as *Sports Illustrated* and *The Sporting News*. Never before had a baseball player appeared on the cover of all four periodicals in the same month. Readers devoured stories about the reluctant hero who squirmed when journalists reminded him of his greatness. In the midst of his finest season, Mantle continued professing that he could not understand why he received so much attention. But whether he liked it or not, "he was now public property."[15]

Mantle's bank account benefitted from the attention and Scott's connections. Scott's career in baseball began well before Mantle arrived in New York. When he became the Yankees' traveling secretary in 1947, Scott never thought that he would one day become baseball's most successful agent. But George Weiss believed that his responsibilities as traveling secretary required that he also act as the team's private eye, spying on players who broke curfew or shared a room with a woman. Scott refused to be Weiss's snitch, and his loyalty to the players cost him his job.[16]

After Weiss fired him on October 24, 1950, Scott left the Yankees but stayed in baseball, offering to manage the players' business interests for a modest 10 percent fee. He convinced them that if they performed well, he could help them earn money from television appearances, testimonials, and merchandising. Phil Rizzuto, Yogi Berra, Hank Bauer, and Eddie Lopat agreed immediately. "Those first players signed with me out of friendship," Scott said, "and I'll never forget them for it." The players trusted him because he was honest and direct. As he told them, "If I don't make anything for you, then I make ten percent of nothing. I get my fee only on the business I can line up for you."[17]

Gradually, Scott signed more Yankees—including Mantle in 1953—and other New York players too. Willie Mays, Duke Snider, Roy Campanella, Pee Wee Reese, Monte Irvin, and Bobby Thomson joined his list of clients. By 1956, he represented nearly ninety major-league players, most of whom were well known in New York—whether or not they played in the city—the headquarters of the nation's advertising, publishing, and television firms. But Scott would not sign just any player. He wanted stars. "If a guy bats .250," he told a reporter, "I can't do anything for him."[18]

Selling Mickey Mantle to Madison Avenue was easier than selling beer at Yankee Stadium. The more home runs he hit, the higher his stock rose, and the more fees Scott collected for appearances and testimonials. In New York, Yankees players commanded the highest endorsement fees. "People buy winners, not losers," Scott explained. Throughout the season, the savvy agent worked the phones, letting sponsors know that for $5,000 his client would lend his name to a product for a year. Soon, Mantle's likeness appeared in ads for more than ten companies, including Wheaties ("Champions are made not born"), Wonderbread ("Helps build strong bodies 12 ways!"), GEM razor blades ("'GEM gives me more clean shaves than *any* other blade,' says Mickey Mantle"), Batter Up pancakes ("Mr. Batter Up, Mickey Mantle, says, 'Make everyday a Batter Up day. I do!'"), Viceroy cigarettes ("Mickey Mantle, New York Yankees' home run champion, says: 'Viceroys are richer tasting . . . smoother by far! From my very first puff—man, it was Viceroys for me!'"), and Rawlings ("Make your next glove a Mickey Mantle—a glove that's already set a new record in preference and performance!"). Together, Scott and Mantle were the most successful branding partners since Christy Walsh discovered that Babe Ruth could sell soda pop, candy bars, and cars.[19]

Advertisers were eager to pay for Mickey's services because they understood customers were not drawn merely to the product. They bought a brand, what David Ogilvy, "the father of advertising" described as "the sum of a product's attributes." Mantle's public image, his brand, was representative of Middle America, the innocence and strength of the heartland. He was a winner, the face of American sports. Ogilvy understood the advantages of transforming a symbol or a character into a brand. "Don't bunt," he advised fellow admen. "Aim out of the park. Aim for the company of immortals."[20]

With his bright smile, Mickey was the perfect face for national advertising. His appeal derived from his small-town roots and folksy lifestyle, seemingly unchanged and uncorrupted by life in the city. "Mick is a kid from a small town who doesn't ever want to become a big-city guy," Billy Martin said. "He's most comfortable when he's home with his buddies in Commerce. He feels they understand him better. When I was in the Army, Mickey visited me at Fort Carson, Colorado, and all my buddies thought he was the greatest guy in the world. He's the most modest, unassuming, kindest guy I've known."[21]

Sportswriters portrayed Mantle as the antithesis of Babe Ruth, who was remembered as an overgrown adolescent who possessed an insatiable appetite for whiskey and women. Mantle, on the other hand, "seldom drinks and still is not at ease with a cigar," the *New York Journal-American*'s Hugh Bradley wrote, failing to mention that he endorsed Viceroy cigarettes. Bradley insisted that there was no truth to rumors of Mantle's late-night carousing. "I know what I'm talking about," he wrote. "There are no secrets on a ball club."[22]

The New York beat writers acted as if they were on the Yankees' payroll, protecting Mantle's wholesome image. And Mantle fully understood that the code between players and writers insulated him. "In those days," Mantle reflected years later, "there was an unwritten rule among the baseball reporters: If the way you spent your free time didn't hurt the club, then it was off the record."[23]

Journalists sanitized his private life, manufacturing the Mantle myth. "The Mantles definitely are not club folks," Dan Daniel explained, neglecting the fact that Mickey regularly frequented Toots Shor's, the Copacabana, and Danny's Hideaway without his wife. Columnists portrayed him as the ideal husband and father. Teenage sweethearts, Mickey and Merlyn were "happily married" with two young sons, living the dream of suburban affluence in their summer home in River Edge, New Jersey. Advertisers trumpeted the fairy tale of domestic tranquility. "If we had gone knocking on doors looking for the typical young American family which had been clean-scrubbed and was handsome to boot, we couldn't have turned up a finer one than the Mantles," said an adman from Madison Avenue.[24]

America might have known Mickey as the greatest baseball player in the game, but at home he was just a husband and father. "We hardly ever discuss [baseball]," Merlyn said. "When he comes home he plays with little Mickey or we go to a drive-in movie. I like to go to the games, but I don't feel I know enough about baseball to discuss it with Mickey." The Mantles were portrayed as prototypical 1950s family: "Mr. Mantle" worked in the city, and "Mrs. Mantle" stayed home and raised the children. Mrs. Mantle was "strictly down-to-earth and unaffected by her husband's fame," a reporter noted. "The red-headed ex-drum majorette is the kind of gal who has to be reminded that her spouse is Mister Big in Baseball."[25]

In the city, far enough away from home, the Yankees front office knew a different Mickey Mantle. In early June, the team's executives learned that the FBI was investigating an attempt to extort $15,000 from the premier player. The blackmailers claimed that Mantle had

Family man—this is the image of Mickey Mantle created by the New York and national media in 1956. Mickey with his wife, Merlyn, and his sons, Mickey Jr. and David, living the suburban dream in New Jersey. Mickey was also living another, less publicized life. *Courtesy of Getty Images.*

been caught in "a compromising situation with a married woman" and threatened to go to the tabloids. Mickey claimed that the report was a lie. He admitted that he had "shacked up" with many women in New York but claimed he had "never been caught."[26]

GEORGE WEISS WAS NOT afraid of resorting to gimmicks to put fans in the seats. During World War II, when Major League Baseball suffered through years of abysmal attendance, the Yankees, like most teams, created Ladies' Days, offering gifts and reduced admission to women. As enticements, baseball clubs offered women free cosmetics, flowers, and leggings at the entrance gate. But it would take more than free nylons for the Yankees' female fans to return to the ballpark after Ladies' Day 1956. It was June 9, a Saturday, and the Indians crushed the Yankees 15–8.[27]

Don Larsen pitched his worst game of the season. After starting on opening day, he gradually lost command of his pitches, and Casey Stengel lost his patience. After Larsen surrendered five runs in five innings, including two homers, Stengel pulled him with the bases loaded in the sixth. After the game, the skipper told reporters that he had seen enough of Larsen on the mound. "Larsen has had 10 starts now," he grumbled, "and too many times he's been out of there by the fifth or sixth inning. Maybe it's time for someone else to get a chance." Stengel demoted the pitcher, with his ballooning 5.56 earned run average, to the bullpen, unsure when he would return to the starting rotation.[28]

Larsen's erratic pitching added to the immense stress in his personal life. His "extra-curricular activities," one reporter noted, "are legendary." He enjoyed the life of a bachelor, carousing and drinking well into the night. "Larsen was easily the greatest drinker I've known," Mantle later recalled, "and I've known some pretty good ones in my time." When Larsen arrived at spring training earlier that year, he announced that he would act more responsibly. "I'm through living it up," he declared. "I'm buckling down to business. This time I mean it."[29]

About a month later, though, at around 5:00 a.m., he crashed his brand-new Oldsmobile convertible into a telephone pole. Fortunately, he suffered only a chipped tooth. Reporters didn't press him when he claimed that he had fallen asleep at the wheel, though he later admitted to Casey Stengel that he had visited St. Petersburg's "watering holes."

Writers were surprised that the Yankees didn't punish Larsen. "Fine him?" Stengel said. "He oughta get an award, finding something to do in this town after midnight."[30]

By the time Stengel demoted him to the bullpen, Larsen had stopped speaking to his wife. What nobody knew—not even his teammates—was that he had married a woman named Vivian about a year earlier, after she called him and said that she was pregnant. Initially Don wanted her to put the baby up for adoption, but she refused. He decided that he would marry her but they would not live together. Larsen felt trapped in a marriage he never wanted. "I'm not ready to settle down," he told her. "I prefer to live a free and carefree existence." So he stopped returning her calls, struggling to protect his secret.[31]

DON LARSEN WAS NOT the only Yankee laboring to little effect against the Indians. After going 1–4 at the plate, Mantle's batting average fell below .400 for the first time since May 23. Some New York fans were worried, now that the Indians were only 2.5 games behind the Yankees, but if Mantle was concerned, he didn't show it on the night of June 9, when he appeared on the popular crooner Perry Como's television show.

By the summer, Frank Scott's most marketable client commanded a league-leading $1,000 per television appearance. Before the show, Como's producer insisted that Mickey study the script, suspecting that the star center fielder might be too much of a hayseed to read the teleprompter. Scott maintained that Mickey didn't need that kind of preparation. If he fumbled his lines, Scott promised, then he would refuse the booking fee. Mantle delivered his lines like a Broadway thespian, impressing the host. "He can't miss," Como said afterward. "Everything he says, he says with a smile, and I'd say his smile is fifty percent blush. That makes the audience a pushover."[32]

Television made baseball stars like Mantle into celebrities. People who were not necessarily Yankees fans or even baseball fans knew Mickey Mantle because they had seen him on TV. New Yorkers could watch every one of his home games and most road games, and fans throughout the country could tune in for the nationally televised *Game of the Week*, which often featured the Yankees. By 1956, more Americans had watched him play on the small screen than had seen Babe Ruth or Joe DiMaggio in person. Most fans had only listened to a radio announcer describe the Babe's swing or heard the crack of

DiMaggio's bat. But with television, viewers could witness Mantle's strength, speed, and grace. Seeing him perform convinced many fans that he was the best player of all time—because he was the best player they had ever seen.[33]

Television substantially increased Mantle's income. One paid appearance could earn him a bigger paycheck in ninety seconds than his father made in an entire month toiling in the zinc mines. Playing for the Yankees increased the demand for his services. "The biggest names, of course, are always the easiest to sell on TV," Frank Scott told *The Sporting News*. Earlier in his career, Mantle had shied away from TV appearances, but once he realized how much money he could make just for smiling on camera, he eagerly agreed to visit the studios. "He likes to fondle those checks he's stacking up to take to the bank," Scott said. "He never used to ask how much we were getting for a show. Now he likes to make those big scores."[34]

In 1956, Mantle cashed more checks from endorsements and appearances than any other player in baseball. He earned nearly $60,000 above his regular salary—about double what the Yankees paid him.

But if Mantle kept hitting home runs for the rest of the summer, his endorsement earnings would far outpace his salary. Although he and Willie Mays earned the same player salary, the Giants center fielder, a former MVP, made only about $8,500 in royalties, television appearances, and testimonials, a paltry sum compared to Mickey's. Both men were stars playing in New York, represented by Frank Scott. The difference, of course, was that Mays was black. When a Cincinnati "food outfit" approached Scott about using "All-Stars" for a national advertising campaign, he suggested the ads include four leading black players. The advertising director, horrified by the idea, berated the agent and demanded four white players. Scott balked at the order and called off the deal.[35]

Major League Baseball—and its corporate partners—marketed the game for a white audience. Eager to capitalize on the baby boom and baseball's popularity among America's youth, Topps Chewing Gum, Inc., the premier baseball card manufacturer, presented the players as

In 1956 every kid who opened a package of Topps Baseball Picture Cards wanted card number 135. Holding the Mickey Mantle card made them feel special, like they had touched greatness. *Courtesy of the National Baseball Hall of Fame. Image used with permission from The Topps Company, Inc.*

heroes in order to sell bubble gum. For a nickel kids could buy a package of seven cards and two sheets of gum. As much as newspapers, books, or sports announcers, baseball cards educated children about the sport, race, and American values. In the early years of integration, when Major League Baseball promoted itself as a democratic, meritocratic game offering equal opportunities to black players, the overwhelming number of cards children saw showed white faces. At the same time, as black Latinos broke into the major leagues, Topps whitewashed their images, anglicizing the names of players like Roberto Clemente. Without his permission, Topps transformed the proud black Puerto Rican into "Bob Clemente," recasting him as more "American" and less threatening.[36]

In the 1950s, advertisers feared that white consumers would not buy products promoted by "Negro" spokesmen, which meant more business went to Mickey Mantle than otherwise would have. His emergence as a popular icon occurred at the same time that black players were excelling. Between 1951 and 1959, blacks won eight of the nine National League MVP awards. And yet, corporate sponsors were far less interested in Mays, Roy Campanella, Don Newcombe, Ernie Banks, and Hank Aaron than in Mickey Mantle.

If the National League witnessed the emergence of a generation of black stars, the pace of integration in the American League was much slower. Black American Leaguers were invisible. Some appeared on the field in supporting roles, but they were nowhere to be found when the year-end awards were passed out. During the 1950s Yogi Berra won three MVP awards and Mantle won two, but no black player won the league MVP until Elston Howard in 1963.

National League star Hank Aaron knew the score. "Baseball has done a lot for me," he said. "It has taught me that regardless of who you are and regardless of how much money you make, you are still a Negro."[37]

MICKEY MANTLE WAS IN no mood to spend his day off watching a Broadway play, especially one about the Yankees losing the pennant. On the evening of June 11, after dropping two of three games to Cleveland, Mantle and his teammates boarded a team bus. Most of the guys didn't want to go to the 46th Street Theatre. Some didn't even show up. And Mickey wished he hadn't.[38]

Damn Yankees! was the first—and Mickey claimed the last—play he ever saw. In the opening scene, Joe Boyd, a hapless middle-aged Washington Senators fan, curses the Yankees after watching them defeat his beloved team on television. His wife goes to bed, but Joe continues to grumble about the lowly Senators. He swears that he would sell his soul for the Senators to acquire a young power hitter who could "lick those damn Yankees." Suddenly, the devil disguised as a mysterious man named Applegate makes him an offer he can't refuse: for the price of his soul, the disheartened real estate agent can become a supernatural hitter—Joe Hardy—and save the Senators from futility—if he agrees to leave his wife.[39]

Boyd accepts the offer, but in the end, after living out his baseball fantasy, he misses his wife too much. Breaking the deal with the devil, he returns to his natural form at the precise moment he makes a remarkable game-winning catch to secure the pennant.

Joe Boyd first appeared in 1954 as the protagonist in a novel written by Douglass Wallop, a frustrated Senators fan and closeted "Yankee admirer." In *The Year the Yankees Lost the Pennant*, Joe sells his soul after Applegate suggests that it's almost tragic that he might die and never see another team win the pennant. What matters most to Joe, more than the Senators' triumph, is the demise of the Yankees dynasty. Wallop understood the unlikelihood that the Senators—"First in war, first in peace, last in the American League"—would steal the pennant away from the Yankees. Only the devil could make that happen. Or the Cleveland Indians. On September 18, 1954, six days after the *New York Times* reviewed Wallop's novel, the Indians clinched the American League championship.[40]

It seemed miraculous that the Yankees didn't win the American League pennant that season. Between 1927 and 1953 the Yankees won fifteen championships in sixteen World Series appearances. After winning five straight titles between 1949 and 1953, Casey Stengel's team appeared destined to win the pennant in perpetuity. Disgusted by the Yankees' dominance, a Chicago writer groused, "The day the Yankees lose the pennant will be the greatest since V-J Day." But a year later, Chicagoans celebrated with Cleveland when the Indians won a record 111 games and the AL pennant. The Yankees may have fallen short of making the playoffs, but with 103 wins the Bronx Bombers still had their best record since 1942.[41]

For nearly two decades, since Joe DiMaggio first arrived in New York, baseball fans across the country had cried, "Break up the Yankees!" Club executives, fans, and writers accused the team of being a baseball monopoly. The Yanks won more championships, the *Los*

Angeles Times's Jim Murray charged, because they had "more fans paying more money than any other club in the history of the game."[42]

There was some truth to Murray's claim, but the Yankees' formula for success was not that simple. The New York team consistently generated higher revenues because it drew more fans on the road and therefore received a greater portion of the gate receipts than any other AL club, appeared in more World Series, and profited from greater broadcasting fees. As the biggest road draw in baseball, the Yankees pocketed a greater share of ticket receipts. Furthermore, they did not have to split revenues from local radio or television broadcasts with visiting teams. The owners also agreed to allocate national television receipts based on how often a team appeared on CBS's *Game of the Week*. Fortunately for the Yankees, the network preferred to show their home games more than those of other clubs at a time when the network only paid the home team for telecasts. These inequities further exacerbated the competitive imbalance. By the end of the 1950s, the Yankees were making more than $1 million a year from broadcast fees, while Joe Boyd's lowly Senators only received $150,000.[43]

The whole system seemed rigged in favor of big-market teams. St. Louis Browns owner Bill Veeck lamented that the broadcasting agreement created league-wide disparities. "With all that TV money they're getting," he said, "the Yankees can continue to keep outbidding us for talent. They've signed $500,000 worth of bonus players in the last couple of years, paying them with all that TV money we help provide." Veeck recognized that media revenues had become increasingly important over the previous decade. In 1956, radio and TV income represented 17 percent of total team revenues, up from 3 percent a decade earlier. "None of us is ever going to catch up with the Yankees at that rate," he concluded.[44]

The Yankees' affluence generated widespread antagonism among opposing fans. There was something unfair and undemocratic about the Yankees' accumulated wealth. The Yanks, Douglass Wallop wrote, were "exasperating, irritating, and, if not downright un-American, certainly disruptive of American institutions." Critics believed that the Yankees played with arrogance, and their entitled fans were just as bad, if not worse, than the players themselves. In the public imagination, Yankees fans represented corporate America. They were advertising executives who drove Cadillacs and drank wine in the exclusive Stadium Club. They were aristocrats and big-business Republicans. "Wall Street bankers supposedly back the Yankees," Gay Talese wrote. "Smith College girls approve of them; God, Brooks Brothers, and United States Steel are believed to be solidly in the Yankees' corner."[45]

Yet most Yankees fans were not bankers and business tycoons, of course. The team had countless blue-collar, beer-drinking supporters in the South Bronx. "The Yankee fan," Charles Dexter wrote in 1954, "is faceless and nameless. He comes from all levels of society, from all parts of the nation, and even from foreign lands."[46]

Regular fans identified with the players, knowing that they came from humble beginnings and grew up in neighborhoods similar to their own. An Italian immigrant, Yogi Berra's father came to St. Louis knowing nothing about baseball. Billy Martin grew up fatherless in a penurious neighborhood in West Berkeley, California. Whitey Ford was raised in Astoria, Queens, on a block thick with second-generation Irish, Italian, and Polish families. And Mickey Mantle came of age in a dusty mining town in the heartland. The team's roster represented the country in microcosm, plucked from ordinary circumstances. Together, the Yankee stars embodied a cross section of working-class America.

AFTER HIS TORRID START to the 1956 season, Mickey Mantle seemed destined to win the Triple Crown. The Yankees' beat writers were convinced that he would do it. By June 15, he held a comfortable lead in all three batting categories. Hitting .392, he led Detroit's Charlie Maxwell in batting average by twenty-one points, and he had hit twenty-two home runs, six more than Yogi Berra. Together, Mantle and Berra had earned a reputation as the "greatest one-two punch the Bombers have boasted since Babe Ruth and Lou Gehrig." Only Kansas City's Harry Simpson stood within ten RBIs of Mantle's commanding lead.[47]

Three days later, with Mantle appearing on the cover of *Sports Illustrated*, the magazine announced that "The Year of the Slugger" had arrived. There was no better proof of Mantle's preeminence than his eighth-inning blast that afternoon at Briggs Stadium. With two men on and no outs, the Yankees and Tigers were tied 4–4. Behind the plate, with a brisk fifteen-mile-per-hour wind blowing in from right field, the Detroit catcher told Mickey that the gusts were too strong for him. "Mickey," Frank House said in an Alabama drawl, "you ain't gonna hit one out of here today."[48]

Mantle ignored him, focusing all of his attention on Tigers pitcher Paul Foytack. Then he smashed a letter-high fastball deep toward right field. House rose from his catcher's squat, watching in disbelief as the ball continued to rise until it landed on the second deck of the roof, 110 feet off the ground. When the ball bounded onto Trumball Avenue, several parking attendants rushed onto the busy street to nab it, but they were too slow. A taxi driver spotted the bouncing ball on the pavement, slammed the breaks, and jumped out of the car. He scooped up the souvenir, hopped back into his car, and sped away "as if he had robbed a bank."[49]

After the game, dozens of writers circled Mantle's locker as he relaxed with a cold beer. Detroit's reporters could hardly remember the last time a player had hit a home run out of Briggs Stadium. In fact, only once before—in 1939, when Ted Williams clobbered a ball just inside the foul line—had a player accomplished the feat. While reporters buzzed around the locker room, Mickey's teammates debated which of his home runs had traveled the farthest.[50]

Two days later, he hit two more home runs from the right side of the plate, his twenty-sixth and twenty-seventh of the year. More remarkable than his power display, though, was the spectators' response. The crowd got so excited that the game had to be stopped twice when people ran onto the field. Hoping to get close to Mantle or shake his hand, nearly two dozen fans of all ages, boys and girls, "came pouring out from the four corners" of the stadium during the ninth inning. Watching from the press box the local writers were amazed. "I've seen a lot of famous ballplayers play the game in Briggs Stadium," a telegrapher said, "but never have I seen any demonstration like the one they gave Mantle."[51]

After the final out, a mob flooded the field. "This time," one writer observed, "it was a mass movement. Hundreds of them came out of the stands. From where I sat, they looked like bugs." As the crowd swarmed him, Mantle clutched his hat, breaking for the Yankees' dugout. The groundskeepers had to turn on the sprinklers just to get the fans off the field.[52]

Outside New York, baseball fans didn't care that Mantle played for the Yankees. "To youngsters," the *New York Post*'s Leonard Koppett wrote, "a hero's a hero no matter what team he plays on." Mickey had become a folk hero, "baseball's Paul Bunyan," a larger-than-life figure whose exploits on the field were quickly relayed as tall tales of superhuman power. "Mr. Muscles" was a symbol of might and vigor. From ballparks to bars, from street corners to schoolyards, Mantle was the "most talked about player in the land." "In every ballpark," Koppett wrote, "someone has a story to tell about" Mantle hitting a home run "where no one had ever hit one before."[53]

From Detroit the Yankees traveled to Chicago, where more than 47,000 fans packed Comiskey Park for a doubleheader—the stadium's largest crowd of the year. In this case, the demonstrations Mickey inspired were not joyous and peaceful. In the late innings of the second game, drunken fans heckled and cursed Mantle from the bleachers, tossing food and trash at him. A wild pack of men stormed center field, scaring Mantle until police hauled them away. "How do I know what those fans are going to do?" he asked reporters afterward, clearly alarmed. "They may stick out a hand, they may stick out a knife." Handling fame proved more difficult than hitting a curveball. "If I were to shove a fan out of the way," he added, "I would be hooted out of the park. You should hear what they holler at me. Can't something be done?"[54]

But on the whole the tumult in Chicago was an aberration. Writers filed columns about Mantle's popularity in stadiums throughout the American League. Fans who used to jeer the Yankees, a *New York Times* writer observed, were now cheering the Bronx Bombers all because of Mantle. League president Will Harridge noticed the shift. "Everywhere I went this morning, in the restaurant, in the elevator, and in the barber shop, it was Mantle, Mantle, Mantle." The White Sox's first sellout pleased Harridge too. In the burgeoning television age, when owners and executives feared that too many fans would prefer watching baseball at home, Mantle lured people to the park in a way that no player had since DiMaggio during his 1941 hitting streak.[55]

Comparing Mantle to Ruth, some reporters wondered if Mickey benefitted from a livelier ball. Were his home runs the product of his natural ability? Or were baseballs being manufactured differently than in the past? Harridge adamantly denied that the balls were "juiced." "The specifications for their manufacture is the same, hasn't changed in years," he said. "The workmanship, due to improved machinery, is probably superior, but, I repeat, the specifications are the same."[56]

The president of Spalding, the major leagues' ball manufacturer, agreed. "There definitely has been no change in the baseball for a number of years," Walter Gerould said. In truth players were hitting more home runs in 1956 because of the players' increased size and bat speed and their strategy at the plate. Twenty years earlier, the average baseball player stood two to three inches shorter and weighed ten to twenty pounds less, depending on the position. Standing five foot eleven and weighing 196 pounds, Mantle was built like a heavyweight boxer with nearly identical proportions to Rocky Marciano's.[57]

"The Muscle Men" of the 1950s did not choke up on thick-handled bats like Ty Cobb or Rogers Hornsby, who poked the ball across the infield. Instead, they swung from their shoestrings using lighter, slender-handled bats that bent "like a reed when swung hard" and could easily snap but could produce blurring velocity through the strike zone. When Babe Ruth hit sixty home runs in 1927, he swung a sledgehammer—Black Betsy, for instance, weighed forty-two ounces, nearly ten ounces more than the toothpick Mantle used.[58]

Mantle may have used a lighter bat than the Babe, but Yankees coach Bill Dickey, who played with Ruth, said that it didn't matter what kind of wood he used or if the balls were juiced. "Regardless of whether the ball is dead or lively, if Mantle hits it right, it goes a long way. Mickey has more power than Ruth or Gehrig had. I've never seen anyone who could hit the ball so far."[59]

Some writers suggested that the best players were hitting more home runs than the stars of the past, but that was inaccurate. The game's strongest batters—Mantle, Mays, Duke Snider, Eddie Matthews, and Ted Kluszewski—were not hitting more home runs than Gehrig, Hank Greenberg, or Jimmie Foxx. But more players were hitting home runs. In 1946, major leaguers hit 1,215 homers. Remarkably, a decade later they tallied 2,249—nearly 90 percent more. Why? Giants executive Garry Schumacher suggested that players valued the home run more than ever before. "Players have found that the long ball pays off and they're going for it, even at the expense of averages and base hits."[60]

Schumacher was right. Increasingly, since the 1930s, hitters had swung for the fences, striking out at a higher rate. During the Depression, 41 percent of regular players hit .300 or better, but in the 1950s that number fell to 19 percent. In 1936, the typical player hit .284, but twenty years later he hit .258. The latest strategy emphasized getting men on base and driving them home with the long ball, and power hitters like Mantle were in great demand. National League president Warren Giles explained that scouting had changed after World War

II, when teams increasingly searched for young men who could pull the ball. The primary question scouts asked was, "How far can he hit the ball?"[61]

In the summer of 1956, no one hit the ball farther than Mickey Mantle. He was distinct in other respects too. On July 1, at Yankee Stadium, in the second game of a doubleheader against Washington, "the Switcher" hit home runs from the left and the right side of the plate. This was not the first game in which he homered from both sides. Earlier in the season, on May 18, he had victimized two White Sox pitchers at Comiskey Park. But this time he belted a dramatic game-winning two-run homer in the bottom of the ninth. When he pounded his twenty-ninth home run, the crowd erupted. The fans had paid to see Mickey hit a homer, and he had delivered beyond their expectations.[62]

After the contest, a reporter asked him how it felt to win the game with a walk-off home run. "It's the greatest feeling in the world," Mantle said with a boyish grin. "Going around the bases that last time, you feel like a king."[63]

CHAPTER 7

The Gods

"If Mantle fails to become the 10th Triple Crown winner in modern baseball history, the man most likely to frustrate him is [Ted] Williams, the man who won the Triple Crown in 1942 and 1947."

—HAROLD KAESE,
Boston Globe, July 4, 1956

The debate was over, at least for the season. Everyone knew who was the best player in baseball. It wasn't Willie Mays or Duke Snider or Hank Aaron. It was Mickey Mantle. "This season, Mantle has come finally to a point where he is generally regarded as the best baseball player in the world and is given a serious chance to become the best ball player of all time," wrote *Newsweek*'s Roger Kahn.[1]

By early July, Mantle had become something more than the game's greatest player. He had become a national attraction. At a time when fans still mailed their All-Star ballots to newspaper offices and radio and television stations, Mantle received more votes than any other player. He was the only All-Star to break 200,000, earning 15,000 more than Yogi Berra, 30,000 more than Stan Musial, 70,000 more than Ted Williams, and 160,000 more than Willie Mays.[2]

His value to the Yankees and the American League could be measured with every home run. "The home run hitter, not the bunter," Shirley Povich explained, "fills the parks." While the typical American League game averaged about 12,000 fans, when the Bronx Bombers traveled to those same cities, some 22,000 spectators clicked the turnstiles to see "Mr. Box Office." In nearly every American League city—Baltimore, Boston, Chicago, Cleveland, Kansas City, and Washington—the Yankees' opponents set attendance highs when Mickey came to town. "Just to watch Mickey Mantle swing a bat is worth the price of admission," the New York Times announced.[3]

Mantle's monumental feats both shaped and reflected American culture during the mid-1950s, an age of instant gratification and consumerism. The decade was one of broad prosperity, a boom time of construction and expansion. Everything seemed to be getting bigger and better: rising skyscrapers disappeared into the heavens, ribbons of highways knit the country together, two-story shopping malls sprouted on the outskirts of towns, and split-level homes sprang up on spacious lots. America's astounding economic growth spurred massive consumption. Advertisers challenged notions of thrift that had been commonplace before the 1950s. Americans were encouraged to buy now and pay later. Young adults with little memory of the Great Depression eagerly purchased chrome-trimmed cars, television sets, and household appliances on credit. "Never has a whole people spent so much money on so many expensive things in such an easy way as Americans are doing today," Fortune announced in 1956.[4]

The widespread fascination with Mantle's awesome power at the plate revealed American reverence for the "bigger is better" philosophy. "The American public is aggressive," Ford's director of styling, George Walker, observed. "It's moving upward all the time . . . and that means bigness. When the American workingman gets a little money he wants a bigger house and he wants a bigger car." Consumers demanded wider automobiles, larger refrigerators, bigger television sets—and longer home runs.[5]

In the summer of 1956, Mickey Mantle, an American colossus, personified and fulfilled the country's most fervent desires.

"FENWAY PARK, IN BOSTON, is a lyric little bandbox of a ballpark," John Updike once wrote. "Everything is painted green and seems in curiously sharp focus, like the inside of an old-fashioned peeping-type Easter Egg." Unlike the vast Yankee Stadium, Fenway's cramped boundaries created an intimacy between the fans and players. Sitting at field level along the baselines, spectators enveloped the grass. The narrow foul territory made life difficult for pitchers since many foul balls that fielders would have caught in other stadiums instead fell into the stands.[6]

The stadium's peculiarities tested the players' talents. The outfield wall itself was asymmetrical and irregular. The deep gap where center and right field merged formed a triangle. A ricochet off the wall just to the left of the bullpen could transform a baseball into a pinball and turn a routine double into an inside-the-park home run. Although Fenway's deep right field made it difficult for left-handers to pull home runs, the high left-field wall, only 315 feet from home plate along the foul line, almost dared right-handed hitters to pummel it.

In 1956, though, there was only one reason for Red Sox fans to visit Fenway: Ted Williams. For the previous three seasons—and for the rest of the decade—the Red Sox played mediocre baseball, never finishing closer than twelve games behind the pennant winner, which was usually the Yankees. In 1952, when Ted joined the marines, the Red Sox entered a rebuilding phase, reconstructing the roster with a "cargo of youthful innocents." After Captain Williams returned from Korea late in the 1953 season, appearing in only thirty-seven games, the Red Sox, he said, "were no longer a factor." He hardly recognized the new kids in the clubhouse. Gone were all his old buddies: Bobby

Doerr, Johnny Pesky, and Dom DiMaggio (Joe's brother). Without them, playing baseball just wasn't as much fun.[7]

During spring training, Williams was asked whether he could still handle the bat as brilliantly as before. "Let's face it," he said, "I'm 37 years old. I won't hit .350 forever." He was unsure how much longer he would play at all. Two years earlier, shortly after breaking his collarbone during a tumble in the outfield, he had threatened to retire. Now, weighing thirty pounds more than the beanpole who came to Boston in 1939, he moved a little slower, dealing with the aches from twelve full seasons and two military stints. It was time, he said, to face reality. Few players could still hit at his age. "Foxx was all through at 37," he reminded reporters. "Greenberg was all through. DiMaggio was all through." But did Teddy Ballgame really believe that he was all through too?[8]

A few minutes before his pessimistic self-evaluation, he had displayed the same boundless arrogance that led him to once declare, "I'm the best goddam hitter in the world." Standing in the batting cage, he was speaking to the pitcher, to the writers, and to himself, always in his naturally stentorian voice. He turned to a writer and wagered that he could hit a ball over the right-field fence. Williams gave the writer favorable odds: "Two and a half to one. Twenty-five bucks to 10." The writer agreed. Ted had seven fair balls to win the bet.[9]

Williams grinned, relishing any opportunity to prove a writer wrong. "Hey Sully," he shouted to pitcher Frank Sullivan. "I'll give you $12.50 if you groove it." Everyone in the Red Sox camp stopped what they were doing, riveting their eyes on Williams. In the still of the Sarasota sun, he muttered to himself, "Over the wall." Standing fairly erect, he held the bat almost perpendicular to the ground, firmly gripping it with his fingers. Sullivan threw three fastballs, but Williams failed to pull them. Then, on the fourth pitch, Ted eyed a fastball right where he wanted it. Cocking his hips, he stepped forward with his right foot, uncoiled his body, and snapped his arms and wrists in a graceful motion. *Whack!* The ball sailed high into right field until it dropped over the wall. "There," Williams barked. "Into the lousy trailer camp."[10]

Whatever hopes the Fenway faithful had for the season quickly vanished in early April when Ted slipped on a shower clog, injuring the arch in his right foot. For more than five weeks, he didn't start a game, though he occasionally pinch-hit. Sitting on the bench, he grew restless. By the time he returned against the Yankees on May 29, sportswriters had discovered that Mickey Mantle stories sold more newspapers than reports about an aging and injured Williams. Boston columnists suggested that the Yankee slugger had replaced him as the best hitter in baseball. "When the ballplayers start to talk about another player like the Sox were talking about Mantle tonight," the *Boston Globe*'s Cliff Keane wrote on June 19, "you know he's great. They're talking about him the way that they used to talk about Williams years ago." After Mantle hit two more home runs the following day, Harold Kaese's *Globe* column headlined, "Red Sox Need Homers from Ted to Win."[11]

Williams accepted the challenge. The next day, he hit his first home run of the season—and a brief, spectacular rivalry was born. It was classic Teddy Ballgame, crusty and resilient, motivated by the doubters. For years, Boston columnists had written Williams off. This would be the year, they said, that his body betrayed him. But he always roared back, Updike wrote in 1960, "back from Korea, back from a broken collarbone, a shattered elbow, a bruised heel, back from drastic bouts of the flu and ptomaine poisoning. Hardly a season went by without some enfeebling mishap, yet he always came back, and always looked like himself."[12]

Williams refused to concede his self-proclaimed title as the best hitter in the game. His fierce inner pride, his single-minded determination, drove him during every at bat. Failure at the plate was unacceptable. It made his blood boil. That fury, he believed, made him a better hitter. Cursing beneath his breath, he stepped into the batter's box demanding perfection. He told his younger teammate Jimmy

Piersall, "Kid, there's only one way for you to become a hitter. Go up to the plate and get mad. Get mad at yourself and mad at the pitcher."[13]

By the time the Yankees rolled into Boston on July 4, Ted Williams was hotter than a habanero. In the previous fifteen games, he had hit .431, raising his season average to .375, two points better than Mantle. Suddenly, Mickey found himself competing for the batting title against the last Triple Crown winner. Williams wouldn't admit it publicly, but he had made up his mind. He wanted one more batting title. About a month earlier he had told writers that he couldn't hit fastballs anymore. Yet no one his age had ever looked better. "At thirty seven, an age when most ball players have hung up their spikes," Al Hirshberg wrote, "Williams is still the most feared hitter in the business."[14]

In the first game of the Independence Day doubleheader, Williams faced Yankees starting pitcher Johnny Kucks. Carrying a 3.19 earned run average, the slender twenty-two-year-old right-hander from Jersey City had recently learned that he was on his way to his first All-Star game. A sinker ball pitcher, Kucks could still picture the gopher ball that he had floated over the plate against Williams the previous season. If Johnny wasn't careful, Ted would make him pay again. Pitching against Williams, he recalled, was difficult because Williams had complete command of the strike zone, laying off balls that skimmed the edges of the plate—and because if he didn't swing at a close pitch, umpires gave him beneficial calls. One time, when a catcher argued that a called ball was actually a strike, the umpire reminded him, "Mr. Williams will let you know when your pitcher throws a strike."[15]

In the bottom of the seventh inning, with two men on base, two outs, and the score tied 2–2, Williams stepped to the plate. He looked at the pitcher, beginning his routine muttering. "When I hit," he said, "I think to myself, 'Boy, I've got to be quick with the bat, quick with my hands, quick with the bat.'" He repeated, "Quick with bat, quick with my hands." He expected Kucks would throw a mixture of sinkers and sliders. When Kucks began his sidearm delivery, Williams anticipated the pitch and walloped a three-run homer. The Red Sox took the lead, 5–2.[16]

Billy Martin wouldn't let the Yankees give up. In the ninth, they fought back, taking a one-run lead on Martin's two-run homer. In the bottom of the inning, Boston's Jackie Jensen hit a game-tying single into shallow center field. Still tied in the bottom of the eleventh, Boston center fielder Jimmy Piersall came to the plate with men on first and second. Facing Yankees reliever Tom Sturdivant, Piersall looped a single toward Mantle in center field. Mickey charged toward the rolling ball and scooped it up. As he stepped into the throw, his right cleat stuck into the turf, twisting his right knee. He managed to fling an off-balance throw to Berra at home, but Boston's Billy Goodman had already crossed the plate for the game-winning run.[17]

Afterward, Mickey hobbled around the locker room. This injury appeared much worse than the one he had suffered in April. He had not missed a game all season, but there was no doubt that he would skip the second game of the doubleheader later that night. As Mickey unwrapped "several yards of bandages" around his injured right leg, he listened to Gus Mauch tell a group of writers that he had sprained lateral ligaments behind his knee. "Tomorrow we'll look and see if there's any swelling," the trainer explained.[18]

"Won't swell," Mantle grumbled in frustration. "Sure of that."

"Well, maybe it will, and maybe it won't," Mauch replied.

"No, it won't," Mickey insisted. He cringed at the thought of another injury, especially when he was having the best season of his life.

"Well, let's hope," Mauch said, masking his pessimism.

The following afternoon, Mickey boarded a 2:00 p.m. train out of Boston with a swollen knee. Sportswriters speculated that he would miss at least a week. With the All-Star game only five days away, there was little chance that he would play in the Midsummer Classic. Later that night, he visited the Lenox Hill Hospital on the Upper East Side, where he received the news: he hadn't torn any muscles or ligaments,

By 1956 Boston Red Sox great Ted Williams was entering the last act of his playing career, but his competitive fires burned just as intensely as they had in 1941, when he hit .406. He believed that he was still the best hitter in the game and was determined to stop Mantle's bid for the Triple Crown. *Courtesy of the National Baseball Hall of Fame.*

but he had sprained his medial collateral ligament and would have to wear a single-hinge brace until his leg healed.[19]

The All-Star break couldn't come soon enough for the Yankees. Although they had won five straight games leading into it, Billy Martin joined Mantle on the bench with a nagging hamstring injury. It was terrible timing for Martin, who had finally broken out of a slump, hitting .350 over his last eleven games. To make matters worse, Yogi Berra was nursing a sore left ankle after a foul ball caromed off him. And that wasn't the worst of it. Berra's batting average had plummeted seventy-six points since June 14, the worst slide of his career. Hitting .281 was certainly respectable, but he wasn't swinging well enough to justify his $55,000 salary, the highest on the club. Yet there was good news too. A few days after hurting his leg, Mickey made an announcement: "I feel good," he said. "I'm ready anytime."[20]

Team doctors authorized him to return to the field if he played with a brace on his right knee. On July 8, the last game before the break, he started against the Washington Senators. Testing his leg in center field, he played four innings and managed a single in one of his three plate appearances. Casey Stengel, however, worried that Mickey was rushing back. The skipper wanted him to sit one more day, but Mantle wouldn't listen. "What are you going to do?" Stengel asked a group of writers. "He is a cripple and insists on playing."[21]

A BAG OF BATS sat at the edge of Ted Williams's hotel bed. No possession mattered to him more. In Washington, DC, on the eve of the All-Star game, while most players spent the night on the town, he declared in the early evening that he was going to order a big steak and go to sleep. He needed rest. "Williams," Mickey Mantle later recalled, "was the one guy on the American League team who took the All-Star game seriously."[22]

No one who really knew Ted was surprised that he preferred to spend an evening alone with his bats. Unlike Mickey, who loved rooming with Billy Martin, Ted refused to share quarters with another player. When the Red Sox traveled on the road, he didn't join his teammates for a game of cards or a round of beers. He'd much rather be by himself, honing his bats with a bone, grinding down the wood. After wiping away the dust and rosin, he would weigh them on his own scale to ensure that they had not absorbed any moisture from the humid summer air. If they were too heavy, he'd ask the clubhouse attendant, Johnny Orlando, to put them in the dryer.[23]

Williams lived by a routine. Before every game he stood in front of a large hotel mirror, usually wearing only an undershirt and his underwear, swinging a bat. He wanted to see how he looked with the bat in his hands because he had to look good. "My name is Ted Fuckin' Williams and I'm the greatest hitter in baseball," he would declare through clenched teeth. He'd swing the bat and repeat his mantra. "My name is Ted Fuckin' Williams and I'm the greatest hitter in baseball."[24]

While Williams spent the night imagining a stellar All-Star game performance, Mickey barhopped with Whitey Ford and a few friends from other clubs. He later admitted that he treated the mid-season break "as a three-day party." He was unconcerned about rehabbing his leg or resting his body or about the exhibition game the next day. He cared only about his night out in the nation's capital. In Washington, the FBI learned a year later, a prominent bookie arranged dates at a brothel "for members of the New York Yankees," including Mantle.[25]

If Mickey lived everyday like it was his last, Ted lived for tomorrow. Mantle abused his body; Williams treated his like a temple, avoiding cigarettes, alcohol, and late-night escapades. When Ted first started dating, he let every woman know that he followed a self-imposed curfew. "I don't care what we do," he'd say, "just so long as you let me get home by midnight." If Mantle looked at his watch, it was only because he wanted to know if the bar was closing.[26]

Mickey treated his talents like a renewable resource. He didn't worry about wasting them. Over the years, as his body broke down from various injuries, he ignored doctors who prescribed rest and rehab exercises. He assumed that he would recover without much effort. Baseball had always come easily to him. He figured that he could play the game on natural ability alone. So, when the season ended, he stopped thinking about the sport.[27]

Williams, on the other hand, obsessed about building his body. He worked with weights, pulleys, and a hand-sized metal contraption with springs, squeezing it to boost the strength in his wrists and forearms. After games he knocked out one hundred fingertip push-ups. Few teammates ever beat him in a push-up contest. The competition drove him to be better at everything he did—push-ups, pull-ups, hitting. If a reporter suggested that he succeeded on natural ability, he would erupt. "They never talk about practice," he boomed. "Practice! Practice! Practice! Dammit, you gotta practice!"[28]

The central difference between Williams and Mantle was ambition. As a confident young hitter, Ted arrived in Boston dreaming about immortality. "When I'm finished with baseball," he said, "I want to be able to walk down the street and have folks point to me and say, 'There goes the greatest hitter who ever lived.'" When Mickey came to the big leagues, his biggest concern was making the team. He was stunned that the Yankees gave a roster spot to a nineteen-year-old. "I am over-awed," he said in 1951. "I don't really belong here."[29]

Over the years, whenever the Yankees played the Red Sox, Mantle studied Williams at the plate. "I was like everybody else," he said. "When he took batting practice, I got up and watched. He was the best hitter I ever saw." During spring training, Mantle approached Williams to ask him a few questions about hitting. The Boston veteran reminded him to wait for a good pitch. It was the central lesson he offered younger hitters. "Make them pitch to your strike zone," he instructed, "not theirs."[30]

One time before a game, Williams confused Mantle with a series of questions of his own. When Ted asked him which hand was his power hand and which was his guide hand, Mickey had no idea what he was talking about. After listening to him, Mantle tried applying his theories at the plate, but imitating Ted only made batting more difficult. He didn't get a hit for about twenty-five straight plate appearances. While Williams was interested in the science of hitting, going as far as meeting with a physics professor at MIT to learn about the aerodynamics of a curveball, Mantle was all brawn and instinct. "Hell," Mantle said years later, "I just used to go up there swinging."[31]

The Yankee center fielder reminded Williams of Jimmie Foxx, the stout, powerfully built slugger who finished his career with 534 home runs, second only to Babe Ruth at the time. The volatile crack of Mantle's bat against the ball reverberated just like those hit by "the Beast." "It sounded like cherry bombs going off when Foxx hit them," Williams recalled. In Ted's view, Mantle had joined elite company. There were few hitters he admired more than Foxx. But Mantle, Williams suggested, had become more than a power hitter. Mickey had greater discipline in 1956, and it showed. Ted told Yankees beat writer Tom Meany that Mantle had a legitimate shot to finish the season with a .400 batting average, high praise coming from the last man to do it. "Mickey has everything going for him," he said. "He has the speed to beat out bunts, so they can't play him too deep, and the power to drive it past them if they creep in on him. He bats both ways, so you can't play him in any particular field. And he has Yogi Berra hitting behind him, which means the pitchers can't put him on base without leaving themselves open to two runs instead of one."[32]

On July 10, a sellout crowd of about 28,000 packed Washington's Griffith Stadium to see the game's greatest players. When the public address announcer introduced the All-Stars, including six Yankees, no two players received a greater ovation than Mickey Mantle and Ted Williams, save perhaps hometown favorite Mickey Vernon. The game was more than an exhibition; it was a national event, watched by millions on NBC and featured as a cover story by *Sports Illustrated*. And the All-Stars themselves were the elite of America's sporting fraternity. "No athlete in any other sport in any part of the world," the magazine's Robert Creamer observed, "is accorded such widespread and insistent homage as the American major league baseball players." Being an All-Star, like Mantle and Williams, meant that a player had become one of "the gods, and the Pantheon of each league as constructed each July is heaven, the desired perfection dreamed of by the baseball follower."[33]

During the Great Depression, when baseball attendance declined by 40 percent, owners and sportswriters invented new ways to commemorate the biggest stars of the past and present, cementing baseball's place in American life. In 1931, the Baseball Writers Association of America established the modern practice of voting for the MVP. Two seasons later, at the suggestion of *Chicago Tribune* writer Arch Ward, Comiskey Park hosted the "Game of the Century," the first midsummer exhibition played by the biggest stars in the American and National leagues. And in 1936, the charter members were inducted into the Hall of Fame. Three years later, those legends—Babe Ruth, Ty Cobb, Honus Wagner, Christy Matthewson, and Walter Johnson—were enshrined in the hall during a ceremony in Cooperstown, New York, baseball's fabled birthplace. Each of these honors—the MVP award, the selection for the All-Star game, and induction into the Hall of Fame—celebrated individual achievement in the team sport.[34]

Mickey didn't intend to perform like a Hall of Famer in Washington. He looked as though he had enjoyed himself too much the night before. Wearing a brace on his right knee, he fanned in his first two at bats, against Pittsburgh's Bob Friend and Milwaukee's Warren Spahn. Standing in the on-deck circle in the sixth inning, with the American League trailing 0–5 and one man on base, he watched Ted Williams square off against Spahn, a nine-time All-Star and a contender for that season's Cy Young Award. Williams loved facing the best pitchers in the game on such a grand stage. It was his chance to show everyone that he was the best of the best. When Spahn tested his bat speed with a fastball, Williams belted a towering shot toward center field, where Duke Snider watched it fly over his head and drop into the American League bullpen.[35]

Then Mantle dug into the right side of the batter's box. Spahn had gotten the best of him in the fourth inning, but Mantle now had a better feel for his delivery and the speed of his fastball. In the press box, writers expected little from him, especially after two strikeouts. He simply could not pivot on his knee the way he normally did. But when Spahn hung an off-speed slider, Mantle muscled the ball into the left-center-field stands. He drove it "merely with his arms," an impressive display of power that left the crowd thundering with applause. Even he was surprised that the ball had cleared the fence. "I thought it was an outside pitch," he said. "Maybe I shouldn't have swung."[36]

The back-to-back home runs by Williams and Mantle renewed the home crowd's hope for an American League victory. But the AL never scored again, losing 7–3. Besides the homers by Mantle, Williams, Willie Mays, and Stan Musial, the game, Jimmy Cannon complained, was "boring," with no major turning points, no real drama. It was "just a ball game with two for a nickel hits falling flabbily." Afterward, reporters pressed Casey Stengel about losing his fifth All-Star game as American League manager, but he was concerned less about his record than about his starting catcher.[37]

In the sixth inning, Cincinnati's Ted Kluszewski, built like a tight end, fouled a ball off Berra's bare right hand. His pinky and ring finger had turned black and blue, but the indispensable Yankee didn't think much of it. Getting dinged behind the plate was all part of a day's work. After skipping an appointment with the team physician, Dr. Sidney Gaynor, the catcher told writers, "My hand's okay. It's still puffed up, but I can tape it up and I can bat and throw so I'll be able to play."[38]

Although Berra planned to catch after the break, reporters still doubted his health—and Mantle's. Mickey may have hit a home run during the All-Star game, but he didn't look like himself. Writers asked Gaynor, could Mickey continue to pivot on that fragile knee? Could he roam center field with that bulky brace? The doctor had watched Mantle play during the game, noting his agility running down balls in the outfield gaps. With the wry creativity of a Yankees PR man, he eluded the questions with one of his own. "Was he able to run to right field?"[39]

THE YANKEES OPENED THE second half of the season 6.5 games ahead of the Cleveland Indians and the Chicago White Sox and had a chance to extend their lead in the standings with six games in five days. First, they played the Indians in a three-game series in New York, drubbing Cleveland in the first two contests 9–5 and 10–0. The third game, on July 14, however, proved far more challenging, with Indians ace Herb Score on the mound. After Don Larsen surrendered three runs in the top of the fourth, with the Yankees still scoreless, Casey Stengel pulled his starting pitcher for reliever Tommy Byrne, who prevented the Indians from scoring with the bases loaded.[40]

With his team still trailing Cleveland 3–0, Mantle carried his bat to the right side of the plate, favoring his aching leg. Score, a tall, young lefty, was one of the hardest-throwing pitchers in the American League. A year earlier, he had won the Rookie of the Year award, leading the league in strikeouts. Facing Mantle with one out and nobody on base, he took a big windup, turning his body away from Mickey, uncoiled, and fired the ball toward the plate. Mantle swung hard, grunting through his teeth, smashing the ball more than four hundred feet into the Indians' bullpen in left field. It was Mantle's thirtieth home run but only his first since July 1. Two innings later, after he popped up to first base, Elston Howard replaced him in the lineup. For the rest of the day Mickey sat on the bench resting his sore leg.[41]

By July 15, after the Yankees beat the White Sox in both games of a doubleheader, sportswriters declared that the Yankees, leading the American League by 10.5 games, had won the pennant. "Barring a miracle," Robert Creamer wrote, "the pennant race is over, no sudden losing streak or winning splurge from now through that last Sunday in September is going to change the American League entry in the 1956 World Series."[42]

Three days later the Detroit Tigers snapped the Yankees' eleven-game winning streak. But, as Creamer had suggested, it changed nothing. Since June 25, the Yankees had won eighteen of twenty games. After the Yanks fell to the Tigers, the *New York Daily Mirror*'s Leonard Lewin yawned. "Ho hum!" he wrote. "How boring can AL baseball get? No fights with fans. No gutless charges. No foot races. Just another routine 450-foot homer by Mickey Mantle, his 31st . . . and a not so routine defeat for the Yankees."[43]

Although they lost, Mantle thrilled the crowd every time he swung the bat. "Even when he strikes out as he did in the ninth, when a homer would have put the Bombers within one," Lewin wrote, "the fans get a bang of it." With every ferocious cut, fans anticipated another prodigious blast. When Mantle missed, he missed like Casey in Mudville, causing the crowd to tremble with a chorus of "oohs," imagining what might have been had he connected. A year earlier, his failures at the plate brought a shower of boos, but now he had made believers out of those who had once doubted him. This season he gave the fans what they had long desired. Witnessing his past failures and seeing him overcome injuries and disappointment made fans appreciate his greatness as never before. Now they cheered for him even when he faltered at the plate.[44]

Since most writers believed that the Yankees had already clinched the pennant, they focused most of their attention on Mantle. Not until the World Series began in October, they reasoned, would the team be relevant again. Starting in mid-July, baseball fans could open the sports section, skip the game summary, and find a box score dedicated solely to Mickey's plate appearances. Everything a fan wanted to know about his day could be found on page thirty-nine in the July 19th edition of the *New York Daily Mirror*:

Mantle At Bat
1st—Hit 450-foot homer.
3rd—Took third strike.
5th—Hit 450-foot sacrifice fly.
7th—Beat out two-strike drag bunt.
9th—Fanned to end the game.

The Yankees' loss to the Tigers offered little comfort to the team's critics. Anyone who despised them—and the list was long—grumbled, as usual, that the Bronx Bombers simply had far better players than every other club in the American League and probably the National League too. Why were the Yankees so dominant? "Talent!" an American League manager barked. The Yankees' roster was filled with

All-Stars. "Stengel's got players on his bench who'd make a better team than some of the teams we have in the majors right now," the manager complained. It all seemed so unfair.[45]

To make matters worse, the Yankees had a hitter who could single-handedly change the outcome of a game. So why were the Yankees so dominant? The team's executive office secretary believed she had the answer. Smiling, she replied, "We've got Mickey Mantle."[46]

MICKEY DIDN'T KNOW what to say. Throughout July writers asked him why he was having the best season of his career. When Dan Daniel inquired, Mantle searched for an adequate answer but could only offer a question of his own. "Let me ask you that question," he said to the columnist from the *New York World-Telegram and Sun*. "What's your explanation of my improvement?" Mantle preferred to let his performance on the field do the talking. In his mind, baseball was a simple game. Pitchers threw the ball, and he hit it. What else could he say?[47]

Daniel believed his hitting strategy was more sophisticated than that, even if Mickey could not communicate it. "The chief reason is that you have eliminated your blind spot in batting," he said. "Right up to this season pitchers of the American League knew that when you were hitting left-handed, a tight pitch letter high was your weak point." Daniel observed that Mantle began moving away from the plate during spring training, which helped him avoid getting tied up with high fastballs. "You now see the pitch better," Daniel recognized. Mantle could not explain his batting adjustment nearly as well as the columnist. "You've got something there," Mickey said, adding little to the conversation. "I tried stepping back from the plate during the training season, and it felt good. I decided to stay with it."[48]

Even though Mantle was more forthcoming in 1956 than in seasons past, reporters still complained that his overall reticence made their jobs more difficult. "He's not witty," the *Boston Globe*'s Harold

Kaese complained, "not quick on the trigger. He's not fancy, smart, or clever. He has a positive distaste for interviews and photograph sessions." Stengel defended Mickey. "Sure," he said, "I've heard about Mantle's being called dumber than Ned-in-the-Third-Reader." In "Stengelese" that meant he'd heard people call Mantle naive. "If that's so, I could use a few more like him around."[49]

Although interviews with Mantle frequently left writers with blank notebooks, they were grateful that his loquacious manager could talk for a couple hours about him. Seeking their admiration, Stengel courted writers like a politician running for reelection. Those he trusted most—"my writers," he called them—benefitted from private conversations in the clubhouse or dugout. He took the time to learn their names, which paper they wrote for, and whether they had an afternoon deadline or a morning one. The afternoon writers, he understood, needed good material—stories that could fill columns—before the games were played.[50]

Yet Stengel's speech patterns often dumbfounded reporters. He used all sorts of odd phrases that made sense only to him. If he was going to take a nap, he would say, "If anyone wants me, tell them I'm being embalmed." Scouting talent, he called inferior players "road apples," a good fielder was a "plumber," and a rookie was a "green pea." Praising his guys, Casey would say, "He done splendid." He admired tough players, the kind who "could squeeze your earbrows off." He also warned Mantle, Martin, Ford, and the other playboys on the team—the guys who were "whiskey slick"—not to stay out too late chasing women. In fact, he was less concerned about the conquests than the pursuit. "It ain't getting it that hurts them," he said. "It's staying up all night looking for it. They gotta learn that if you don't get it by midnight, you ain't gonna get it, and if you do, it ain't worth it."[51]

At any moment he could launch into a monologue without "subjects or predicates or conjunctions or coherence." He spoke in constant animation, contorting his leathery "gargoyle face" into twisted winks,

waving his arms like an orchestra conductor. Stengel took wide de-
tours when he told stories, bringing his hand over his mouth "long
enough to wipe out an entire sentence." One time when a reporter
asked him a question, Casey offered a forty-minute reply. Exasperated,
the writer said, "Casey, you haven't answered my question." Stengel
replied, "Don't rush me."[52]

Casey was completely comfortable talking to anyone, anywhere,
anytime. Dining cars, bars, locker rooms, and hotel lobbies all served
as his stage. Without a hint of self-consciousness, he would undress
after games in front of reporters. As he unbuttoned his uniform and
took off his pants, he would stop to make a point, flipping his hand.
"He had a lot of gestures," Robert Creamer recalled. Casey had "a
curious way of raising his chin high, his mouth closed in a grim, serious line, his eyes half closed, as he listened to someone else." Then he
would finish stripping, removing his underwear and the jockstrap that
he had worn as if he might have to take the field in a pinch. Wearing
nothing but slippers, the gray-haired sexagenarian marched through
the locker room with a towel draped over his forearm "like a toga,
looking for all the world like a Roman senator on his way to the
baths." As he headed for the showers, the writers trailed behind, listening to him pontificate. Watching him, Creamer thought it was "a
bizarre spectacle, this naked old man parading through a room full of
hard-muscled young athletes, but Stengel never gave a sign that he
recognized the incongruity." And, of course, the conversation didn't
end when Casey began scrubbing himself. If a reporter missed something he had said, Stengel poked his head out of the shower to make
sure that the writer heard him clearly.[53]

In 1956, it was easy to get him to talk about his favorite subject:
Mickey Mantle. He had so much to say about him that Tom Meany
wrote an article for *Collier's* titled "As Casey Stengel Sees Mickey
Mantle." Stengel raved about Mickey. Mantle, he said, could blaze
down the first base line faster than any other player: "The boy can fly!"
He had more natural power than any hitter Casey had ever seen: "He

hit one into those upper right-field stands in Detroit. Seats were flyin' round for five minutes." Mickey was far and away the best switch hitter in the game: "You don't find many fellas with tremendous power from both sides of the plate, which he has shown he has."[54]

Mantle's switch-hitting fascinated Meany. Mickey told him a story about how during a game against Baltimore, Bill Wight, a left-handed pitcher, had run up a full count against him. It was the ninth inning, with a runner on first, nobody out, and the Orioles leading by five runs, manager Paul Richards called for a right-handed reliever during Mantle's at bat. When Mickey noticed George Zuverink trotting out to the mound, he went back to the dugout and pulled another bat from the rack. "I use a 36-ounce bat right-handed and a 32-ounce bat left-handed," he said. Now batting left-handed, he smashed Zuverink's pitch into center field for a double.[55]

Sportswriters and fans debated whether Mantle could hit the ball harder from the right side of the plate or the left. By July, he had hit about two-thirds of his homers from the left side—though because of the prominence of right-handed pitchers, he had had far more at bats on that side—but he hit for a higher average from the right side. "Tell ya how it is," Casey said with an exaggerated wink. "There's some say he hits with more power right-handed and others say, 'No, he does it left-handed.'" The Ole Professor admitted that he didn't really know if Mantle hit the ball harder from one side or the other. "Now, he's a natural right-hander, except at the plate. He throws, shaves, eats, and writes right-handed. Now you'd think a fella'd be bound to have more power one way than another, wouldn't you? But with this kid, I dunno."

Mantle's ambidexterity impressed Stengel less than his "physical courage." By the third week of July, Mickey had stopped wearing the brace on his right knee, but he was still an injury risk. Ever since he first twisted his right knee on a drain cover in the 1951 World Series, Mantle had been one false step away from a career-ending sprain or tear. Stunned that Mantle could play at such a high level, Casey said,

Casey Stengel wanted hard-nosed winners, not choirboys, on his team. Mantle, Yogi Berra, and Hank Bauer suited him perfectly. They helped continue the Yankee dynasty. *Courtesy of the National Baseball Hall of Fame.*

"Thing too many people overlook about him is that he's been doing all he has been doing this year as a cripple." Mickey still had to have his right leg wrapped from the top of the right ankle all the way to the top of his thigh. Gus Mauch wrapped the bandage so tight that it nearly cut off Mickey's circulation, numbing his leg. It took the trainer so long to mummify him that Mantle would get taped before the first game of a doubleheader and wear the same wrappings for the second game too.[56]

Given Mickey's pain, it's remarkable that he didn't ask Stengel for more days off. But that wasn't his way. He was a product of a mining culture. If a man didn't go down into the mine, he didn't get paid. The laborers who toiled in the Blue Goose mine prized stoicism as much as they valued strength. Complaining was a sign of weakness. Who didn't work when sick or hurt? His father never complained about the aches he suffered toiling in the ground, so Mickey never considered grousing about his own discomfort. Besides, he was paid to play a game. Dwelling on injuries and allowing them to keep him out of the lineup just wasn't an option for a man who grew up in Commerce.

FOR SEVEN CONSECUTIVE GAMES, from July 22 to July 29, Mantle failed to hit a homer. He had scorched so many pitchers that none wanted to test him anymore. When he batted, pitchers nibbled around the corners of the strike zone; some bounced the ball at the plate; others hoped to get him to swing at junk a mile outside. A year earlier, he would have become frustrated and chased bad pitches, but now he was more focused. He remained patient at the plate, maintaining his batting average at .370, seventeen points ahead of Ted Williams.[57]

Reporters quizzed Mantle about his home run drought. Did it bother him that his lead over Ruth's 1927 pace was slipping? "I don't hope to beat Ruth's record or even give it a close battle, especially now that the pitchers won't give me a chance," he said. He admitted that he would have preferred to win the Triple Crown because it would prove that he had become a better all-around hitter. Besides, no switch-hitter had ever led the American League in batting average.[58]

On Monday night, July 30, Mantle broke his power slump and made sure that Casey Stengel would never forget his sixty-sixth birthday. At Cleveland Stadium, in the top of the second inning, Mantle faced Bob Lemon with the bases loaded. Lemon tossed a ball right over the plate, and Mantle crushed it more than four hundred feet into the right-field bleachers for his first grand slam of the season. A year earlier, he had hit .203 against the Indians' rotation, the best staff in the American League; this season he was batting .371. Later that evening, he hit a two-run home run—his thirty-fourth—off Bob Feller. For the sixth time of the year, he had hit two home runs in one game. The second kept him well ahead of Ruth's record pace.[59]

Still, Ruth had hit an incredible number of home runs in the last month of the season, so even with Mickey out ahead of him at a corresponding point in July, it was far from certain that he'd be able to match or break the Bambino's record. As for the Triple Crown, however, that seemed all but wrapped up, which was perhaps the more impressive feat, especially so soon after the season's midpoint. By the end of July he owned a commanding lead in all three hitting categories. Although he had only hit seven home runs that month, he still led all hitters by nine. And not only did he lead Williams by a wide margin in the batting-title competition, but he had eighty-nine RBIs, eleven more than the American League's next best run producer, Cleveland's Vic Wertz.

It seemed that nobody was going to challenge Mantle's hold on the RBI lead—except there was a stir in Detroit. The Tigers' twenty-one-year-old right fielder, Albert William Kaline, had started driving the ball all over the field. The defending batting champion, a handsome young hitter who modeled his swing after Ted Williams's, had started the season nursing a shoulder injury that hindered his hitting through April. It was just the beginning of a season of ailments. The following month he hurt his foot, and in early July he caught the flu and lost seven pounds in three days. His popularity among fans earned him a starting spot on the All-Star team, but he looked nothing like the promising hitter from 1955.[60]

Once Kaline regained his strength after the mid-season break, Detroit's manager Bucky Harris moved him back one spot in the batting order, penciling him in at cleanup. With two All-Stars, shortstop Harvey Kuehn and left fielder Charlie Maxwell, hitting in front of him—each was batting well over .320—Kaline had frequent opportunities to drive home runners. Starting on July 30, he went on a tear comparable, that season, only to one of Mantle's. In seven games he raised his average from .290 to .307 and drove home sixteen runs, eleven of which came against the Yankees during the Tigers' three-game sweep at Briggs Stadium. In just one week, Kaline had cut Mantle's RBI lead from twenty to only eight. "Maybe Kaline can't repeat as the league batting champion," Harris said, "but it looks like he'll give somebody a chase."[61]

CHAPTER 8

"I Love Mickey"

"Only the quiet boy from Commerce, Okla., knows how it feels to be the target of millions of eyes, cameras, and typewriters."

—*THE SPORTING NEWS,*
August 22, 1956

They arrived at major-league clubhouses by the hundreds. Love letters, mash notes, and billets-doux—by whatever name, they offered the same thing: a sexual proposition, a one-night affair, most promising no strings attached. Some players discarded the missives unread and returned to their wives, fiancées, or girlfriends after the game ended. Others willingly accepted the favors offered, sneaking out of their hotels and returning in the early hours before sunrise. Such antics were as much a part of the game as shoestring catches and lazy fly balls.

In 1947, at the end of his first season in the majors, Jackie Robinson received a letter from a woman living in Akron. She wrote that she stood five feet, four inches, weighed 120 pounds, and was attractive. She had won a Miss Akron Beauty Contest and been in many other beauty competitions. Her problem was that every time she heard

Jackie's name, "a thrill goes all through me." "I want you to love me just once," she wrote. "Just once and then I might be satisfied." She knew that he was married and had a son, "but you don't have to be an angel. It would be like heaven just to have you touch me." And, she promised, "I'll love you like you have never had love before." No strings. His wife, Rachel, would never know about it.[1]

Robinson answered the letter. "You are suffering from some kind of mental delusion that can bring you nothing but trouble," he warned. "When I married Mrs. Robinson, I exchanged vows to love, honor and cherish her for the rest of my life. 'Honor' means just that to me," he continued, and he would do nothing to "destroy that very thing that enables me to hold my head up high." Jackie's response unequivocally ended the matter.

Mickey Mantle received countless such letters. But Mickey Mantle was no Jackie Robinson.

His wife, Merlyn, said that during the 1956 season, "lovelorn girls—and older women too" deluged her husband with proposals. Before she became too busy being Mrs. Mickey Mantle, Merlyn answered the fan mail, but it became such a burden that she eventually turned the job over to Mickey's twin brothers and several secretaries from the Yankee organization. The joke was on the randy correspondents, however. "If they only knew that Mickey seldom reads any letters, even the ones from home! We do all our communicating on long-distance telephone."[2]

MERLYN WAS NOT THE only woman he talked to over the phone. Mickey called Holly Brooke in the first week of August, just before going to Boston for two games against the Red Sox. He wanted the self-described showgirl and model to join him in the Hub. Mickey probably had his reasons, though their exact nature has been lost. The two had vague business connections. During Mantle's rookie season the hustler Alan Savitt had signed the ballplayer to a promotional contract. Although his former agent was out of the picture by 1956, aspects of the deceptive contract lingered. Most prominent among them was Holly Brooke.[3]

Back in 1951, Savitt had tried to convert Mantle's signature on the contract into cash, not by making endorsement deals but by selling percentages of the arrangement. Most of his associates were as broke as he was, but one person he represented, Brooke, had the wherewithal to come up with $1,500, which he assured her would buy 25 percent of the Mantle deal. But she wisely distrusted her own agent. Savitt might have no deal at all with Mantle. Besides, she later wrote, "a girl ought to look over her investments *before* making 'em though—at least that's my motto—and I'd never set eyes on Mantle."

Savitt introduced Holly to Mickey at Danny's Hideaway. By the end of the dinner—or at least the next night—she judged Mickey a sound investment. Mantle was equally as impressed with her—a beautiful redhead, seven years older than him and a hundred years more experienced. Within a week or two she was his steady companion. With his fiancée Merlyn back in Oklahoma, Mickey spent much of his free time with Brooke, treating her to drinks and dinners at Danny's Hideaway and quick breakfasts at the Stage Deli after spending nights together. "Plenty of times we'd sit in my car in the wee small hours of the morning and watch the sun rise over Manhattan," she recalled. "Those all-night rendezvous might come after an afternoon baseball game," but, she confessed in sensational tabloid style, "the Mick was never too tired for a night game."[4]

For Brooke, Mantle was a better lover than financial investment. "*Mickey* was collecting too many dividends on *my* investment," she observed. "I was beginning to wonder who owned a piece of who?" Although he told her not to worry about the deal—that "the Yankees will take care of it"—by 1956 she was having doubts. That summer, it was difficult to open a newspaper without seeing something about Mickey Mantle in it: his aw-shucks, country-boy smile appeared on magazine covers; his buttoned-down Madison Avenue image graced advertisements; and he charmed television audiences like a practiced performer. Perhaps Holly Brooke wanted a dividend on her 25 percent.[5]

Or maybe Mickey just wanted her. A baseball season is long and grueling—a seemingly endless string of games played under a blistering sun, long train rides between cities, and lonely nights in hotel rooms. Booze and an occasional "Baseball Annie" might relieve the stretches of monotony, but never entirely. Mantle called her toward the end of a brutal road trip. The Yankees had played three games in Chicago, three in Kansas City, four in Cleveland, and three in Detroit—thirteen contests in as many days. And they would not get a day off for another full week. Furthermore, going into Boston they had dropped six in a row. Poor batting and only slightly better pitching had marked the slump. Holly had been there for Mickey when he had been sent down to the minors in 1951. She had visited him in Kansas City, Columbus, and other minor-league towns when his spirits had flagged, and he felt the need for a woman in the night. Perhaps Mickey wanted Holly to lighten the pressures of a season once again.

While Mickey spoke on the phone, Holly heard "Come On-A My House" playing on the radio in the background. It was their song. But she no longer danced to Mickey's tune. "Here I was five years after I'd made that deal and I had yet to get my money back," she would soon write. "No one could say I hadn't watched over my securities . . . and then some. But it had all been in vain." She stayed in New York while he went to Boston. With Mantle at the height of his popularity, she knew that she could leverage his fame to recoup part of her investment.[6]

Mickey would soon find that while sports stars could also be celebrities, sports stars and celebrities were not always treated the same. Sportswriters carefully crafted an image of him as a family man with a winning grin who joyfully played a boy's game and then went home for a glass of milk. The sports journalists who knew him best largely hid that he wasn't remotely like his public persona and was instead an often moody, angry, hard-drinking, philandering, flawed man. They sold Mickey like political columnists sold America during the Cold

War. Mickey and his nation stood for revered ideals. Yet, as his popularity transcended sports, he would soon find himself at the mercy of tabloid journalists and their muckraking publications. They scoured celebrityland for the cracks in the facade, searching for contradictions between image and reality, and Holly Brooke had just the kind of information that they bought and sold.

ALTHOUGH SPORTSWRITERS AVOIDED reporting on players' personal lives, they could be unforgiving toward recalcitrant stars or lesser performers. Mickey's button-lipped style early in his career, his angry outbursts and general distrust of reporters, won him no popularity contests with the Yankee beat writers. But in 1956, when he learned a few of their names and smiled as he gave several bland comments after a game, they started to fawn over him almost as much as they did Yogi Berra and Casey Stengel. Above all, they needed daily copy. The ball players fed the beast or suffered the consequences. If Mickey still needed an example of how the system worked, he got one during the Yankees' early-August series against the Red Sox.

It's possible, if not likely, that if Ted Williams could have played baseball in empty stadiums, with no reporters present, he would have spent his career in quiet contentment. The game would have been akin to trout fishing—only Ted with his bat facing a pitcher rather than with a reel matching wits with a fish. Unfortunately, he played before passionate, opinionated Red Sox fans and a bevy of sportswriters famous for their sharp wits and critical eyes. They wanted more from their star than consistent, year-after-year play. They demanded something over and beyond Hall of Fame greatness. And Ted, a product of a tough childhood, emotionally fragile and inhumanly stubborn, was "goddamned" if he was going to give it to them. "The newspaper guys in this town are bush," he complained in 1956. Not to put too fine a point on it, he called several of them "gutless, syphilitic cocksuckers." He blamed them for whipping up the Boston fans against him, but that did not mean that he forgave the Red Sox faithful for their fickleness. "Some of those fans are the worst in the world. What do they want from a guy? I've hit over .340 for 17 years in this league, and every time I walk up there, they give me the business. What do they expect me to do, smile at them?"[7]

On August 7, during an afternoon game at Fenway Park before a standing-room-only crowd of 36,350, the stadium's largest since the end of World War II, Williams exploded as unexpectedly as a piece of buried ordnance. It was a blustery day. Winds played tricks with the ball, and intermittent rains peppered the players and made the field slick. The weather turned the contest into a pitchers' duel between Don Larsen and Willard Nixon. Going into the top of the eleventh, the score was still 0–0. With two outs, Mantle came to the plate and hit a fly ball to short left field. With rain in his face, Williams charged the ball but failed to secure it in the webbing of his glove. As it bounced onto the grass, Mantle rounded first and streaked for second. A chorus of boos let Ted know that he was personally responsible for a two-base error and, perhaps, the game.[8]

Yogi Berra, the next batter, lined a much more treacherous shot at Williams. The ball looked like it was headed for the wall but was knocked down by the wind. Sprinting into left center Williams made a magnificent catch at the scoreboard. And just as quickly boos became cheers. Ted hadn't lost the game; he had kept Boston's hopes alive.

But Williams's moods were not as capricious. He never thought he deserved to be booed in *his* Fenway Park—not after hitting .406 in 1941 and establishing himself as the greatest batter in the game—and as he ran back to the dugout, he was hot, angry at the fans, sportswriters, and anyone else in his line of vision. At the first base line, he spit at the spectators behind Boston's dugout; before descending to the bench, he issued another volley of phlegm toward the distant sportswriters; and, not wanting any part of Fenway to escape his wrath, he stepped out of the dugout and lobbed a glob toward the Yankees' dugout and the fans between home and third. "Oh, no," Red Sox announcer Curt Gowdy winced, "this is bad."[9]

After what Red Smith dubbed his "great expectorations," Williams retreated into the tunnel between the dugout and the clubhouse and assaulted a water fountain. It was, noted utility player Billy Consolo, "one of those big metal water coolers, bolted to the concrete wall. Ted just knocked it over, ripped it off the wall. Water started spurting everywhere." It flooded the tunnel, almost requiring scuba gear to make it back to the clubhouse.[10]

Williams was not through. In the bottom of the eleventh inning, Boston loaded the bases, and he came to the plate again. An angry Williams was a fearsome sight for any pitcher, and reliever Tommy Byrne was not about to give Ted anything to hit. Byrne hoped that Williams's rage would make him chase a bad pitch. But even a furious, spit-launching, water-fountain-busting Williams had the best batter's eye in the game. He laid off balls outside the strike zone, and given Williams's emotional instability, the umpire was not about to call anything close against him. On this note of anticlimax, Byrne walked home the winning run. As he moved away from home plate, Williams flung his bat toward the heavens. Some said it ascended thirty feet in the air; others claimed it climbed more than fifty.

The Red Sox locker room was funereally silent. "Kid, that wasn't a good thing to do," manager Pinky Higgins told Williams. Ted's teammates watched silently, as nervous as Byrne had been just minutes before. It was quiet enough to hear a jock hit the ground. Team owner Tom Yawkey had listened to the game on the radio in New York, and he fined Williams $5,000 for his actions, an enormous amount at the time. But Ted had no real regrets. Although he would not meet reporters face-to-face, he did talk with a few through a closed door. Why did he do it? "I just can't help it," he said. And he wasn't a bit sorry for the spitting—just for the $5,000 fine. He had two things he wanted to get off his chest, and he made the reporters repeat them to be sure they got them right: "First, I'd spit at the same people who booed me today. Second, I wouldn't be at the ballpark tomorrow if I could afford a . . . $5,000 fine every day."[11]

The Williams's spitting incident was news for weeks. All of a sudden, Ted was exhibition number one for what was wrong with pampered athletes and what was troubling the Great American Game. He was excoriated by reporters and defended by fans, ridiculed by Boston scribes and praised by the man on the street. Ted Williams's mind became of greater public interest than Albert Einstein's. "They're interviewing psychiatrists now on me," he told a reporter. "I am the spitting cobra." Untroubled by their star's saliva glands, most of the Red Sox faithful now stood by him. "Ted has gone through two tough wars and numerous injuries which would have killed lesser men and has come back to have some of his greatest years," noted a letter to the *Boston Globe*. "Certainly fans have the right to boo players, especially if they are not performing as they should but there is a limit as to what a man can take."[12]

Williams made his case even more eloquently the next night against the Orioles. Once again more than 30,000 spectators crammed into Fenway. They had come to see the "Splendid Spitter," and he reveled in the moment, even if it had cost him $5,000 to push Mantle's pursuit of Babe's record into the wings. As soon as they saw him, the fans began to cheer, and they continued to sound their support every time he came to the plate or caught a ball. With the game knotted at 2–2 in the sixth inning, he knocked a home run into the right-field pavilion. As he crossed home plate and headed for the dugout, he put a finishing touch on his previous day's antics by covering his mouth with his right hand.[13]

Ted was back. He had made his point. And even though he was just shy of his thirty-eighth birthday, he was not about to concede any batting titles to Mickey Mantle.

NOT LONG BEFORE THE tie-breaking homer, while still in the field, Williams wandered over to the scoreboard operator and asked if anything was happening. Mickey had hit another home run against the Senators. Once again in Griffith Stadium he had victimized Camilo Pascual. It was his thirty-eighth of the season. The next day he belted his thirty-ninth—his fifth since the beginning of the month. But with the Yankees heading into a four-game series against Baltimore, *New York Journal-American* columnist Hugh Bradley cautioned restraint. "Mickey Mantle hasn't hit a homer against the lowly Orioles this year," he wrote. Furthermore, the Birds had held him to a mere .219 batting average. Perhaps manager Paul Richards had some "magic formula." "I wish it was true," he said. "It would make my life a lot more pleasant." But the story was "bunk."[14]

Orioles catcher–first baseman Gus Triandos was more forthcoming. "Our guys throw about everything they have in the way of pitches, including sliders, curves, screw balls, knucklers and fastballs," he explained. "They try to keep him from getting set." Maybe that was the secret—keeping the slugger from digging in at the plate. Mickey wasn't sure what it was. When quizzed on the subject, he smiled, then speculated, "Maybe the answer can be given better after the next four games are completed. . . . I'm not worrying—at least not yet."[15]

Mickey was right. Baltimore pitchers had no secret formula. He hit his fortieth home run during a Saturday game, becoming the first Yankee to reach that mark since DiMaggio tallied forty-six in 1937. The shot put him eleven games ahead of Babe Ruth's record pace. The next day Mickey celebrated by hitting another homer against Baltimore. He had never hit forty homers in a year, and now on August 12, with more than a month and a half remaining in the regular season, he had eclipsed that mark. He had made a believer of Richards. "Mickey Mantle is a better player than Ruth," the manager gushed. "Baseball has been looking a long time for a super player. Now it can stop looking because Mantle is that player."[16]

LIKE RUTH HAD IN his own time, Mantle was outgrowing his sport. Every part of the entertainment industry clamored for his attention.

After playing the Sunday doubleheader against the Orioles, he rushed to Midtown Manhattan to appear on *The Ed Sullivan Show* (Sullivan had recently been in an automobile accident, and comedian Phil Silvers was filling in for him). The variety show was a TV staple. By 1956 television had begun to reshape American culture. With more than five hundred stations and sets in almost 40 million homes—or 85 percent of the total—it had become a $1 billion a year industry. The tube alternately informed, enlightened, and entertained the nation, and in the 1956–1957 season *The Ed Sullivan Show* was the second most watched program, attracting just short of 15 million viewers a week. No other variety program—and only *I Love Lucy*—topped its numbers. The show made some careers and confirmed others. Less than a month after Mantle appeared, Elvis Presley sang and gyrated for the first time on the program.[17]

Mantle appeared with singer Teresa Brewer to perform their recently released "I Love Mickey," a bouncy tune extolling "the fella with the celebrated swing." Songs about famous athletes had a long tradition. During the Yankee Clipper's *annus mirabilis* of 1941, Les Brown and His Orchestra had a hit with "Joltin' Joe DiMaggio," and in 1949 the tune "Did You See Jackie Robinson Hit That Ball?" showed up in record stores. Most strikingly, in the 1930s heavyweight champion Joe Louis inspired almost as many songs as Jesus, including Memphis Minnie's "He's in the Ring (Doin' the Same Old Thing)," Carl Martin's "Joe Louis Blues," and Cab Calloway and His Orchestra's "Let's Go Joe." But "I Love Mickey" was something else, because Mantle actually performed it. Whenever Brewer sings "I love Mickey," he chimes in, "Mickey who?" and she responds, "You know who!"[18]

There is nothing innocent about "I Love Mickey." The singer might exhibit a schoolgirl's crush on the ballplayer, but her desires are decidedly mature. That her "love letter" was more public than the usual ones received by Mantle, Robinson, and other players did not alter its intent. She wants to "pitch a little woo" with him, "steal" him home, and "pop right in his arms." There is no acknowledgment that he is a married man with young children. Brewer, the "Baseball Annie," knows precisely what she wants, and it is not to watch Mickey hit a baseball.

Mantle's "Mickey who?" response casts him in the role of incredulous dupe, clueless about her intentions. He simply can't decipher her double entendres or fathom her impure intentions. This image of Mickey as an inexperienced rube dominated the media's treatment of him. Except for his preternatural talent and rippling muscles, he was the suburban man-next-door—faithful husband and loving father. In an *American Weekly* feature, he explained that what fans initially interpreted as arrogance was actually reticence. "I was never very handy with words, and I'd always been a little shy among strangers," he said. "I could say things that needed saying, but if 'yes,' 'no' or 'maybe' filled the bill, I never bothered saying much else." The leap from Commerce to New York was simply too great, and it took him some time to adjust to the frantic pace and Gotham's shrewd characters.[19]

But as with hitting a big-league fastball, he had become accustomed to the speed of the city and found his place. In the popular narrative, at least, the Broadway nightlife was not for him. He had given all that up for a suburban home in River Edge, New Jersey. "When I'm not playing ball I like to spend all my time with Merlyn and the children, Mickey, Jr., who's three, and the baby, David." And once the season concluded, he hightailed it back to Commerce. "The bright lights don't attract me anymore."[20]

That, anyway, was the Mickey Mantle being packaged and sold on the newsstands. It was a well-worn story but appealing nonetheless. And it was perfect for television. While Mickey was pursuing the ghost of Babe Ruth, NBC's Kraft Theater developed a drama based on his life to be aired on the evening of the World Series opener. *The Life of Mickey Mantle* was billed as a warts-and-all biopic detailing his close relationship with his father as well as his early struggles in New York, initial failures as a Yankee, and troubles with Merlyn. But the warts turned out to be mere smudges, and any flaws in his character were conveniently explained as unfortunate misunderstandings. For instance, after ten days on the road, he returns home, and his wife asks, "How was the trip?" Mickey grumbles something and retreats into silence. When Merlyn tries again, he snaps, "What do you want me to talk about?" With tears in her eyes, she pleads, "Mickey, talk to me. If you only knew how lonely I am when you are away." Untouched by the exchange, he ends the conversation: "Why don't you leave me alone? I got nothing to say."[21]

An example of a cold, distant husband? Not exactly. It is later revealed that Mickey has been exhausted by chasing Ruth's home run record and frustrated by the nagging questions of sportswriters. Would he surpass the Babe? Would he win the Triple Crown? How did it feel to hit the ball so hard? The same questions day after day have ground him down. But by the end, the biopic has resolved all his professional and personal problems. It closes with Mickey, his arm around his wife, talking comfortably to a group of reporters.

The show even airbrushes Mantle's escapades with his Yankee teammates. Troublemaker Billy Martin is never mentioned. A more innocent scene replaces Mantle and Martin's late-night drinking and carousing, a constant source of friction between Mickey and Merlyn. One night after a road trip Mickey returns home particularly late, drawing complaints from his wife. The real culprit, it turns out, is not Mickey or even Billy but Jerry Coleman, another teammate. In the case of the wayward ballplayers, Coleman had convinced Mickey to stop off for an ice-cream soda before heading home to Merlyn.[22]

The Life of Mickey Mantle, as well as the feature articles, effectively transformed the temperamental Mantle into a misunderstood puppy. Mickey wasn't uncommunicative; he was shy. He wasn't an insensitive husband; he was a great teammate. Although Dan Daniel labeled the biopic "corny" and "overdramatic"—he said it was "hardly [selling] Mantle to the public as Mantle is"—it never intended to portray the real ballplayer. At a time when youth culture seemed vaguely threatening—when Marlon Brando and James Dean appeared on-screen as inarticulate, misunderstood, and even dangerous juveniles; when Elvis

Presley shook up the music industry, undulating like a belly dancer and peddling "race music"; when psychiatrist Frederic Wertham ominously asserted that the comic book industry was subverting the morals of American youths; and when Beat writers offered alternatives to the dominant corporate, unimaginative, capitalist ethos—the Mantle corn served as an antidote. Mickey's fresh face and his Homeric feats at the plate reassured Americans that there was nothing wrong with the country's kids. Not when they had heroes and role models like Mickey Mantle.[23]

ALL MICKEY HAD TO do to remain the hero for Cub Scouts, Boy Scouts, and Little Leaguers, as well as their dads, who served as troop leaders and coaches, was not stumble. His private lapses presented no immediate problem. He had become the darling of the media. Sportswriters and columnists ignored his nocturnal drinking sprees with Billy Martin and Whitey Ford, and, at least so far, the gossip rags seemed more interested in the bad habits of movie stars than those of athletes. But reporters were a fickle lot. In the past, if Mickey had gone cold at the plate or failed to deliver in a clutch moment, they had attacked, nibbling away at his image like piranhas. Hero or goat, Mickey Mantle would be their story. All the favorable press—and the money from endorsements, television deals, and appearances—depended on how well he swung a bat. As long as he chased Babe's record and maintained command of the Triple Crown race, then his star would only continue to rise.

But Mickey faced competition. Ted Williams, spitting, cursing, and complaining his way through the season, was not ready to concede anything to a younger star. Publicly he praised Mickey, calling him the greatest power hitter since Ruth and the best bet to break the Babe's home run mark. He confided to sportswriters that he was getting old. Gone were the days when he was "the Kid," the skinniest, feistiest hitter in baseball. But if the Kid had put on a few pounds, if he was more prone to aches and injuries, he nevertheless refused to accept that anyone could hit better than he could. The magic was still in his eyes and hands, and he still yearned for greatness. He still meant what he said in 1941: "I wanna be an immortal."[24]

Williams, always motivated, was a genuine threat. A few more hits by Ted and a few less by Mickey, and the race for the batting title would be on in earnest. Even at Yankee Stadium, the fans sensed it. *They wanted it.* During an August game in New York against Baltimore, the public-address announcer reminded the spectators that the next series was against the Boston Red Sox—"and Ted Williams." The stands erupted—not for the battle between the first-place Yankees and the fourth-place Red Sox but for the one between Mickey and Ted. On August 12, Mantle's league-leading average stood at .371; Williams, at .354, was well behind but still in the hunt.[25]

Mickey was eleven games ahead of Ruth's pace and unconcerned about Williams for the batting title when the Red Sox arrived in the Bronx. The first contest attracted the largest crowd, for a night game, of the Yankees' 1956 campaign. More than 52,000 spectators, including President Dwight Eisenhower, packed into Yankee Stadium, loud, expectant, craving to see Mickey continue his campaign for baseball's most sacred record. Mantle liked the drama of the noise and the moment, the sight of Ike in the stands, and a full house cheering his name.[26]

Hank Bauer and Billy Martin also enjoyed the big stage. Bauer led off the game with a 440-foot triple, and Martin drove him in with his eighth home run of the season. As Billy strutted into the dugout, Mickey said, "Now I'll have to hit one to keep pace, huh?" And he did. In the third inning he crushed a ball over the fence. "He really hit that one hard," Martin marveled after the game. But Yankee beat writer Leonard Koppett was fascinated more by the crowd's reaction than by Mantle's power. Mickey had captured their imagination. When he connected with the pitch, the sound and activity in the stands were different, alive with "a sort of hysterical satisfaction." And when Mantle walked in his last at bat in the eighth inning, Yankee Stadium seemed to visibly deflate.[27]

"Did you see how as soon as Mantle got his last turn at bat 10,000 people got up and left?" a visitor said in the clubhouse. "That's how it used to be with the Babe, remember?"[28]

The Mick and the Babe—the two seemed to be the subject of every reporter's questions. Mickey was now thirteen games ahead of Ruth's pace, and with each step toward the record, the focus on him increased. He had become a sort of scientific experiment, apparent evidence of the notion that every generation produces bigger, stronger, and faster athletes. As Mantle stayed ahead of Babe's pace, Red Smith claimed, "medical journals were snooping into his reflexes, publishing diagrams of brain and nerve and muscles to show what happened when he took aim on a curve."[29]

And while the scientists speculated, American League pitchers bemoaned their fates. What was the best way to pitch to Mantle? The question crept up in dozens of newspaper columns. Most followed the trail blazed by Carl Erskine, who had had success against Mantle when the Yankees faced the Dodgers in the 1953 World Series. Erskine threw an overhand curve that broke straight down, befuddling Mickey. Although few hurlers possessed such an effective pitch, most likewise favored an approach based on breaking and off-speed pitches. The problem was that too often the tactic didn't work. Mickey could hit almost everything.[30]

Boston's Willard Nixon boasted a lifetime 10–5 record against the Yankees, but even he feared Mantle. He took a cautious approach. "You can't afford to give him a good pitch unless you're sure he's going to be completely fooled," he said. "Even then it's dangerous." He recalled one confrontation. "I was throwing breaking stuff, as usual, and I certainly wasn't planning to let him sock a long blow. In fact, I was hoping for a grounder. But Mickey connected with a knuckler that was almost at his shoe tops and there was nothing to do but watch it disappear." It was as if the strike zone meant nothing to Mantle. "I've seen enough to know that home run hitters can't be choosy," he told columnist Joe Williams.[31]

It always came back to the same question: Could he hit sixty-one? It was a heady time. "Can the Kid Make It?" asked a headline in the *New York Times*. Hank Greenberg, Jimmie Foxx, Hack Wilson, Ralph Kiner—they had all made it into the mid-fifties and fallen short. But, John Drebinger wrote, Mickey had a rare quality. He fired the imaginations of hard-core fans and people who couldn't tell the difference between a baseball and a softball. "The fever again is gripping one and all. Even case-hardened observers, who vowed long ago they never would concede the thing could happen until it actually had, are finding it difficult to remain cool, calm and collected."[32]

Could he do it? Matching the Babe through September would be a challenge, Mickey's friend and teammate Hank Bauer thought. Ruth's 1927 September had been epic, and at the same time, Mantle would have to face "a lot of lefthanders" in Yankee Stadium, making it more difficult to hit balls out of the park. "I figure if he has 50 by the end of the month he'll make it," he predicted. Could he do it? From Bauer to the reporters in the press box, to the fans in the stands, to the people on the streets, everyone believed he had a slugger's chance.[33]

THEN MANTLE WENT COLD. On August 17 the Yankees began a four-game series in Baltimore. Memorial Stadium was a "hitters' graveyard" where long fly balls died in the enormous outfield. Mickey had not hit a homer there all year. In the August series, Orioles pitchers buried him. In four games he went 2–17, failed to hit a home run, and watched his batting average slip. Still, Mickey maintained a comfortable lead in the batting competition with Williams.[34]

Mantle was still making news, but now it was driven by his failures. Even before the disastrous Baltimore series, sportswriters noted that although Mickey was eleven games ahead of Ruth's pace, he was statistically behind it. Mantle was averaging one homer every 2.71 games;

in 1927 Babe had average one every 2.57 contests. In short, he had to pick up his production. Now, however, he was clearly falling behind, and he had to contend with the added pressure of headlines announcing his failures. "Mantle Fades in Homer Race: Blanked in 3 Straight Games," trumpeted the *Detroit News*. "Yanks Tired for Stretch, Mantle Looks Tiredest," echoed the *New York World-Telegram and Sun*. "Pressure to Mount on Mantle," pitched *The Sporting News*. Mickey, reporters agreed, faced more pressure than Ruth had. Hank Greenberg astutely observed than he and Jimmie Foxx had been lucky when they challenged the record. They hadn't played in the New York fishbowl. As long as Mantle was in pursuit of Ruth and the Triple Crown, nothing he did on the field would go unobserved. Everything would be meticulously reported, analyzed, and quantified.[35]

"Frustrating game, baseball," Mickey would later write. "When you're on a hot streak, hitting seems like the easiest thing in the world. The ball comes up there looking like a great big balloon and you think you're never going to make an out. But when you cool off and go into a slump, the ball comes up there looking like a golf ball and you get the feeling you're never going to get another hit." And the ball was still miniscule when Mantle faced Cleveland's formidable pitchers. He went 1–4 against Herb Score and 0–3 versus Early Wynn. After the game, another Indians pitcher, Bob Lemon, told reporters that he didn't know what was wrong with the slugger. "Previously he always has been able to blast curves just as well as fast ones. So no pitcher can really be confident." But as long as the slump lasted, pitchers from Boston to Chicago silently celebrated.[36]

BACK IN NEW YORK Mickey escaped the glare of publicity by retreating to an unchanging, unthreatening place. During the hours before a game, the locker room was off-limits to anyone but the Yankees family. Warm and inviting, bright and spacious, the chamber was the envy of professional baseball. Broad pathways of tan carpet protected the brown square tiles on the floor. "When I first came in here, I couldn't believe that we were actually supposed to walk across the carpeting in our spikes. It was like walking through your parlor," Mickey recalled. And the lockers themselves were large and afforded an unusual degree of privacy.[37]

The Yankees let their guard down in the locker room. Some, especially the younger ones, sat silently, worrying about their performance and fearing the consequences of a few bad games. Others, particularly Billy Martin and Whitey Ford, talked loudly, joking, laughing, insulting anyone within an earshot. Since there was often a buffet, most had a sandwich before a game and a few beers afterward. *New York Post* columnist Leonard Shecter recalled Yogi Berra at these feasts. Berra, he thought, was a self-made star on the diamond but a media-made celebrity off the field. Unlike other reporters Shecter wasn't seduced by the litany of Yogisms. He found the catcher to be consistently profane and occasionally crude. And Berra was at his worst at the buffet table. "The other players always complained that Yogi Berra would stand naked at the clubhouse buffet and scratch his genitals over the cold cuts."[38]

Mickey, like most of his other teammates, wore thigh-length cotton drawers around the locker room. When on a hot streak, he was as affable, if not as loud, as Martin and Ford, but during a slump or when injured, he became withdrawn, moody, and apt to "turn his back even on well-wishers." Shecter believed he was instinctively self-protective. He "always doubted himself and, most of all, his knowledge of the game." Unlike Ted Williams, a student of baseball who had made a science of hitting, Mickey regarded his prowess with the bat as some sort of strange voodoo, a natural force that could leave him as mysteriously as it came. Intuitive rather than thoughtful, instinctive rather than analytical, Mickey reacted to a slump like a farmer did to a tornado: he hunkered down and waited for it to pass. Shecter thought that it was "possible that Mantle was incapable of even the minimum amount of concentration the finer points of baseball require."[39]

Mantle might have regarded the clubhouse as a safe haven, but it was fraught with potential dangers. His locker was next to Billy Martin's, a point of worry in the front office. Some of their hijinks were sophomoric. A few seasons before, they had set off on a quest to take a picture of every teammate on the john—with the exception of Joe DiMaggio, who was regally off-limits. Armed with a Polaroid instamatic camera, they became toilet dwellers, hunters looking to bag their next prey. As soon as they snapped a photo, they taped it to the wall in the training room. Remembering the bathroom adventures and other escapades, teammate Gil McDougald said, "Mickey and Billy would do all these things and start giggling until they had tears in their eyes. . . . Some of the other guys wanted to wring their necks, but they were like two kids. People would just smirk and say, 'There they go again.'"[40]

Sometimes their hijinks became dangerous. Passing the time during their monotonous train travels, Mickey and Billy stripped down to their undershorts and wrestled in the aisles of a Pullman car. Given Mantle's weight advantage, Martin always started the contest attempting to snare the bigger man in a hold but usually ended up flat on his back calling mercy. Occasionally, though, he got the best of Mick. "I fixed him once," Billy said. "I put my fingers inside his mouth, got him by the gums. He threw me, but he couldn't eat for two days."[41]

When they weren't wrestling, they played a sport called "nose poker." At the end of a head-to-head poker hand, the winner chose a card from the deck. If he pulled a ten card, he got to swat it ten times at the loser's nose. A skilled handyman swiping the celluloid card back and forth could produce a red nose, not to mention tears. "Once the train gave a lurch," Mickey said. "Whitey caught me right on the chin with his left fist. That bled me."[42]

Their antics were likely fueled by something more than just youthful energy. Both drank too much. After games they downed beer in the clubhouse, turned to harder alcohol during dinners at Danny's Hideaway and rounds at Toots Shor's, and guzzled a "hair-of-the-dog" hangover cure the next morning. This concoction was dangerous enough, but an assortment of pills made it positively combustible. Childhood demons haunted both men, but Martin's were more apparent. In 1956 sportswriter Al Stump spent several weeks with Billy collecting material for a feature article in the *Saturday Evening Post*. He concluded that the physical and especially emotional demands of playing big-league baseball were too much for most young men, and Martin, "the most unhappy young man in the major leagues," was a case in point. Combative on and off the field, plagued by family and marital troubles, subject to manic highs and lows, he suffered from insomnia, hypertension, and melancholia.[43]

Billy's solution to his problems was pharmaceutical. Insomnia and a lack of appetite caused him to lose weight and flag during the late innings of games. He turned to sleeping pills. They seemed to do the job, and his performance on the field improved, but increasingly he fought bouts of depression. Daily trips to St. Patrick's Cathedral on Fifth Avenue helped some, but so too did "nerve pills." Billy told Stump, "I took over three hundred goof balls [a combination of amphetamines and barbiturates]. Even then, most nights I'd be walking the floor until daylight." The combination of sleeping pills and antidepressants was not a long-term solution. He needed something to make him feel better and energize him for games.[44]

By the 1950s baseball had just what Billy and other listless players required. To be sure, not all baseball players suffered from Martin's string of afflictions. But during a 154-game season involving extended road trips, fatiguing train rides, day games contested under the hot sun, doubleheaders, and nagging injuries, they all tired at one point or another. Some had trouble sleeping in strange beds; others missed their wives and children when on the road for a week or two. Like Martin, many players didn't sleep well. They showed up at the ballpark bone weary and irritable. Baseball seemed less a game than an ordeal. The answer to a whole host of troubles was a little green pill.

Ballplayers called them "greenies," though they were not always green. Some were orange. The pills were amphetamines. The most prevalent brand, Dexedrine, was green; another favorite, Benzedrine, was orange. Stimulants and sports share a history that goes back to the ancient Greeks, and modern high-performance athletics has a long history of doping. And athletes recognized early on the benefits of amphetamines. By 1939 cyclists—as well as long-distance truck drivers—had discovered the miracles of Bennies. But it was during World War II that the gospel spread. German storm troopers blitzed into Poland and France emboldened by amphetamines, and every army used phentermine and methamphetamine drugs during the war. Physicians lauded their ability to push soldiers beyond the normal limits of the human body, staving off fatigue and instilling confidence.[45]

In the years after the war, family doctors prescribed amphetamines for a wide variety of maladies. They were hailed as a way to shed unwanted pounds and as an answer to general ennui. As authorities on the drug Lester Grinspoon and Peter Hedblom observed, "Never before has so powerful a drug been introduced in such quantities in so short a time, and never before had a drug with such high addictive potential and capability of causing irreversible physical and psychological damage been so enthusiastically embraced by the medical profession as a panacea or so extravagantly promoted by the drug industry."[46]

Ballplayers may not have been able to spell "ennui," but they knew a performance enhancer when they experienced one. Some had used amphetamines during their military service, but they did not have to introduce their teammates to them when they returned home. Greenies were already prevalent; candy jars full of them awaited players who needed a pick-me-up before a game. Pittsburgh slugger and future Hall of Famer Ralph Kiner recalled that after a stint in the navy, he returned to the Pirates; when he complained of fatigue between a doubleheader, a trainer offered him some Bennies. As he remembered, "All the trainers in all the ballparks had them."[47]

"Don't go out there alone" became the common admonition in the locker room. Every training room had colored pills—vitamins, "pep" pills, amphetamines, and painkillers. Players downed them like jelly-beans. For some they became the breakfast of champions, certain to cure a hangover, turn a road trip into a joy ride, make an ache disappear, and get you ready to play the game. Whatever the truth—and there is no clear answer—players were convinced that with the help of their little green friends, they swung faster at the plate, moved quicker toward a ground ball, concentrated more sharply, and performed better. And theirs was the ultimate performance business. Especially for players like Billy Martin, who was prone to slumps at the plate, energy, aggression, and field generalship were the recipe for staying in the major leagues. He had an extended family, child, and ex-wife who depended on his big-league salary. He approached amphetamines like he did drink: if one would make him feel good, he'd order a double and go from there. The side effects of overusing the drug—high blood pressure, abnormal heart beat, irritability, insomnia, anxiety, heightened aggression, and even psychosis—did not concern him, though he did fall into the dangerous cycle of using uppers to perform and downers to sleep.[48]

Martin told Stump about his pill use, an admission that did not endear him to Yankees general manager George Weiss. In that sense Billy was a rarity. In the 1950s and 1960s, most players did not broadcast that they took greenies before games, though some later mentioned it in candid memoirs. It was their secret, an aspect of the game that ran counter to its all-American image. Since Mantle was reticent to talk about anything with reporters, he followed baseball's code of silence. But it seems unlikely that he would have denied himself the perceived benefits of the pills. In 1961, for instance, when Mickey felt physically run-down, Yankee announcer Mel Allen told him to visit Dr. Max Jacobson—the notorious Dr. Feelgood frequented by wealthy Wall Street insiders, jet-setters, A-list celebrities, and even the new president and First Lady of the United States—for a quick lift. Jacob-

Whitey Ford, Mickey Mantle, and Billy Martin saw themselves as the Three Musketeers, dashing athletes who played one game during the day and another at night. To the Yankees management, they were perpetual troublemakers whose escapades constantly threatened to get out of hand and tarnish the squeaky-clean image of the team. *Courtesy of the National Baseball Hall of Fame.*

son gave Mantle a shot of amphetamines mixed with vitamins, human placenta, and eel cells. Far from curing Mickey's blues, the shot led to a series of complications. But the episode was evidence that he was willing to experiment with an untested drug.[49]

We can't know what Mantle was ingesting in the summer of 1956, but we have a clear idea of Martin's consumption, and we know that the M&M boys were racing around the locker room like spirited colts, playing practical jokes on their teammates, and behaving like circus clowns. For the two troubled players, it was all great fun, and they probably never considered that someone might get hurt.[50]

Then, on August 22, during Mickey's slump, the *New York Daily News* ran a story with the headline "Mantle Denies Leg Injury." The tale that he and the Yankees denied was that Mickey had broken his leg in some clubhouse horseplay. He hadn't, but the antics were real enough, and the scenario was all too believable to George Weiss. Mickey, Weiss knew, was a natural-born follower with a liking for rough-humored bad boys. Billy was just the sort of "bad influence" that attracted the slugger. And, as Roger Kahn commented, "a non-conformist fits the Yankees the way a teetotaler fits Toots Shor's."[51]

CHAPTER 9

The Best in the Game

HARRIET: "What will you hope to accomplish, Roy?"
ROY: "Sometimes when I walk down the street I bet
    people will say there goes Roy Hobbs, the best there
    ever was in the game."
HARRIET: "Is that all?"
ROY: "Is that all? . . . What more is there?"

—BERNARD MALAMUD,
The Natural, 1952

Every day that Mickey remained mired in a slump, Ruth's record drifted further beyond his reach, and Ted Williams crept closer to him in the race for the batting title. What made it all the more frustrating was that he did not have the foggiest notion of how to end his hitting woes. Williams, of course, would have known how to climb out of the hole. Teddy Ballgame understood that slumps stemmed from fundamental flaws. Great batters tried to hit the ball hard up the middle, hit it in the air, and maintain discipline in the batter's box. "If I'm hitting the ball hard and not getting hits, I didn't worry," he once explained. "I would say, 'The law of averages is going to catch up with this.'" So he concentrated on smacking the ball with authority into the outfield because he knew that a fly ball was less likely to be an out than a grounder. He also understood that he had to wait for the right pitch and not chase balls outside the strike zone. "A great hitter should walk three times for every strikeout," he insisted. Williams, in short, avoided prolonged slumps by mastering every nuance of hitting—where to hit a ball, when to go after a fastball, when to lay off of a curve, how to shift his weight, and how to adjust his hands. Nothing about hitting was too unimportant for him to analyze.[1]

Mickey, however, relied more on muscle memory, the valuable but mostly unconscious retention of previous swings located deep in the fibers of his arms, legs, and torso, rather than technique. And muscle memory *was* critical. It let him know if a swing felt right or wrong. Yet knowing that a swing felt wrong did not help him make the next feel right. That took a more conscious understanding of the mechanics of his swing, the very thing that Williams had and he did not. In the meantime, he pressed, swinging too hard, going after unhittable pitches, and compounding his travails by forming bad habits. In August 1956, Mickey knew only that the baseball looked like a golf ball, and he desperately wanted it to appear as large as a full moon.

Mantle's slump instilled hope in the Yankees' American League rivals. Although the Bombers' lead over Cleveland bounced between seven and nine games, if Mickey faltered, his team might—just might—fall apart. "Mickey has been the man who has carried the club all season," argued Indians general manager Hank Greenberg. "Unless he returns to hitting solidly, Casey Stengel will be in real trouble." Greenberg's forecast appeared a touch too dire; yet New York journalists fretted that perhaps Mickey was nursing a slight injury after all. They had seen it before—the long stretches of early or mid-season brilliance followed by late-season mediocrity. When a hitter as talented as Mantle stops hitting, it gives rise to all sorts of apocalyptic musings.[2]

He continued to struggle. Following two disastrous series against Boston and Baltimore, he managed one hit in seven at bats and struck out three times in two games against Cleveland. Then, in the opening game of a doubleheader against Chicago, he again failed to get a hit, going 0–3 with two strikeouts. In eight games, between August 16 and 23, he had three hits in thirty-one at bats, an abysmal .097 average. Mantle's slump seemed to be affecting his team. The Yankees had dropped five of their previous eight games. The club's failures mystified Stengel. "I'm just disgusted," he remarked after the game. "We had no pitching, no hitting. We looked awful. Even the defense looked bad."[3]

In the nightcap against Chicago, the Yankees' struggles continued, though Mickey rebounded in a 4–6 loss. In his first time at the plate he legged out a bunt, using his speed to record a hit. In the fifth inning he clubbed a 457-foot triple off the center-field fence. And he finished the evening with a ninth-inning home run. The "tape-measure job" into the upper left-field seats was his first homer in ten games. It kept him slightly ahead of Ruth's record pace, but given Babe's memorable September, his chances of breaking the record seemed remote.[4]

A bunt, a triple, and a home run—in one of the mysteries of baseball a slumping batter had once again found his groove. Mickey was hot, and now he felt like he was swinging at softballs. In the final eight games of August, he went 16–32, batting an even .500. Five of his hits were home runs. Once again he was the darling of New York, belting homers in Yankee Stadium and making appearances on television shows. And as his home run tally increased, so did his fee for walk-on appearances. In June he received $1,000 for a brief stint on TV; now he earned $1,500 to take a bow on such programs as *The Arthur Murray Party*.[5]

But even in the middle of a streak, the ghost of Babe Ruth loomed, seemingly just out of reach. An illustration in the *New York Post* depicted Mickey's plight. Looking toward the heavens, Mantle says, "It's Tough Babe!" A voice from the clouds answers, "Keep Swinging Kid!" Going into the Yankees' final game in August, Mantle's home run total stood at forty-six, still fourteen short of Ruth's record. But he took heart from the Yankees' schedule. They were headed to Washington for three games—and Mickey hit in Griffith Stadium like he owned it.[6]

MANTLE'S PURSUIT OF THE home run record was the story of the season. For many fans, especially fair-weather ones, Mickey Mantle *was* baseball. His exploits kept interest in the game high; he gave people something to talk about and reason to turn to the sports section each day. With Mickey chasing Ruth and the reenergized Dodgers closing in on the Braves in a tight National League pennant race, baseball became more exciting with every game. The demand to see Mantle was so great, suggested sportswriter Jerry Nason, that the entire American League owed him a bonus.[7]

Even President Dwight Eisenhower wanted another chance to see him swing the bat. On Friday, August 31, he quit work early, took a two-hour nap, and made a surprise late-afternoon visit to Griffith Stadium to watch the Yankee slugger. Before the contest Ike asked to meet the player everyone was talking about, and Mickey, cap in hand, made a brief visit to the president's box. They were introduced and huddled for a few minutes. Initially Ike urged Mickey to "hit two home runs for me tonight." Then he amended his request: "I hope you hit a home run. But I also hope Washington wins." It was less an executive request than a plea from the country's highest-ranking sports fan.[8]

Mantle did his part, punishing Camilo Pascual for the fifth time of the season. In the seventh inning he cracked his forty-seventh homer over the high right-field wall. The Senators, however, failed Ike. Although outfielder Jim Lemon hit three home runs into the left-field bleachers—a feat that only Joe DiMaggio had previously accomplished in Washington—the Senators lost to the Yankees 6–4. Still, the president thoroughly enjoyed the ballpark atmosphere. He beamed

In 1956 President Dwight Eisenhower proved Mickey Mantle's good luck charm. On three occasions with Ike in the stands, Mantle homered. In this photo, taken on August 31, Eisenhower asked Mantle to hit a homer for him. The slugger graciously obliged. *Courtesy of Getty Images.*

at every home run, rising out of his seat and leading the applause. With an election on the horizon, he sought to affirm his love for the Great American Game.[9]

At the beginning of September, the Yankees were coasting toward the American League pennant, but Mantle's quest to break Ruth's record and win the Triple Crown teetered uncertainly. He remained four games in front of Ruth's 1927 pace, but with twenty-nine games remaining he had to belt thirteen homers to tie the record and fourteen to break it. It was a daunting prospect. By September the season's toll on players' bodies was beginning to show. For the Yankees, it was time to give players like Mantle, Yogi Berra, and Whitey Ford a respite to rejuvenate their sore legs and arms before the World Series. But rest for Mickey was a dream. He essentially had to hit a homer every two games to surpass Ruth, and his grip on the Triple Crown was by no means secure.[10]

History was not in his corner. Of course, in 1927 the Babe had entered September on pace for a fine season (by his standards) and finished the month in Valhalla. After tallying forty-three homers by the end of August, in September he hit seventeen more in twenty-nine games, including six in the first seven games of the month and four in the last five. Other stars had approached but fallen short of Ruth's achievement. In 1930 the Chicago Cubs' irrepressible star Hack Wilson had begun September with forty-six homers. He finished the month with fifty-six. In 1932 the Philadelphia Athletics' slugger Jimmie Foxx had started the last month of the season with forty-eight dingers and ended up with fifty-eight. And in 1938 the Detroit Tigers' power hitting Hank Greenberg had gone into September like Ruth with forty-three homers. He too had a magnificent final month, but ended the campaign with fifty-eight.[11]

Greenberg and Foxx understood the obstacles and pressures Mantle faced. "Mickey's difficulties will come in the last four or five days," Greenberg warned. "Everybody will be more conscious of his attempt to break the record and the pitchers will be more careful." Foxx agreed. Mantle, he judged, "had the tools to do it," but he was uncertain about the Yankee star's "temperament." To break Ruth's mark, Mickey would need to avoid slumps, remain healthy, and most of all filter out all the noise about the Great Bambino, the September curse, and the magic of the number sixty. No one in a generation had done it. Many in baseball believed no one could.[12]

Ruth's record was not the only mark in Mantle's sights. The Triple Crown was also within reach, forcing him to be more disciplined at the plate. Consistent excellence at the plate won the batting title and, in conjunction with teammates who got into scoring position, the crown for RBIs. Altogether Mickey faced an unprecedented September of opportunities, challenges, and pressures. Before that month baseball fans and reporters only demanded that he play great. But now they wanted him to accomplish what Lou Gehrig, Joe DiMaggio, and even Babe Ruth had not. To satisfy their lofty ambitions, Mickey would have to be the best who had ever lived.

THE TOWERING HOME RUN that thrilled President Eisenhower was Mantle's only hit of the day in Washington. In his other four trips to the plate, he walked, grounded out, and struck out twice. His homer accounted for his only RBI. In Briggs Stadium later that night, Al Kaline led the Tigers to a comfortable 6–1 victory over the Athletics. The sensational young batter collected three hits and five RBIs. A month earlier it appeared as if Mickey would stroll to the Triple Crown. His .371 batting average and thirty-five home runs put him far ahead of his competitors. He even had a comfortable lead in RBIs, owning eighty-nine to Kaline's seventy-two. But by the end of August his advantage had shrunk to 118–107—still impressive, but with Kaline driving pitches to every field, far from safe.[13]

Al Kaline was something close to Mantle's doppelgänger. Not that he looked like Mickey. Physically he was lean and bandy-legged, a Walter Mitty compared to Mantle's heavily muscled Adonis. The resemblance went deeper. Both had suffered through the pain and uncertainty of osteomyelitis; Kaline's illness had led a surgeon to cut two inches of bone out of his left foot. And both were sons of struggling blue-collar men who believed that their sons' mastery of hitting a ball offered the only path out of poverty. Mickey's dad worked in a lead mine, Kaline's in a Baltimore broom factory. And both fathers suffered from illnesses. Like Mantle, Kaline's dad and uncles played semiprofessional baseball and tutored their boy in the finer points of the sport. And partially as a result, both boys excelled almost immediately. Before Kaline was ten he was playing in pickup games with grown men in a vacant lot in Baltimore. At eleven he threw a softball 173 feet, 6 inches. In four varsity years at Southern High, he hit .333, .418, .469, and .488, earning a berth on the All-Maryland team each year and winning the Lou Gehrig Trophy at the annual Hearst All-Star Game in New York.[14]

Al was a phenom. Detroit's legendary scout Al Katalinas watched him play at fifteen and recalled, "He was one of the golden boys." Baseball was his ticket out of the working-class east side of Baltimore and to a better life. In the summer he played in multiple leagues, across multiple age groups. Relatives drove him from one game to the next while he changed uniforms in the back seat of the car. There was no time to be a kid, no freedom to go swimming with the neighborhood gang or to the beach with a girl. "You're gonna have to work hard and you're gonna have to suffer if you're gonna be a ballplayer," his dad told him. "You're gonna have to play and play all the time." And he did. Sweating in the heat and humidity of Baltimore summers, grinding at the plate against pitchers years older than him, practicing hitting until his hands were blistered and bleeding, Al Kaline made the most of his immense talents.[15]

Baltimore was not like remote Commerce and scouts soon learned of Kaline's skills. The rules of the day mandated that a team could not sign a player until he graduated from high school, so Katalinas requested a meeting with him at one minute after midnight on the day after graduation. Kaline was on a date, but the scout met with the boy and his father in the morning and sealed the deal. Kaline signed a $30,000 "bonus-baby" contract with Detroit that required him to jump directly into the major leagues. Only eighteen, he was playing with and against the best. In 1954, his first full season with the Tigers, he hit .276. The next year he accounted for two hundred hits and raised his average to .340. At the age of twenty! He was the youngest player ever to win an American League batting title. That year he outhit Mantle by thirty-four points and Willie Mays by twenty-one.[16]

His fabulous season had unintended, if predicable, consequences. Like Mantle's sudden appearance in a Yankees uniform, Kaline's early batting crown brought with it impossibly high expectations. The praise

In just his third full season, Detroit Tigers outfielder Al Kaline was already a sensation. He had won the American League batting title in 1955 and, after a slow start in 1956, went on an RBI-producing tear comparable only to Mickey Mantle's. His hitting prowess kept pressure on Mantle's hold as the RBI leader until the final game of the regular season. *Courtesy of the National Baseball Hall of Fame.*

was immediate and staggering, though not quite on the same level as the response to Mantle, in part owing to the fact that Kaline did not play in New York. "There's a hitter," said Ted Williams. "In my book he's the greatest right-handed hitter in the league." Paul Richards, Baltimore's field manager and general manager, agreed, predicting, "That kid in Detroit, Al Kaline, won't fall short of Joe DiMaggio." Another experienced manager concurred. "The fellow is amazing. You ask yourself four questions. Can he throw? And the answer is yes. Can he field the ball. And you answer yes. Is he active on the bases? Yes, you'd have to say yes. And then, can he drive in runs? The real test. And again you say yes. So he is an amazing fellow."[17]

Now, in September 1956, Kaline, as shy and reticent as Mickey but just as determined to excel, was tracking the Yankee slugger. Although his batting average was far below Mantle's, he was gaining ground in RBIs. All he needed was a great September and perhaps a slight stumble by Mickey. And why couldn't he catch him? In 1956 there was still no reason to question Williams's judgment that Kaline was the game's premier right-handed hitter.

Williams, of course, was not about to confer the title of the game's greatest overall hitter on Kaline. Nor was he inclined to concede the batting crown to Mantle. For Ted, Mickey and Al were kids, talented certainly, but they had not been through the fire. He had fought in two foreign wars, and at home he had battled Boston scribes and fans. He had come up to the big leagues in 1939, when Mantle was eight and Kaline five. And he believed he knew more about hitting—and was better at it—than any man alive. Most players agreed. "He's the best hitter I ever saw," Mantle confessed.

Entering September with his team out of contention, Williams sought to salvage his own season. On August 31, while Mickey was entertaining the president, the Red Sox were getting mauled by the Orioles. But Williams went 3–5, raising his batting average to .346, eighteen points behind Mickey. Teddy Ballgame was ready for another run at the batting title.[18]

WITHIN EARSHOT OF columnist Red Smith, the guys were talking about sports. The tight National League race between the Brooklyn Dodgers and the Milwaukee Braves, the upcoming welterweight title rematch in Syracuse between Carmen Basilio and Johnny Saxton, Johnny Sullivan breaking Willie Troy's jaw in St. Nick's Arena—they touched on all the topics of the day. Then one of them "brought out a sleeper." "What ever became of Mickey Mantle?"[19]

"Maybe it was a trick question but it was a live one," Smith observed. "Ten days ago Mr. Muscles was making bigger headlines than Nasser," the Egyptian president locked in an international crisis with Great Britain, France, and Israel. "As of now . . . he is a strapping young man who also plays with the Yankees, same as Yogi Berra and Hank Bauer and that implausible old gentleman, Mr. Enos Slaughter." No longer, it seemed, was he the toast of the town, the darling of

Toots Shor's, and the savior of baseball. Now he appeared sadly mortal, struggling to stay in front of Ted Williams and Al Kaline. It seemed, at least to Smith, that there was no room on Mount Olympus for anyone but Ruth.

Maybe, thought the *Boston Globe*'s Harold Kaese, Mickey was another victim of the September curse. "A few days ago," he wrote on September 10, "it was the National League's pennant race against the American League's Mickey Mantle. Now it is no longer a contest. All that's left is the National League pennant race." At the moment he needed it most, when his name seemed to be on everyone's lips and his every movement was being scrutinized, Mickey had lost his power. In the first twelve days of September he failed to hit a home run, and now with seventeen games remaining, he needed to hit thirteen just to tie the Babe—a 1,000-to-1 shot, Kaese believed.[20]

For the Boston columnist, the real question was whether Mantle could still capture the Triple Crown. Williams had moved within eleven points of him in the batting contest, and Kaline was only four behind in the RBI race. But Mickey shouldn't feel ashamed. "He has had a fine season," wrote Kaese, pointing out that "better batters than Mantle"—including Ted Williams—had stumbled in September. In the last weeks of the 1949 season, "when pitchers are sharp and strong, the ball is colder and deader, and shadows fall darkly over home plate," Williams had lost the batting title to George Kell by .0002 points (.3427 to .3429)—just one more hit and Ted would have secured the batting title and the Triple Crown.[21]

A fine season? Better batters than Mantle? What had happened? How had Mantle become mortal? And how had he done so in such a beguilingly quick fashion?

The pressure to produce like he had all season, the burden to outduel baseball's greatest legend, proved stultifying. After entertaining President Eisenhower so royally on August 31, Mantle experienced a "September jinx," a term for an unexplainable slump. He later said that in early September he "couldn't get a homer if the pitcher told me what was coming." "Where was President Eisenhower when I really needed him?" he quipped.[22]

He started September badly, going 0–5 in two games against Washington and 3–8 in a doubleheader versus Baltimore. At the end of the second contest, the Baltimore-born George Herman Ruth Jr. had caught Mantle. That is, Mickey had lost his lead against the Babe. In 133 games both men had hit forty-seven homers, and to make matters even more dire for Mantle, Ruth hit two in his 134th contest. As if he needed any more pressure, he now knew he had to clout his forty-eighth and forty-ninth against Boston on September 5 or fall behind Ruth. It was a "phantom race," Red Smith declared, but a race nonetheless—and increasingly, he believed, one that Mickey had little chance of winning. Ruth's late September surge was simply unique. In the last ten games of the season he swatted eleven homers, a feat that Mickey was not likely to duplicate. "However," Smith speculated, Mantle "is already almost dead sure of winning the batsman's triple crown, a three-ply title which always escaped Ruth."[23]

Mickey did not hit two against the Red Sox. Nor did he hit one. Instead, he began to press, swinging hard at pitches just off the edge of the plate. It was the classic vicious cycle: the more he slumped, the more he pressed, and the more he pressed, the more he slumped. He had become a favorite of American League pitchers who rarely gave him anything to hit and watched him swing anyway.[24]

Mantle looked completely lost at the plate. "Some said that the pressure about Ruth's record was wearing me down," he said later. "But I didn't even think about hitting a homer. All I wanted was a single— anything. That batting average was dropping every day and I couldn't even bunt. I would jab it back at the pitcher or pop to the third base-man." He didn't know what to do.[25]

The days passed in a funk of broken bats and dented water cool-ers. In a string of six games he managed just two hits in twenty at bats. No home runs, no RBIs, and a batting average dropping like the Dow Jones during a recession. Ruth's record seemed a mere mirage in the distance. And suddenly the race for the batting and RBI crowns was on.

At the end of the Yankees' September 12 game against the Athletics, Mickey was batting .352 with 47 homers and 118 RBIs. Ted Williams had increased his average to .349. Al Kaline, leading the streaking Tigers to nine wins in eleven games, had upped his RBI count to 116. Once again, after so many spectacular months, it seemed that Mickey's season would end in disappointment and frustration. September, Harold Kaese thought, "may be the month when Mantle loses several things, including the Triple Crown, the batting championship, the home run record and a 1957 salary of $100,000."[26]

THE BREEZE AT Kansas City's Municipal Stadium was blowing strongly toward center field on September 13 when Mantle came to the plate with no men on. He had doubled in the first inning and was reading right-hander Tom Gorman well. Now in the third, with the Yankees holding a two-run lead, he hit a ball toward the left-center wall. It was not a blast that rocketed out of the park but the sort that climbs high and rides the wind long enough to get over the fence. The dwindling group of sportswriters who were still following the Mantle-Ruth story noted that Mickey needed thirteen homers in the Yankees' last fourteen games to break the record, and they all agreed that the mark was out of reach. Still, a double, a homer, and a victory made for a good day. Perhaps the slump was over. Even more than to break Ruth's record, Mickey wanted to win the Triple Crown.[27]

But the slump continued. The next day, after a train ride from Kansas City to Detroit, the Yankees played the Tigers in a doubleheader. Mickey went 1–5 and 0–4. "Key to Mantle's Woes: He Just Can't Buy a Hit," headlined the *Detroit Free Press*. "It's just one of those tough streaks that come to every hitter, no matter how great," explained Yankees coach Bill Dickey. "Nobody knows what causes a slump, or how to cure it." It just proved to Dickey that Mickey was human, subject to the same boom-and-bust cycles as any ballplayer.[28]

Dickey had to do all the talking because Mickey wasn't answering reporters' questions. When asked about his hitting woes, he shrugged, took a swig of beer, and headed over for a private conversation about winning another pennant with teammates Joe Collins and Hank Bauer. Distant from reporters, the Mantle of 1955, it seemed, had returned to the locker room. Later on, after the season was over, he would open up about the pressures he had faced. Now he just wanted a cold beer and the company of teammates.[29]

No wonder he was not talking. That day he had learned that his batting average had slipped behind Williams's league-leading .352. But Ted had problems of his own. Because he had missed so many games with a foot injury at the beginning of the season, there was some doubt that he would get the requisite four hundred official at bats needed to qualify for the batting title. It was going to be tight, a fact not lost on the pitchers who had to face the Red Sox. Normally the most judicious of batters, a hitter whose eye was so precise that umpires hesitated to call a strike if he let a pitch pass without swinging, Williams had to go after marginal pitches if he was going to reach four hundred. In short, he expanded his own carefully guarded strike zone. Pitchers rejoiced, celebrating by presenting him with a steady diet of low, high, inside, and outside balls. With so little to hit, he struggled.[30]

On Sunday, September 16, the Yankees played a twin bill in Cleveland, home of several of the best pitchers in the American League. They faced Bob Lemon in the first game and Early Wynn in the second. Both would later be inducted into the Baseball Hall of Fame, and in the past each had given Mickey fits. But not on this day. Breaking out of his slump in a solid if unspectacular fashion, he collected three hits in seven at bats, including an eighth-inning home run off Wynn in the second game.

Mickey attributed the homer to advice from Stengel and Dickey. "I never knew what was wrong until [they] took me aside and proved it to me that I was lunging at the ball and striding too long in the box," Mantle said. Ted Williams preached that a batter's lead foot should stride eight inches toward the mound. Any longer, the batter loses balance and gets in front of the pitch, resulting in a swing and miss, a foul ball, or a weakly hit ground ball. A ten-inch stride moved Mickey's arms away from his body's core and robbed him of his power. He didn't need the longer stride; in fact, he generated more power and made better contact with a shorter step.[31]

Success in Cleveland made the next day's train ride west to Chicago more enjoyable. The victory against the Indians eliminated them from the pennant race and brought the Yankees within one game of clinching another World Series appearance. Instead of fretting about his slump, Mickey relaxed, even finding time to read the sports pages. He noticed that the day before at Ebbets Field Sal Maglie had pitched the Dodgers to a 3–2 victory over the Cincinnati Reds. For the first time since late April, the Bums had moved into a half-game lead in the National League. Maybe, just possibly, the Yankees would play in another Subway Series and get an opportunity to avenge the previous season's defeat.[32]

Confident again, Mickey looked even better against Chicago than he had in Cleveland. A well-attended Tuesday-afternoon game quickly became a pitcher's duel between Whitey Ford and twenty-game-winner Billy Pierce. After nine innings the contest was tied 2–2, and neither pitcher gave up a run in the tenth. Bauer opened the eleventh with a deep fly out to left field, and Martin followed with a strikeout. That brought Mantle to the plate. Earlier that day he had singled, grounded into a double play, and struck out twice, but he remained committed to the shorter stride. Now, batting right-handed at dusk, he struck. He pounded the first pitch into the upper left-field stands, not as far as the 550-foot monster he hit off Pierce the year before, but it was enough to give the Yankees a 3–2 lead. The score held in the bottom of the inning, and the franchise won its twenty-second pennant. Mantle also became the only Yankee other than Ruth to hit fifty home runs in a season.[33]

After the contest, he reminded reporters that the win was more important to him than his home run. "It's something I'll always remember," he said of number fifty. "I was glad I got it because it helped Whitey win his nineteenth game. You know, he's trying to get twenty this year." Mantle's comment demonstrated what made him so likeable among his teammates: here he was with a chance to win a Triple Crown, and yet he never acted like he was more than just one of the guys. He was the consummate teammate, selfless and enthusiastic about winning above all else.[34]

Drinking celebratory beers before departing, the Yankees considered the upcoming World Series. Stengel seemed unconcerned with the outcome of the close National League race. "Bring on the National League," he cried. "Our club has been great at times and it has been lousy, but it's a first class club and it's in condition so we're not afraid of anyone in the National League."[35]

The real celebrations came later. During the twenty-hour train ride back to New York, the Yankees guzzled champagne. Casey told them to go slow and conserve energy for a bash in the city. "They should have their wives with them when they celebrate," he insisted. But not all the Yankees agreed with him. Whitey was only one win away from his twentieth of the season, Mickey had hit number fifty and broken out of his slump, and Billy Martin never needed much of an excuse to drink. Besides, they had won the pennant. That was worth several celebrations.[36]

HE WAS DREAMING ABOUT the Triple Crown, or, more precisely, about losing it. Mickey was dreaming about it at night and thinking about it all day. He didn't know how he got so wrapped up in the chase and hoped it would never happen again. "It's too nerve-wracking," he would say at the end of the regular season. But when the Yankees arrived in the evening of September 19 at Grand Central Station, he was in the race and determined to win it.[37]

Going into the last ten days of the season, his Triple Crown bid was a three-horse race. Ted Williams threatened Mickey's chances of winning the batting title, while Al Kaline encroached on Mantle's RBI lead. Williams's .355 batting average was five points ahead of Mantle's, but the Splendid Splinter had only 372 official trips to the plate. He needed twenty-eight more in his eight final games to reach the required four hundred. Four at bats per game was not an unreasonable goal, but it meant that he would have to break his number one rule of hitting: "Get a good ball to hit." At the beginning of Ted's major-league career, the great Rogers Hornsby had impressed the point upon him. A good ball, Williams explained, was one in his "happy areas," the spots in the strike zone where he could hit for the highest average. But now to reach four hundred he had to go after balls in his unhappy regions, especially ones low and inside and low and outside. He estimated that he could only bat .230 to .270 on balls headed for those portions of the strike zone.[38]

The question was whether Williams would change his approach. "I can't swing at a bad pitch," he insisted. "If I go for a pitch that's an inch to the outside, those pitchers will start feeding me pitches two inches outside and keep increasing the margins until I'm a bad-ball hitter. Then I'm just a bad hitter." His fetish for swinging only at good pitches so dominated his thinking that many believed he just couldn't give in to the creeping malady. Arthur Daley of the *New York Times* openly wondered, "Can Williams go counter to principles that are as much a part of him as his reflexes?" He doubted it.[39]

Making matters worse for Williams, six of Boston's remaining games were against the Yankees. Throughout the season Yankee pitchers had baffled him. In thirty-six at bats he had managed only eight hits, a miserable .222 average. Bill Dickey had devised a strategy for pitching to the Boston hitter. The rules were iron clad:

Get ahead of Ted Williams—pitch to him.
Get behind him—walk him.

No 'sucker' pitches to the guy.

Keep the ball low and inside if possible.

Simple enough, but difficult to execute. Yet so far the Yankees' throwers had gotten the best of him.[40]

Not only did he have trouble hitting New York's pitchers, but they now had an added incentive to throw him junk. They could eliminate Williams from the batting race simply by walking him. If Ted wanted to swing at bad pitches, all the better. *New York Times* sportswriter John Drebinger feared the possibility of a conspiracy. Certainly it would not rise to the level of the Black Sox Scandal, but, he commented, "this wouldn't be a sporting thing to do."[41]

Meanwhile, Al Kaline was behind Mantle in the RBI contest, but he was on a tear. In Briggs Stadium, before fewer than 1,500 fans on a cold, windy September 19, he accounted for four RBIs on a home run and three singles against the Orioles. In the standings, the game advanced the Tigers to within one and a half games of fourth place, an inconsequential change. More importantly, Kaline's 4-RBI performance drew him to within 1 of Mickey's league-leading total of 123. For the remainder of the season, Kaline could swing freely, knowing that the Tigers were simply playing for personal statistics.[42]

Mantle's dilemma was whether to swing much at all. Now that the pennant was won, Stengel had lost interest in the remainder of the team's games. "I don't care about the other clubs in the league and whether they're playing for second or third money," he told reporters. Late September was a time to bring up some promising minor leaguers, a chance to see how they handled big-league pitching. He also wanted to rest Bauer, Slaughter, and a few other senior players. And of course, Casey planned to protect Berra and Mantle for the Fall Classic. "Think I wanna go into another series without Mantle or Bauer? And how would it be if Berra was hurt catching in these remaining games?" Such catastrophic possibilities boggled his imagination, disturbing his sleep as much as the Triple Crown did Mantle's.[43]

New York had nine contests remaining in the season, including the two three-game weekend series against Boston. With Mantle and Williams vying for the batting title, even Casey hesitated to put his slugger on the bench. The first series at Fenway Park might determine the victor. Almost 25,000 spectators passed through the turnstiles to witness the Friday-afternoon duel between Mickey and Ted. A frosty slugfest, the game dragged on for three hours and twenty-three minutes before Boston won 13–7. Fans witnessed two records: the Yankees set a new American League mark for home runs in a season (183) and a dubious major-league standard for stranding players on base in a single game (20). But the records and the game's outcome were secondary to the encounter between Williams and Mantle.[44]

Ted walked only once and registered four official appearances at the plate, slapping two singles and raising his average from .355 to .356. It was a fine game. Mickey, however, was magnificent. He went 3–5, batted in two RBIs, and hit a towering 450-foot homer into the center-field bleachers. Joe Looney of the *Boston Herald* wrote that it "soared majestically until it struck a foot from the top of the center field wall at the section 36." On contact, center fielder Jimmy Piersall took two quick steps back and stopped in his tracks, admiring the ball as it caromed off the wall toward the outstretched hands of a group of spectators. It was Mantle's first home run at Fenway that season and number fifty-one overall. Only seven players in the history of the game had hit fifty-one or more homers in a year. In addition, his three hits raised his average from .350 to .353, only three points behind Williams.[45]

Fittingly, Saturday's contest was televised nationally on CBS's *Game of the Week*, and though it had none of the fireworks of the previous contest, it had even more drama. After eight innings, Yankee pitcher Don Larsen had surrendered only four hits, and his team led 2–1. But in the bottom of the ninth he ran into trouble. A Boston player reached first on an error, and Larsen walked two others. With two outs and Williams coming to the plate, Stengel sent in reliever

Tommy Byrne. His first pitch was a fastball over the heart of the plate in the happiest of Williams's happy areas. He hit it flush. "The torpedo-like smash," wrote Looney, struck Byrne on the inside of the left ankle and ricocheted over to "the almost unsuspecting Bill Skowron" at third base. Moose fired the ball to first to finish the 1–5–3 game-ending putout.[46]

"I don't think I fooled Ted a bit," Byrne confessed after the game. "It was a fast ball right down the middle, but it came back twice as fast. First thing I knew my ankle was stinging." So was Williams as he kicked the dirt on the way to first. Perfect ball, hit hard up the middle—and an out on the scorecard. Ted went 0–4, and his average tumbled to .353. Mickey finished the day 2–3, bumping his average to .354. By a thousandth of a point he was back on top.[47]

CASEY WAS NOT A worrier for nothing. Ballplayers get hurt during games. Byrne had a nasty ankle bruise after the contest. It could have been worse. The night before, infielder Andy Carey was beaned sliding into third base. He was taken to a local hospital. On his release the next day, doctors told him to take it easy for a while. And then in the meaningless 2–1 game, Mickey hit a ball to right field, rounded first, and sprinted toward second for a double. He felt a tick of a pull in the groin of his left leg. Not too bad. But bad enough for Casey to pull him out of the game a few innings later. It could have been worse. That's what Casey always said. It could be worse, and sometimes it was.[48]

Triple Crown or no Triple Crown, Stengel wanted Mantle healthy for the World Series. Yet he was sympathetic to Mickey's ambition to accomplish a feat that not even Babe Ruth had. Only one Yankee, Lou Gehrig, had won a Triple Crown, and it had been a decade since Ted Williams had completed one. And no one had won a Triple Crown and hit fifty home runs. Mantle had a shot at baseball immortality, and Casey did not want to completely take the bat out of his boy's hands. So he devised a strategy. He would remove Mantle from the starting lineup, allowing him to rest his legs on the bench, and pick choice spots to pinch-hit him. If there was a chance to get him in the game with runners in scoring position, Casey would send him to the plate.

Mantle loved to watch Ted Williams hit, and on Sunday, September 23, he got a chance to do just that. Resting in the shade of the dugout, he spent most of the game as a spectator, admiring Williams's swing. Ted went 0–3. His average fell another three points to .350.[49]

Mickey got his opportunity in the ninth inning. With runners on the corners, Stengel sent him in to pinch-hit. Mantle responded with a line-drive single into right field, scoring the runner on third. The hit raised his batting average to .356, giving him a more comfortable lead over Williams, and kept him ahead of Kaline in the RBI competition by 127–123. Although Boston sportswriter Bill Cunningham complained that Stengel had "been wanting to wrap Mantle in cotton" and suggested that Mickey's "injury" might be an excuse to keep him off the field, Casey's strategy seemed sound. Limiting his star's plate appearances would effectively freeze his batting average near the mid-.350s, making it almost impossible for Williams to catch him. But it would also reduce his opportunities to drive in runs, which might give Kaline hope.[50]

Sandwiched between the two Boston series were three road games against Baltimore. Sitting in the dugout, Mantle had time to reflect on his circumstances. "Kaline was healthy and I wasn't," he said years later. "He could have a big day or two and pass me in RBIs. Williams could get hot and pass me in batting. My home-run lead was safe, but I was in danger of not getting the Triple Crown I wanted so badly."[51]

Once again, he felt betrayed by his body. He was so close to the end of an incredible season. To stumble now would be difficult to endure. But it seemed to be happening. Casey sent him to pinch-hit in all three games in Baltimore. Mickey drew a walk in the first, fouled out in the second, and popped out in the third. Since a walk does not count as an official at bat, he went 0–2 in the series, and his average ticked down to .354, still four points higher than Williams. Kaline had only inched closer in RBIs. Mickey led 127–124. Both races would be decided in the last weekend of play.

WILLIAMS HATED YANKEE STADIUM late in the season. Mostly it was the afternoon sun, the way it created long shadows and knifed into the eyes of left-handed hitters. For a man who took everything personally, the sun seemed to conspire against Theodore Samuel Williams himself. He thought that the Yankees' management should turn the lights on during afternoon games in late September, but he knew why they didn't: they wanted to give an edge to their pitchers. Not that they needed the advantage. Mantle and Berra and the other Yankee hitters were accustomed to the sun and shadows. "But Williams, purest that he was," wrote David Halberstam, "thought that anything that diminished a hitter's ability subtracted from the game."[52]

Mickey didn't care about the hitting conditions. He only wanted to play. And he would, because Casey had said so. "He ought to be ready," the Professor announced. "Those four days off shoulda done him some good . . . an' I know the other fella [Williams] didn't hurt him much while he was out." That settled it. On Friday, September 28, the two finest hitters in the game, the two most celebrated players in baseball, would begin the series that would determine the batting championship.[53]

On a chilly afternoon before 16,760 spectators, Yankee pitcher Don Larsen kept the ball low and Williams off balance, making the brilliant hitter look ordinary. Three times he got Ted to hit ground balls at Billy Martin, and two of them led to double plays. Williams hit the ball hard but finished the day hitless and frustrated, his average falling from .350 to .348 and his chances of catching Mantle fading into the shadows of Yankee Stadium.[54]

In four appearances at the plate, Mickey only managed one hit. In the third inning with no one on base, former Yankee pitcher Bob Porterfield got careless and grooved a pitch. Mantle caught it perfectly, driving the ball into the lower right-field seats for his fifty-second home run. Although his batting average dropped to .353, the homer gave him 128 RBIs for the season. In Cleveland that afternoon, Kaline failed to knock in a run during the Indians 2–1 win over the Tigers.

With his slugger gaining some breathing room, Stengel decided to return Mantle to pinch-hitting duty for the final two games. The first of the contests decided the batting title. In thirteen innings, the Red Sox won 7–5, and Williams reached the four hundredth at bat he needed to be eligible for the batting title. But to do so he chased bad pitches, and he paid the price. Once again, Yankee pitching frustrated him. His 1–6 performance lowered his batting average to .345, too far behind Mantle to catch up.

Still, he didn't concede a "damn" thing when it came to skill with the bat. As far as he was concerned, Mantle had two advantages. First, he didn't have to hit Yankees pitching. Second, he had the speed to bunt and reach first on slow infield grounders. "If I could run like that son of a bitch," he said, "I'd hit .400 every year."[55]

Casey picked the perfect time to pinch-hit Mantle. In the bottom of the eighth inning, the Yankees loaded the bases, and Stengel sent him into the game to drive home a few runners. Enjoying the best season of his young career, reliever Ike Delock was on the mound. He tried unsuccessfully to tempt Mantle into swinging at a bad pitch. Mickey held his ground. If Delock wanted to be coy, he was happy to accept a walk and a cheap RBI. It was his 129th.

Before fewer than 3,000 spectators in Cleveland that afternoon, Kaline had knocked in his 125th and 126th, staying within range of

Mickey and guaranteeing that their race would go down to the final game of the season.

ON SUNDAY, SEPTEMBER 30, 1956, war was brewing in Egypt, and President Gamal Nasser vowed to fight to the bitter end if the West forced its plan for the Suez Canal on his nation. General Anastasio Somoza Garcia, president of Nicaragua, had just died from bullet wounds. At home, Americans were still talking about Elvis Presley's recent television appearance on *The Ed Sullivan Show*. Some 54 million people—82.6 percent of the television audience—had watched Elvis sing "Hound Dog," "Love Me Tender," and several other selections. But on the last day of the month, there was even more chatter in New York about baseball. That day would determine whether Mickey won the Triple Crown and whether the Brooklyn Dodgers would get the chance to defend their World Series title. Up one game against the Milwaukee Braves, the Bums sent power pitcher Don Newcombe to the mound against the Pittsburgh Pirates' Vernon Law.

At Yankee Stadium, the center of attention was a player who might not even participate in the game. Bob Cerv, who had come up to the Yankees the same year as Mickey, took Mantle's place in center field. Spectators sat listlessly on the chilly, overcast afternoon, watching a game that didn't matter. In the first half of the contest, the lead went back and forth. Then, with the Red Sox ahead by a run, the Yankees struggled even to get a man on base. Starting in the sixth, the crowd began to chant, "We want Mantle! We want Mantle!"

Mickey sat silently in the dugout. Casey was not about to send him in to pinch-hit unless there was a chance to knock someone home.

In the ninth inning, with the Yankees trailing 4–3, Jerry Lumpe singled to center field and advanced to third on an error. Casey waved Mickey to the plate to replace pitcher Jim Coates. Immediately, a roar erupted from the 18,587 spectators in the stands. Stiff from sitting for several hours, Mickey took his place on the left side of the batter's box. Rookie pitcher Dave Sisler threw a pitch that fooled him. He began to swing, then tried to check it. Too late. His bat made contact with the ball, rolling it slowly toward short. On contact, Lumke broke hard for home. Shortstop Billy Klaus fielded the ball cleanly, saw he had no play at home, and fired it for the putout at first. Mickey was nowhere near the bag when the ball smacked into the first baseman's glove. Rather than risk aggravating his pulled groin, he moved toward first almost as slowly as he had walked to the plate.[56]

Neither the putout nor the game-tying score mattered. Mickey's off-balance hit had driven in a run. He had gotten RBI 130, increasing his lead over Al Kaline, who was playing that afternoon in Cleveland.

"KALINE GET ANY YET?" asked Yankee pitcher Tommy Byrne.[57]

Boston had won the game; yet there were no losers in the Yankees' clubhouse, though there was some nervous chatter. No one seemed to care that Brooklyn had beat the Pirates in a thrilling contest and that there would be another Subway Series. For the Yankees, the story of the moment was in Cleveland. The Tigers and Indians were still on the field. Mantle and his teammates only knew that the game was moving into the late innings and that in the sixth Kaline had tripled, knocking in two runs and raising his RBI total to 128, two behind Mickey. He was bound to get another crack at the plate, maybe a couple.

Mickey paced the locker room. How did he feel? a reporter inquired. "Me, why I'd feel swell if only I could find out whether I can win this thing." Thinking for a moment, he then added, "I ought to be satisfied with the batting title, which is really something, but I'm all tied up in this triple crown business now and have to find out."

It was maddening. He went back to pacing.

Teammates told him not to worry. He would win. Mickey wasn't so sure. Failures and losses, injuries and deaths had defined his life more than successes and victories.

He got dressed and waited.

Someone came in with news from Cleveland. The game was over. Kaline had grounded out in the ninth without getting another RBI. "Good," said Yogi, "then Mickey gets it."

For the first time in what seemed like months, Mantle smiled—relaxed, satisfied, fulfilled. Fifty-two home runs, a .353 batting average, and 130 RBIs. He led each category in both leagues. He was only the fifth player in history to accomplish that feat, the others being Ty Cobb (1909), Rogers Hornsby (1925), Lou Gehrig (1934), and Ted Williams (1942). Mutt Mantle probably never even dreamed that big.

A reporter asked Mickey what it meant to him. He struggled with his response. He didn't have the words. He was easily tongue-tied and not given to any sort of introspection. How could he tell the worldly reporters of New York City about Mickey Mantle? He had inherited a dream, his father's dream, and it pushed him and nurtured him. One hundred thousand or more pitches thrown between his tiny home and shed, within sight of the Eagle-Picher chat mountains in Commerce. Hundreds of games on dusty, alkali fields that turned his eyes as red as a rat's. The pain and uncertainty of osteomyelitis, an affliction that could have killed him. The high-and-inside hole in his swing that got him sent back down to the minors. The failures and injuries and boos that dogged him as a young Yankee. The shadows of Ruth and Gehrig and DiMaggio that blocked the sun from his face. And now this—the Triple Crown. The realization of his old man's dream. How could he possibly summon some Yogi-like quip? How could he wrap his life into a neat, pithy statement and deliver it to them on a silver platter?

What did it mean to him? It meant anxiety at night and worries during the day, playing injured and struggling through slumps, hitting tape-measure home runs and winning games, laughing with his friends and drinking at Toots Shor's. It meant being a big-league ball-player living a big-league life. Boiled down to its essence, it meant that in 1956 he was the best player in the game.

He couldn't, and didn't, put it into words. But that big, wide-faced Mickey Mantle grin said it all.

YEARS LATER IN DETROIT a young kid taunted Al Kaline, who had come so close to Mantle in 1956. "You're not half as good as Mickey Mantle," he shouted. Kaline, a good and decent man, took it in stride. "Son," he explained, "nobody is half as good as Mickey Mantle."

OFFICIAL PROGRAM - FIFTY CENTS

Yankees

YANKEE STADIUM

WORLD 1956 SERIES

Dodgers

EBBETS FIELD

Everyone in New York wanted a ticket to the 1956 Subway Series. During the 1950s, there was no greater rivalry in baseball than the feud between the Yankees and Dodgers. This was the last time that vendors ever sold a World Series program featuring the two New York clubs. After the 1957 season, Dodgers owner Walter O'Malley moved the team to Los Angeles, marking the end of an era for New York. *Courtesy of the University of Notre Dame Special Collections.*

CHAPTER 10

Aristocrats and Bums

"Now come baseball's final moments. The Barber has thrown his last pitch. The Dodgers have won. . . . Mantle has his triple crown. . . . The season is over and now it is the World Series. This should be the climax, the ultimate in the extravagant drama that claimed the rapt attention of so many Americans this year."

—ROBERT CREAMER AND ROY TERRELL,
Sports Illustrated, October 8, 1956

Billy Martin could still see the blood on his hands. Losing the 1955 World Series had shattered him. Cursing and shouting, he had burst into the dressing room and pulverized his locker, slicing his knuckles. He couldn't tolerate failure. When he had finally calmed down, he retreated to the showers, hiding the tears. He hated himself for crying, but he couldn't suppress the pain. For an hour he had avoided reporters and his teammates. "I didn't want the fellows to see me," he said. "I couldn't stop crying. I don't want to feel that way again."[1]

Martin dreamed about another shot against the Dodgers. On the eve of the 1956 World Series, he told the *New York Post*'s Milton Gross, "I've been itching for a year to get back at them." He replayed one particular moment from the previous series over and over again in his head. In the sixth inning of Game One, with the Yanks leading 6–3, Martin hit a triple off Don Newcombe. After Don Bessent replaced Newk, catcher Roy Campanella visited him on the mound, warning the reliever that Martin played like a gambler with house money. "Watch that man," he said loud enough for Martin to hear him. "He's got a notion."[2]

Billy was not especially fast. And it would have been foolish for him to try to steal home with a right-handed pitcher on the mound and a left-handed batter at the plate. But Campy remembered that Martin had called him "spike shy," an intolerable insult to any catcher. Squatting behind home plate, Campanella peered at Martin out of the corner of his eye. Sure enough Billy broke toward home after the second pitch. Barreling toward Campy, he slid feet first. When they collided Martin threw an elbow, but Roy got the best of him, slapping his throat with a hard tag. Martin sprung to his feet, clenching his fists, glaring at Campanella. He hardly heard the umpire call him out.[3]

Now, a year later, he hoped that he would meet Campy again. He tried stealing home plate five times during the 1956 season. "I was practicin' for Campanella," he said. "Does he still tag 'em high on the pants?" If he had an opportunity to steal home, there was no way that an umpire would determine the outcome. "I'll not only go across the plate ahead of any throw, but [I'll] carry Campy with me."[4]

Those were fighting words. For the past decade no rivalry defined Major League Baseball more than the one between the Yankees and Dodgers. Nearly every October it seemed that the Yankees—and their arrogant fans—tortured all of Brooklyn. Yankees supporters delighted in reminding Brooklyn natives that the Dodgers were losers. Bums. Failures. Even the Giants won the World Series once, they said. Dodgers loyalist Bill Reddy recalled one painful October evening at a New York tavern when a Yankees fan taunted him. "You Goddam Dodgers," the man slurred, "you lay down like dogs." Incensed, Reddy interrupted the heckler with a shot across the jaw. In Brooklyn, mocking a man's baseball team was like insulting his family.[5]

Brooklyn, a resident journalist noted, developed in the "long shadow of its more glamorous and vertical neighbor." Manhattan seemed to be more important, the epicenter not only of New York but of America. It had the biggest and best of everything—Broadway, Wall Street, Times Square, the Empire State Building, and Yankee Stadium. Dwarfed by the city, Brooklyn appeared drab, devoid of monuments to human ambition and replete with the hard-pressed. If Manhattan offered the fairy tale of fame and fortune, Brooklyn offered cheap rent. "All the underdogs in the world live here," novelist Thomas Wolfe once reflected. "The dishwashers, the fellers who run the subway train, the fellers in cafeterias, the elevator operators, the scrubwoman, the fellers who work in chain grocery stores—they all live here."[6]

In the mid-1950s, Brooklyn was in decline. The signs were everywhere. Manufacturing jobs disappeared, and so did the workers. At its peak, the Navy Yard, once the largest single employer in the borough, employed more than 70,000 people, but by the onset of the Korean War, the number of jobs it provided had dropped by almost half. And as middle-class residents left for the suburbs, the borough's tax base—and its social services—suffered. "The Eisenhower era bragged of the good life for all, a time of abundance and prosperity," Pete Hamill later wrote. But in Park Slope, where his parents lived, affluence "didn't touch the Neighborhood. The prosperous were gone to the suburbs; among those who stayed, money was still short."[7]

Yet in 1955 the Dodgers had given Brooklyn a reason to celebrate. For years, the borough had thirsted for a championship, only to be turned away at the well. Finally, after losing to the Yankees five times in the World Series, Brooklyn parched no longer. On October 4, 1955, the Flatbush faithful raised their glasses, bottles, and flasks, saluting the men who ended the drought. It was the most exciting moment in Brooklyn since VJ Day. Dodgers fans flooded the streets, cheering and yelling, "We did it! We did it!" Taxi drivers blared their horns; church bells pealed; factory whistles blew.[8]

We did it. The chant revealed the close ties between the Dodgers and Brooklyn. In a land of a thousand accents, Brooklyn never perfectly represented the melting-pot ideal, but at Ebbets Field Italians, Irish, Poles, blacks, and Jews shared a common language as they cheered for their Dodgers. The players were the idols of the borough, heroes of aspiring big leaguers who dreamed that they too would someday represent Brooklyn. In October, whenever the Dodgers competed in the World Series, teachers turned on radios so that kids would not miss an inning. After school let out, children raced home, hearing Red Barber or Vin Scully's voice echoing through open brownstone windows. Some stopped on their way and stood in front of appliance stores, watching the games on television. Most kids knew the Dodgers by their nicknames—the Duke, the Little Colonel, Campy, Oisk, Newk, and Skoonj—like they were relatives or neighbors down the street. In Brooklyn, kids bragged to their friends about running into a Dodger at the local grocery or how they had followed a player home after a game. The sight of the players in the neighborhood, out of uniform, made Brooklyn feel a little smaller, like a village, and the Dodgers more familiar, like a factory-town team.[9]

For Brooklyn's working-class residents, the Yankees were New York's team—or, more accurately, Manhattan's team, even though they played in the Bronx. Across the East River the fans from the city lived a world apart. If the Yankees were perceived as corporate America's team, the Dodgers belonged to the blue-collar ethnics of Brooklyn, "dem bums" who wore denim and white T-shirts in the boisterous bleachers of Ebbets Field. "When we played the Yankees," future radio and television host Larry King observed, "it was us poor Dodger fans against the rich." Yankees fans "were different from us. You would never wear blue jeans to a Yankee game. And the Yankee fans didn't scream. They clapped, like at the opera."[10]

In the 1950s, being a baseball fan went to the very core of a New Yorker's identity; whom one rooted for revealed one's neighborhood, heritage, and cultural values. Doris Kearns Goodwin recalled of growing up on Long Island, "In each home, team affiliation was passed on from father to child, with the crucial moments in a team's history repeated like the liturgy of a church service." Every autumn, New Yorkers argued about baseball in bars, subways, delis, drugstores, and stadiums. And legions of Dodgers fanatics made sure that Yankees fans who came to Ebbets Field understood that they had entered enemy territory.[11]

During one October series, when a Yankees fan cheered too enthusiastically, a Brooklyn man said, "Why don't you go back where you belong, Yankee lover?"[12]

Then the intruder made a mistake. "I got a right to cheer my team," he said. "This is a free country."

"This ain't no free country, chum," the Dodgers fan replied. "This is Brooklyn."

IT SEEMED THAT EVERY October America fixed its gaze on New York. In the postwar era, between 1947 and 1956, a New York franchise appeared in every World Series but one. And in 1956 the Yankees and Dodgers met in the Fall Classic for the fourth time in five seasons. The Subway Series defined the city and affirmed New York's centrality in American life. It had become New York's own weeklong holiday, though one characterized by drama and suspense.

Some fans outside the Big Apple had grown tired of New York's baseball supremacy. "In the corn and rutabaga belts, in the rolling mill and pressed steel valley of the Midwest and in the highly cultured city of Boston," Jimmy Powers reported, fans grumbled that another Subway Series was "bad for baseball." Critics complained that the dominance of New York's teams made baseball too predictable. But the rivalry between the Yankees and Dodgers still generated national interest. Tourists traveled to New York, packing the city's hotels in the hope that a concierge or a doorman could help them score tickets. Viewers from Portland, Maine, to Portland, Oregon, watched the televised series on NBC. Shortwave radio networks made it a global event, bringing the games to American servicemen stationed in Europe, South America, and the Pacific.[13]

On the eve of the series, journalists cast their predictions; most believed the Yankees would win. Bookies set the betting odds at 3–2 in favor of the Bronx Bombers. Although the Dodgers had won the last series in seven games, sportswriters noted that the Yanks had played without "the most formidable slugger of modern times" at full strength. Mickey Mantle, Arthur Daley contended, could "swing this series all by himself."[14]

Before Game One, reporters asked the players how the teams matched up against each other. Mantle ordinarily let his bat do the talking. But he couldn't contain his exuberance. "In my opinion," he said, "the Dodgers will be a whole lot easier to beat than the Braves." Dodgers shortstop Pee Wee Reese couldn't believe that Mickey would insult his team; the Yankee star hardly ever offered an opinion about anything. But it didn't matter what he said, Reese suggested. The entire series would come down to whether or not the Dodgers' pitchers could neutralize the Yankees' power hitters. "If we can stop Mantle and Berra," Reese said, "we can beat them. And I think we can."[15]

The scouting report on Mantle, however, offered the Dodgers little room for optimism. Mantle, *Sports Illustrated* reported, "could beat you a dozen ways." He had "tremendous power" from both sides of the plate and could run the bases better than most players in the league. He could "hit it over the fence or bunt for a hit." In other words, he could do it all. "Pitch him high and tight," scouts advised, "slip in [an] occasional curve, move the ball around—and pray."[16]

THE MORNING EDITION OF the *New York Post* said it all: "Today's the Day!" On October 3, 1956, Yankees fans awoke and tuned to WMGM radio, the team's home station, eager for the latest reports about the Subway Series. The Weather Bureau predicted a perfect day for baseball: sunny, clear skies, and temperatures in the low sixties. In coffee shops and diners throughout the city, baseball fans debated the strengths and weakness of the Yankees and Dodgers over breakfast. In Brooklyn, officials prepared for the president's thirteen-car motorcade. Ike was expected to land at La Guardia Airport around 11:30 a.m. Unlike his opening-day appearance in Washington, Dwight Eisenhower's visit to New York a month before the election was well publicized in advance. His entire route was published in the city's newspapers, a tactic designed to generate enthusiasm for Eisenhower in New York and link him to the prestige of the World Series.[17]

Two buses of reporters and photographers, dozens of police motorcycles, and three secret service vehicles followed Eisenhower's caravan from La Guardia to Queens and then over the Interboro Parkway into the Democratic enclaves of Brooklyn. Motoring along Bushwick Avenue, Ike stood in the open-top car, looking resplendent in his brown suit, smiling and waving his fedora as schoolchildren waved back and shouted, "Root for the Dodgers!"[18]

By noon, an hour before the opening pitch, animated crowds had descended on Ebbets Field. Streams of people scrambled up the cobblestone slope of Bedford Avenue. Once again they looked at the familiar features of the stadium: the redbrick building, with its distinguished arched windows, looked like an old warehouse. Eager fans pushed their way through the turnstiles into the rotunda entrance. The scent of beer, cigars, and Stahl-Meyer frankfurters met them in the grand marble lobby.

From the grandstands spectators looked out over the greenest grass in Brooklyn and a reddish-brown dirt infield outlined in bright white chalk. In the lower boxes, fans packed into narrow seats, close enough to the field that they could see the expressions on the players' faces. In right field, the uneven wall featured a manual scoreboard and a forty-foot-high screen. Colorful advertisements decorated the lower wall. Abe Stark's clothing store ("Hit Sign, Win Suit"), Esquire boot polish, GEM razor blades, Van Heusen shirts, and the Brass Rail Restaurant paid for, and presumably profited from, the famous billboards. Out in left and center field, spectators squeezed into the bleachers, sitting on wooden planks. With the left-field line 343 feet and center field 398 feet from home, the Dodgers' powerful right-hand batters had no trouble hitting home runs. And since the right-field foul pole stood only 297 feet from home, left-handed hitters frequently pulled the ball over the Schaefer Beer sign onto Bedford Avenue.[19]

Shortly after 12:30 p.m., President Eisenhower's limo entered through the center-field gate. More than 34,000 fans rose to their feet as the Fourteenth Regiment band played "Hail to the Chief." Five members of Ike's cabinet joined him, including Secretary of State John Foster Dulles. So too did Mayor Robert Wagner, Governor Averill Harriman, and former president Herbert Hoover. Even the Duke of Windsor—the former King Edward VIII—made an appearance. Casey Stengel and Dodgers manager Walter Alston greeted the president at home plate. Then Eisenhower shook hands with Baseball Commissioner Ford Frick, the presidents of the National and American leagues, club owners Dan Topping and Walter O'Malley, and Brooklyn borough president John Cashmore. Eisenhower grinned as he shook hands with every player on the Yankees and Dodgers. For the first time since 1936, when Franklin Roosevelt campaigned for reelection, a president was attending the World Series. But now television offered Americans around the country an opportunity to actually see him celebrating the Great American Game.[20]

The president's appearance at Ebbets Field affirmed that no other American sporting event mattered as much as the World Series. No heavyweight boxing match or football or basketball game could contend with the significance of the Fall Classic. In 1956, more than a decade before the first Super Bowl, *Sports Illustrated*, the major sports weekly, published fifty-five feature stories about baseball and only five about pro football. And professional basketball received so little attention from the national press that one might have guessed that all the games were played in Alaska. The World Series, however, was so important that about a month before the election, the staffs of Eisenhower and his Democratic opponent, Adlai Stevenson, discussed whether both candidates would attend Game One in Brooklyn. Ultimately, Stevenson surrendered the stage to Ike. The World Series, then, was not just about baseball; it had become the most visible political platform in all of American sports.[21]

Standing adjacent to the Dodgers' dugout, from his box seat, AA-33, Eisenhower placed his hand over his heart, joining the chorus of fans who sang "The Star-Spangled Banner," a tradition that dated back to the 1918 World Series, when the world was at war and the owners in organized baseball wanted to demonstrate that the sport boosted morale and promoted patriotism. By 1956, amid the Cold War, singing the anthem at sporting events had become a ritual intended to unify Americans against the godless Communists. Baseball stadiums were among the most visible spaces where citizens could demonstrate loyalty to their country. Being a good American president, Eisenhower understood, meant showcasing your patriotism and your faith in democracy. After opera singer Everett McCooey finished singing the national anthem, Ike tossed the ceremonial first pitch to Roy Campanella. It was time, the umpire declared, to play ball.

In the top of the first inning, Sal Maglie's worst fear came true. The son of an Italian pipefitter, the Dodgers' thirty-nine-year-old hurler was nicknamed "the Barber" for the way he used to shave batters with high, hard pitches near the chin. Now he relied less on speed and more on a variety of breaking balls. In September, during the National League pennant race, his breaking ball had mystified the Milwaukee Braves, giving Maglie his first no-hitter. But the stakes were significantly higher facing the Yankees in the World Series. After Hank Bauer grounded out to third and left fielder Enos "Country" Slaughter reached first on a single, Mickey Mantle approached the left side of the plate.

Mantle had read the scouting report on Maglie. "He knows where he is going to throw every pitch," Mickey said. "He is thinking with you on every pitch. Worst of all, he never gives you a good ball to hit."

On an 0–1 count, Maglie threw a low, hard slider inside. Mantle crushed it. The ball took off toward deep right field, cleared the tall screen, and bounced off the hood of a car parked on Bedford Avenue. Mickey's majestic shot impressed the Brooklyn crowd so much that a "spontaneous cheer" broke out across Ebbets Field.[22]

The Dodgers struck back in the second inning when Jackie Robinson hit a solo home run off of Whitey Ford. After Gil Hodges singled, Carl Furillo smacked a double, driving home the tying run. Then, in the bottom of the third, Hodges hit a three-run homer, giving Maglie a comfortable 5–2 lead. After giving up a solo shot to Billy Martin in the fourth, Maglie settled down and went on to complete the game, striking out ten Yankees in total. With New York trailing 6–3 in the ninth, with one runner on base and two outs, Mantle stepped to the plate. He eagerly swung at the first pitch, bouncing a hard grounder to second for an easy 4–6–3 double play.[23]

Losing the opener to the Dodgers disappointed the Yankees, but the possibility of losing Mickey Mantle troubled them. Late in the game he seemed to be playing unusually deep in center field. When two short fly balls fell in front of him in the eighth inning, reporters noticed that he reacted cautiously, limping back to his position after returning the ball to the infield. Was Mantle injured? Was it his hamstring again? Had he pulled his groin muscle? Refusing to acknowledge whatever pain he felt, Mickey denied that he was hurt. But he was a terrible actor. "I'm all right," he told inquisitive writers. The *New York Post*'s Leonard Koppett remained unconvinced. "Mickey looked neither as fast nor as smooth as he usually does. He may not have a bad leg—but he ran like a man who has."[24]

RAIN SOAKED EBBETS FIELD the following morning. The Yankees lounged around the clubhouse, hoping the sun would break through. Around 11:00 a.m., Mantle began to change into his uniform. Five minutes later Commissioner Frick postponed Game Two.

In the Dodger's locker room, starting pitcher Don Newcombe grew restless. He had prepared to pitch and didn't want to wait. Newcombe worried that the delay would hamper his rhythm. Dressed in his white uniform, he stepped into the dugout, looked out at the cloudy gray sky, and headed toward the outfield. Jogging in the rain, he began to sweat, which relieved his anxiety, at least for an afternoon.[25]

On Friday the sky cleared, and Newcombe took the mound. In 1956 he was the most dominant pitcher in baseball, winning twenty-seven games, the inaugural Cy Young Award, and the National League's MVP Award. Standing six foot, four inches and weighing 240 pounds, he intimidated batters with his imposing frame and a fastball that made professional batters look like Little Leaguers. He threw so hard that hitters swore the baseball looked like an "aspirin tablet coming toward the plate." Using a smooth, three-quarter overhand pitching angle, Newcombe, Robert Creamer observed, threw "violently, falling off the mound a little toward first base." When the ball smacked Campanella's mitt it made a loud popping sound, bruising Campy's left hand.[26]

Newcombe was especially eager to pitch in the World Series. He had lost all three of his previous postseason starts—all against the Yankees. Critics called him a "choker." Even Mickey Mantle, the most reticent star in baseball, had taunted him before the series. "If Newcombe thinks he can throw a fast ball past me, he's got another think coming." Newk didn't back down. "Mantle has a weakness for a fast ball," he said. "I know where it is and he knows I know. If I get it where I want to, he's not going to hit it."[27]

Early in the game the Yankees shook Newcombe's confidence. After surrendering one run in the first, he fell apart in the second. The Yankees battered him for five runs, four of which came on a Yogi Berra grand slam that bounced across the gas station parking lot on Bedford Avenue. He pitched so poorly that before he could even retire six batters, Walter Alston replaced him with Don Bessent. Frustrated, he trudged toward the dugout and headed straight for the clubhouse, his elbow throbbing—no one knew that he had pitched with immense pain. He changed into his street clothes and stormed out of Ebbets Field. When he reached the parking lot at the corner of McKeever and Sullivan, an attendant sneered, "What's the matter, Newk? Did you have another bad day? Did you run into some competition?"[28]

Newcombe snapped. He had heard enough boos. His fury was shaped by the racism he experienced as a black man off the field and the epithets hurled at him in stadiums around the country. Seething, he punched the man in the stomach. A police officer intervened and took both men to the station, where the attendant decided not to press charges.

Meanwhile, back at Ebbets Field, Don Larsen took a commanding 6–0 lead into the bottom of the second. He had pitched well throughout September, winning four games in the final month of the season. Now, in the World Series, in less than two innings he had allowed only one hit but had walked four batters. Stengel had no patience for his wildness. After Don gave up a run, Casey yanked him. Stunned, Larsen could not believe it. Two innings? Casey couldn't even let him pitch two innings? "I don't give a damn if I ever pitch for the Yankees or Stengel again," he vented in the locker room. "He had no business taking me out of there."[29]

Perhaps Larsen was right. The Dodgers shelled six subsequent Yankee pitchers for twelve more runs, winning 13–8. Ultimately, the Yankees' abysmal pitching cost them Game Two. At three hours and twenty-six minutes, it was the longest game in World Series history. Stengel had used more pitchers in a single series game than any manager before, but none of them could end his team's misery. After the game, Brooklyn's most devoted fans marched down Flatbush Avenue with broomsticks, calling for a sweep. The last time the Yankees had failed to win a game during the World Series, Warren G. Harding lived in the White House. The following morning, Yankees fans relived the pain when they read the back page of the *New York Daily News*'s bold headline: "MURDER AT EBBETS FIELD."[30]

THROUGHOUT THE SERIES America's most popular ballplayer wrote an exclusive column for the *New York World-Telegram and Sun*. The Yankee slugger revealed his inner thoughts, analyzing each game. It was a rare opportunity for fans to watch baseball from the player's perspective—in this case, from that of the *real* Mickey Mantle. At least that's what the newspaper wanted readers to believe. But like Babe Ruth long before him, Mantle had little to do with the copy. In fact, with few exceptions, most baseball players depended on ghostwriters to manufacture an image that appealed to fans. And Mantle's column was no different. At best a reporter interviewed him and created a voice that conformed to public perceptions about Mantle, the modest star uncomfortable with celebrity. "I am from Oklahoma," he declared, as if readers had short memories, "and I still can't quite understand why there are some people who will pay money to have a ball player show up and say hello" on a television show.[31]

Playing in the World Series for the fifth time in six seasons—in addition to his exploits on and off the field—had given him a national profile. Fans became accustomed to seeing and reading about him and the Yankees nearly every October. But before 1956 the Yankees were really Yogi Berra's team. He was the club's most important player. During that season, though, Mickey had superseded him. Yet, if Mantle was going to secure his place among the Yankee legends and truly fulfill his promise, he needed to lead the Bronx Bombers to glory. The Triple Crown winner couldn't afford to sputter at the plate or let aches and pains sideline him. Losing the World Series again to the Dodgers would blemish his remarkable season.

After the Yankees dropped Game Two, Mantle's column appeared to reveal a man humbled by defeat. He even thanked Dodgers fans "for their kindness" in not booing the Yankees off the field. Decades later, however, in his autobiography about the season, he portrayed Dodgers fans as an angry mob chasing the Yanks out of town. "The bus ride home from Brooklyn was what you might imagine," he wrote. "Thousands of fans lining the street, cursing us, throwing fruit and vegetables at the bus, clenching their fists." But in 1956 Mantle's ghostwriter didn't pen a word about Brooklyn fans carrying clubs and pitchforks. Criticizing baseball fans—even those from Brooklyn—would have undermined his mass appeal.[32]

Returning home to Yankee Stadium renewed Mickey's optimism. He hit well on the road but even better at home. In 1956, he hit .336 away from the Bronx and .369 at Yankee Stadium. By no means did he think the season was over. A year earlier the Yankees had won the first two games of the World Series, but the Dodgers came back to win the championship in seven games. "We can come back, too," he declared.

Early on Saturday afternoon, October 6, excited Yankees fans packed into "D" trains bound for 161st Street and River Avenue. The Transit Authority added additional express cars to accommodate tens of thousands of fans heading to the Bronx. It was a cool autumn day, and men wore fedoras and bomber jackets with newspapers under their arms; women sported swing coats, matching hats, and fashionable long gloves. Nearly 74,000 fans filed into the stadium, more than double the number who attended the previous game at Ebbets Field. Desperate for a victory, Yankees supporters pinned their hopes on Whitey Ford, one of the most reliable and effective pitchers in the American League. The slight southpaw, a handsome blond with a boy's face, took the mound with boundless confidence. He didn't overpower hitters; rather, he relied on his command of three pitches—fastball, curveball, and changeup—to induce groundouts. Carrying a 2.52 earned run average and a 19–5 record, the American League's best left-handed pitcher studied opposing batters, mastering their tendencies, strengths, and weaknesses. "My greatest asset as a pitcher," he said, "is knowing the hitters."[33]

Ford had studied the Dodgers closely. But they were just as familiar with him. In three innings of the first game of the series, Brooklyn had battered the lefty. He had given up five earned runs, six hits, and two homers. Yet in Game Three, he looked like a different pitcher, poised and sharp. Although the Dodgers scattered eight hits against him, Ford limited the damage to three runs—two earned—over nine innings. Enos Slaughter, a balding forty-year-old outfielder, drilled a three-run homer off Roger Craig in the sixth inning, leading the Yankees to a 5–3 victory.[34]

Mickey managed only one hit in Game Three—a bunt single. But the next day, in the sixth inning of Game Four, he launched a 450-foot moonshot into the center-field bleachers, arousing ebullient cheers throughout Yankee Stadium. His solo homer gave the Yanks a 4–1 lead; the following inning, Hank Bauer clubbed a two-run homer. In his first World Series start, Tom Sturdivant, the Yankees' sophomore pitcher, kept the Dodgers off balance, throwing a devastating knuckleball that danced, dipped, and fluttered across the plate. Mystified, the Dodgers swung at the darting ball like an angry chef trying to swat a fly.[35]

The Yankees' 6–2 victory erased the Dodgers' series lead. The next day's game at Yankee Stadium would be pivotal. The winning team would need only one more victory to celebrate the championship. Don Larsen's mediocre performance led him to doubt that he would start another game in the series. But Stengel hadn't completely given up on him. "He wasn't throwing over there in Brooklyn," the Ole Professor said. "He was just pushing the ball. Maybe he was thinking too much about those fences. He can pitch a lot better than that," he added. "You'll see."[36]

STANDING IN FRONT of his locker on Monday, October 8, at around 10:30 a.m., Don Larsen looked at his cleats and discovered a baseball in one of them. It had become a tradition in the Yankee clubhouse for third-base coach Frank Crosetti to arrive early and place a ball in the starting pitcher's shoe. When Hank Bauer entered the room, he asked Crosetti who would take the mound. The answer stunned him. "Oh, shit," Bauer said. Larsen couldn't believe it either. He stared at the ball for a moment, his mind racing. Stengel had taken a big gamble on him, and he knew it.[37]

Conflicting accounts about Game Five have been passed down over the decades. Some suggest that Larsen arrived at the Yankees clubhouse with a throbbing headache from a night of bar hopping. Others, including Larsen, contend that he nursed a few beers with his friend, Art Richman, a sportswriter for the *New York Daily Mirror*, before returning to his hotel room at the Grand Concourse shortly before midnight. Toots Shor bragged that on the eve of Game Five, Larsen guzzled drinks at his restaurant and that he introduced him to Supreme Court chief justice Earl Warren. Bob Cerv, a reserve outfielder, later recalled closing down a bar with Larsen and parting ways at 4:00 a.m. On the morning of Game Five, Cerv claimed, he phoned Larsen to make sure he rolled out of bed. Larsen picked up the receiver, groaning from a hangover, "Noooooo."[38]

Mickey Mantle, whose memories often bordered on fiction, clouded by years of hard drinking, remembered that night differently. He recalled that he and teammate Rip Coleman met up with Larsen at Bill Taylor's restaurant on West 57th Street in Manhattan. According to Mantle, though, Larsen downed mugs of ginger ale. Perhaps Larsen enjoyed the carbonated soft drink, but it's difficult to imagine him turning down beers with the boys, especially since he doubted that Stengel would call on him the next day. When Mantle left Taylor's around 10:30 p.m., he remembered that Larsen "was cold, stone sober." Whether Larsen ended the night that way is impossible to know and ultimately unimportant. What matters is that in an era characterized by a "drink hard, play hard" ethos, the exaggerated tales of Larsen's exploits on the eve of Game Five make his performance on the field appear all the more extraordinary.[39]

Sal Maglie demanded Larsen's very best. The winning pitcher from Game One retired the first eleven Yankees with ease. In the fourth inning of a scoreless game, he had not yet given up a hit when Mickey Mantle approached the plate with two outs. Sal threw two straight pitches on the outside corner, one called a strike, the other a ball. His third pitch, again on the edge of the plate, was called a strike. He tested Mantle once more; Mickey ripped a foul ball into the stands, his timing slightly off. Then Maglie threw another pitch off the plate. Ball two. Maglie tried zipping the next pitch past him, but Mantle fouled it off again. With every pitch the stakes grew. Each man calculated the other's next move. Was Mickey looking for another fastball on the outer edge of the plate? Could Maglie surprise him with an inside pitch?

Squatting behind the plate, Campanella quietly shifted his feet, positioning himself closer to Mickey, and called for a curveball inside. Maglie nodded at Campy and delivered the pitch. *Crack!* The ball flew down the right-field line, curving just inside the foul pole. The Yankees' radio broadcaster, Mel Allen, followed its flight. "It's going . . . going . . . GONE! How 'bout that?!"[40]

"Mighty Mickey" had delivered at a pivotal moment. A home run in such a crucial game affirmed his iconic status. Soon enough, though, he would be tested again, challenged to preserve the very lead that he had created.

In the top of the fifth inning, the scoreboard showed that Larsen had not yet surrendered a run, hit, or walk. Nor had a Dodger reached base on an error. Larsen had changed his pitching delivery. Instead of throwing from a traditional windup, he rocked back and propelled himself forward, making it harder for the Dodgers to time his delivery. Throwing with the nonchalance of a boy skipping stones across a pond, Larsen had never looked so comfortable on the mound. Exercising pinpoint control, he consistently threaded first-pitch strikes. Only once—in the first inning against Pee Wee Reese—had he thrown more than three balls to a batter. In the fifth, after Jackie Robinson flied out to right field, Gil Hodges, a devastating pull hitter, threatened Larsen's perfect game. On a 2–2 count, Larsen fired a hard slider. "The ball was flat when it drifted" across the plate, he admitted later. Hodges uncorked his body, extended his arms, and lofted the ball into deep left-center field.[41]

Larsen knew he was in trouble the moment Hodges hit the ball. He figured it had a chance to at least reach the warning track near the outfield fence, and like everyone else he wondered about the condition of Mantle's leg. Mickey quickly backpedaled, pivoted, and sprinted toward the left-center-field wall, his head up, eyes tracking the ball. As it began dropping, he extended his left arm, fast approaching the fence. Mel Allen described the drama for his radio listeners: "Mantle digging hard. Still going . . . *How about that catch?!*" Running full speed, Mickey somehow managed to stab the ball. It was, he said later, the best catch he ever made. The remarkable feat seemed to answer all the questions about his health.[42]

By the end of the seventh inning, with the Yankees leading by a slim 2–0 margin, everyone in the stadium knew that Larsen had an opportunity to do something never done before. Pitching a perfect game—"27 up, 27 down,"—meant tossing nine complete innings without allowing a player on base and winning. Prior to 1956, only four pitchers had ever tossed a perfect game and all in the regular season, the last in 1922 when the Chicago White Sox's Charlie Robertson faced the Detroit Tigers. But no pitcher had ever completed a no-hitter in the World Series, let alone a perfect game. Before Game Five began, the odds that Larsen would throw a perfect game were 76,000 to 1. He had a better chance of being hit by a car as he crossed the street on his way to the stadium.[43]

In the Yankees' dugout Larsen's teammates avoided sitting next to him. "By then," he later said, "the guys on the bench wouldn't even look at me." Mel Allen struggled to explain to radio listeners that Larsen so far had pitched a perfect game without actually using the term. Baseball's superstitious culture frowned upon anyone acknowledging what everyone was thinking: if Larsen could protect his flawless outing, it would be the greatest pitching performance in history.

Remarkably, between innings as he smoked a cigarette in the dugout, he turned to Mantle and asked, "Wouldn't it be something if I a pitched two more innings with a no-hitter?" Mantle didn't answer, staring at him as if he were a martian, and then walked away.[44]

Returning to the field in the eighth, Don began to feel added pressure. "It's funny how lonely you feel on the mound at a time like that," he said later. Toeing the rubber, his heart pounding, his arm felt heavier. Narrowing his focus on Yogi Berra's signs, the moment distracted him. The crowd hummed, and he heard a ringing noise in his ears. He could feel the eyes of every man, woman, and child in the stadium fixed on him. He thought about his parents watching on television. "The more I thought about it," he said, "the more my hands began to sweat."[45]

After retiring the side in the eighth, Larsen took the mound for one final inning and prayed. He stood three outs away from accomplishing something that Walter Johnson, Christy Matthewson, Cy Young, and all the other greats never had. Arthur Daley suggested that with each pitch the tension in the stadium grew like a red-faced boy blowing up a balloon. At any moment it might pop. Before the inning began, Yogi patted him on the back. "They're still in the game," he reminded Larsen. "Get the first guy. That's the main thing."[46]

Standing in center field directly behind Larsen, Mantle felt his knees shaking. "I kept praying the ball wouldn't be hit to me," he confessed. As the afternoon sun began fading, shadows fell across the field, making it difficult for Mantle to spot the ball. Seeing Carl Furillo approach the batter's box, Larsen muttered, "Throw strikes." "Throw strikes," he repeated. Behind the plate Berra tried distracting Furillo. "This guy's got good stuff, huh?" Furillo glared at him. "Yeah, not bad," he said. After fouling off two pitches, Furillo took a ball and fouled two more. Then he popped out to right fielder Hank Bauer.[47]

Larsen took off his cap, wiped the sweat from his forehead, and took a deep breath. Two outs to go.

Next up: Roy Campanella. On the first pitch Larsen threw a meaty fastball. Campy frightened the crowd when he connected on a long fly, but it bent foul into the upper-left-field stands. Larsen shrugged it off and snapped a curveball on the next pitch. Campanella bit, dribbling a slow grounder to Billy Martin for an easy out.

Two down, one to go.

Bouncing on their feet, the crowd clapped and cheered, in a state of near rapture. Again, Larsen turned his back to the plate, removed his cap and dabbed the sweat from his brow. He picked up the resin bag, tossed it a few times, covering his right hand in a fine powder, and then wiped his hand on his pants.

Pinch-hitting for Sal Maglie, Dale Mitchell, a left-handed reserve outfielder, was the Dodgers' final hope. Anxious, Mantle's mind teetered between fear and focus. "Please don't hit it to me," he thought. He worried that Mitchell, a slashing hitter, might flip a low, looping fly in front of him. But he was also concerned that if he moved any closer toward home, Mitchell might line one right over his head. Uncertain, he stayed put. Calling the game for the Dodgers, Vin Scully remarked, "Yankee Stadium is shivering in its concrete foundations right now."[48]

Larsen's first pitch, low and outside, missed the plate. The crowd groaned when the umpire called it a ball. Berra signaled for a slider. Larsen delivered strike one. Mitchell swung at the next pitch. Strike two. Then Mitchell fouled a curveball. Larsen took a deep breath and fired another fastball. Mitchell began his swinging motion but checked it.

"Strike three!" the umpire shouted.

It didn't matter that Mitchell thought the ball was well off the plate. The game was over. The crowd erupted. Yogi Berra thrust his right arm into the air, raising the ball like a trophy, and darted toward the mound, leaping into Larsen's arms. The entire Yankee team mobbed them. Fans flooded the field, celebrating with the players.[49]

Don Larsen had entered the record books. It was, Arthur Daley noted, "akin to catching lightning in a bottle." Soon, it seemed that everyone in New York was hailing him as the hero of the series, "the imperfect man" who "pitched the perfect game." Yet the following morning, when fans opened up the pages of the sports section expecting to read all about Larsen's gallant performance, they discovered that his estranged wife had filed a complaint with a Bronx court claiming that since their separation he had failed to pay alimony. Vivian Larsen's lawyer told the press that Don had deserted her. "While this baseball hero is enjoying the luxuries of life and the plaudits of the public," he charged, "he is subjecting his fourteen-month-old baby girl and his wife to the pleasures of a starvation existence." Larsen, however, swore that the marriage existed "in form only" for the sake of the child. They never even lived together, he said. If the Yankees won the World Series, however, he would have no trouble paying alimony. Each player on the winning team figured to receive nearly $10,000.[50]

THE YANKEES HAD WON three straight home games and needed only one more victory at Ebbets Field to win the series. For all the attention justly accorded to Larsen, Mickey Mantle had played a decisive role in the outcome of Game Five. His miraculous catch preserved the perfect game, and his home run, Robert Creamer argued, "cost Maglie the ball game. In all probability, it also cost the Dodgers the Series."[51]

Thanks to Mantle and Larsen, everyone—even the Yankees themselves—seemed to think that the series was over. Pitcher Tommy Byrne admitted later, "I think Don's perfect game may have actually hurt us a little bit. It was such an emotional thing with everyone jumping and yelling and congratulating Don that it seemed like we had just won the World Series. And some of us may have forgotten that we hadn't won anything yet."[52]

After losing Game Five to the Yankees, Jackie Robinson could sense that the end was near. In the winter of his career, he realized that if the Dodgers did not win one more game, his playing days could be over. But he wasn't giving up just yet. In the bottom of the tenth inning of a scoreless pitching duel between the Dodgers' Clem Labine and the Yankees' Bob Turley, Robinson proved that he had one last heroic moment left. With two men on and two outs, he stepped to the plate against Turley, who had already struck out ten Dodgers. After fouling the first pitch into the seats along the third base line, Jackie smacked a fastball into left field. As the ball sailed over Enos Slaughter's outstretched glove, Jim Gilliam rounded third and crossed home plate. The Flatbush faithful exploded with joy, watching the Dodgers swarm Jackie, slapping him on the back and head.[53]

The Dodgers lived to play another day, as the Yankees mourned another loss at Ebbets Field. "Our clubhouse," Mantle recalled, "was like a morgue." Hardly anyone spoke. On the quiet bus ride back to the Bronx, Billy Martin sat next to Casey Stengel, imploring him to replace Slaughter with Elston Howard, who had just returned from the hospital, recovering from strep throat. Slaughter had misplayed Robinson's drive in the tenth inning, Martin thought, and cost the Yanks the game. "If you're going to keep playing that fucking National League bobo out there," Martin complained, "we're going to blow this series. You better put Elston out there." And, he added, "you better get Skowron's ass back on first base."[54]

An eavesdropping reporter could not believe that a ballplayer would challenge the manager's authority the way that Martin had. But Billy knew how to push Stengel's buttons. "You think you know the Old Man that well?" the reporter asked. Grinning, Martin replied, "I'll pick the lineup for you tomorrow."[55]

A YEAR EARLIER THE Brooklyn Dodgers became the second team in history to lose the first two games of the World Series and nevertheless go on to win the championship. In 1921, when the series was best-of-nine, the New York Giants lost the first two games to the Yankees, then won five of the next six. However, in October 1956, the

Yankees did not have the luxury of three more games. They had to win now. Their chances of success looked bleak. Going back to the 1955 World Series, they had lost six consecutive games on the Dodgers' home turf.

Casey Stengel worried that the cigar box that was Ebbets Field turned fly balls into home runs. So he decided to start Johnny Kucks. It was a risk, Stengel realized. Kucks had not won a game since Labor Day and had struggled in two relief appearances against the Dodgers. Yet Stengel figured that Kucks, in his words, could "throw ground balls," which meant that he could prevent the Dodgers from hitting fly balls with a chance of leaving the park. But not even Stengel was sure that it was the right move. When Kucks trotted out to the mound in the first inning, he could see Whitey Ford and Tom Sturdivant warming up on the sidelines.[56]

If Stengel doubted his decision to play Kucks, Billy Martin had full confidence in the advice he had given his boss. Filling out his lineup card, Casey penciled in Moose Skowron at first base and replaced Enos Slaughter in left field with Elston Howard. Perhaps, Stengel thought, Skowron and Howard could make a difference against Don Newcombe, who had pitched miserably in Game Two. The Yanks didn't realize that Newk was pitching with an aching elbow that made it difficult for him to throw a curveball. Not that it mattered much anyway. The Yanks' strategy was simple: sit on his fastball and let 'em rip.[57]

The Bronx Bombers turned Game Seven into batting practice. In the first inning Yogi Berra stroked a two-run homer into deep right field. Then he hit another two-run blast off Newcombe in the third inning. In the fourth, Howard, Martin's preferred left fielder, blasted a home run over the right-field scoreboard, giving the Yankees a 5–0 lead. Walter Alston had seen enough. Newcombe lumbered off the field, his head down, hiding the shame on his face, while all of Brooklyn booed. In the press box, Red Smith heard a wisecrack: "Calling all parking lot attendants."[58]

Skowron didn't disappoint Martin either. With the bases loaded in the seventh inning, he began walking toward the plate when Stengel whistled at him. Moose was certain that the skipper was going to bench him for a pinch hitter. But Stengel simply had some final instructions: "I want you to try to hit the ball to right field. Stay out of the double play." Skowron nodded. If the Dodgers had any chance of surviving the Yankees' assault, Brooklyn reliever Roger Craig had to force Moose into a groundout. When Craig fired a first-pitch fastball, Skowron swung hard and hammered it over the left-field fence, finishing his swing with one hand. The home run sealed the game.[59]

The Yankees slaughtered the Dodgers 9–0. "They just beat the hell out of us," Alston admitted after the game. In the Yankee clubhouse, the players celebrated with champagne and beer, hooting and hollering. Although the final game wasn't as competitive as the series itself, the Yankees' comeback, Dick Young wrote in the *New York Daily News*, was "one of the most amazing turnabouts in memory." How exactly did the Yankees do it? Dominant pitching and power hitting. Johnny Kucks's brilliant shutout performance made him the fifth consecutive Yankee starter to pitch a complete game. The Dodgers scored just one run in the final three contests. The Yankees, on the other hand, battered the Dodgers, pounding twelve home runs.[60]

Throughout the city, New Yorkers saluted the Bronx Bombers. In a time of seemingly rapid social and cultural changes, the Yankees' World Series victory—their seventh in ten seasons—bespoke stability and consistency. The editors at the *New York Herald-Tribune* suggested that the Yankees' crown made "one think that the ways of normalcy are coming back into life, that things haven't changed as much as one sometimes thinks they have changed."[61]

Looking back at the 1950s through the lens of nostalgia, many Americans believe that the decade was a time of innocence, an era when baseball mirrored a country with few problems. But that isn't true. In reality the Cold War exacerbated social and political tensions. In the atomic age, people lived in fear of nuclear attack, harbored paranoia about Communist spy rings, and submitted to periodic air raid drills. Americans questioned the security of the country's most important institutions: the government, the military, and the schools. Yet, in troubled times, Mickey Mantle and the Yankees restored faith—at least in parts of New York—in another institution: baseball. The Yankees' triumph reminded their fans that the National Pastime remained sacred and sound, immune to and untouched by the outside forces that plagued the country. "A world beset by doubts, shifts, and uncertainties," the *New York Herald-Tribune* editors accurately noted, "may take some small comfort in the knowledge that at least it can still count on the Yankees."[62]

Mickey Mantle wished that he had played better in the World Series. Although he only had six hits in twenty-four at bats—a .250 average—he clubbed three home runs. Plus he had made crucial plays in the outfield. What mattered most, though, was that the Yankees won. Even if he had not played up to his impossibly high standards, it was still the perfect ending to his perfect season.

Over the winter New Yorkers would forget Mickey's World Series batting average. But they would remember the timeliness of his home run in Game Five and his remarkable stab that preserved Don Larsen's perfect game. Most importantly no one would forget how the Yankees took back the crown that the Dodgers had usurped a year earlier. "The Yankees," Jerry Mitchell concluded in the *New York Post*, "grabbed the championship of the world from the Dodgers like an aristocrat snatching his wallet back from a bum."[63]

"Now batting, Mickey Mantle." When an announcer uttered those four words, anticipation pulsed through spectators. With him standing at the plate the possibilities seemed endless. He might hit a tape-measure homer or strike out with a body-twisting swing. No player of his generation created such great expectations. *Courtesy of the National Baseball Hall of Fame.*

The Last Snapshot

"It is natural to believe in great men. If the companions of our childhood should turn out to be heroes, and their condition regal, it would not surprise us."

—RALPH WALDO EMERSON,
"Uses of Great Men," 1849

By the end of 1956, Mickey Mantle, only twenty-five years old, had transcended baseball. Sportswriters crowned him simply "the Hero." A living legend, Mickey was, Gerald Holland wrote in *Sports Illustrated*, "everybody's dream miraculously come to life." Holland described him as a character in a Ring Lardner story, the unsophisticated rube who "left the country boy far behind," transformed by his deeds on the diamond and overcoming "his physical handicaps."[1]

Mantle could do it all, Holland wrote. He "could run with the speed of a jack rabbit; he could throw strikes to home plate from deep in the outfield; a switch-hitter, he could blast a ball farther than any man who ever lived. He was Elmer the Great," Lardner's talented but gullible ballplayer from a midwestern hamlet, an innocent man who loved his hometown sweetheart yet also lusted for a Hollywood starlet. In many ways, his story fit Lardner's script, except the public only saw the Hero, unblemished by temptation and weakness.[2]

Playing baseball in the nation's first city, he had become a brand: home run king, Yankee icon, president of Mickey Mantle Enterprises, television personality, and banquet speaker. "He was now," Holland noted, "public property." Millions of kids worshipped him, imitated him, and dreamed that someday they could be him. That meant that he couldn't swear in public, lose his temper on the field, argue with umpires, or embarrass the Yankees, his family, or the millions of parents who placed him on a pedestal. "We fathers can only do so much," a man told him. "It is up to *you* to set the example for our kids."[3]

Whether he liked it or not, Mickey Mantle starred in a feature role as the Hero, America's most beloved sports figure. But the Hero, Ring Lardner understood, was a work of fiction.

MICKEY DEMANDED THE Hero's salary. In 1956, he reportedly earned $32,500, $20,000 less than Yogi Berra. He had clearly proven his value to the Yankees and expected compensation for it. George Weiss had different ideas. In an age before free agency, when the reserve clause tethered a player to one club in perpetuity, Mantle lacked leverage. He could not test his worth on the open market or negotiate with any club executive other than Weiss. When they met in New York in January 1957, Mantle asked the general manager to double his pay. Weiss balked.[4]

Mantle's request paled in comparison to Joe DiMaggio's notorious ultimatums. In 1949, after leading the league in home runs and RBIs, Joe demanded that he become the first $100,000 man in baseball. Weiss caved. Yet he didn't believe that Mantle deserved anywhere near what the Yankee Clipper commanded. Increasing Mickey's salary carried great risk, given his lapses in judgment off the field, Weiss calculated. According to Mantle, Weiss slid an envelope across his desk and said, "I wouldn't want this to get into Merlyn's hands."[5]

Mickey opened the envelope. Inside he found damaging reports from private investigators documenting his late-night affairs. Weiss didn't need to say a word. Mantle understood the silent language of blackmail. If he didn't play by the club's rules, Weiss threatened, he would find himself playing for another team. Fuming, Mickey said he would rather quit baseball than let Weiss trade him. Without another word he stormed out of the office.[6]

Fortunately for Mickey, Yankees owners Del Webb and Dan Topping intervened. They didn't want to alienate the best player in the game. Weiss had no choice. He paid the asking price, but Mickey said later he "never forgot" Weiss's treatment of him. Years later, after a few drinks, Mantle called Weiss the "meanest cocksucker" he had ever known.[7]

For a moment Mickey's secret slept in Weiss's desk drawer. But *Confidential*, described by Tom Wolfe as the "most scandalous scandal magazine in the history of the world," exposed his affair with Holly Brooke. The celebrity gossip rag, then at its peak, reached more than 4.5 million readers—a larger circulation than *Time*—threatening Mantle's brand. In an exposé filled with double entendres, Holly revealed how her business deal with Mickey turned into a torrid affair dating back to his rookie season. She wrote, "Some girls have minks, some own diamonds. I had to be different. I own one-fourth of the most gorgeous hunk of man in the major leagues, Mickey Mantle. And there have been times when he was mine—100%."[8]

Mickey wanted to keep his secret from Merlyn. According to Mantle, about a month before spring training began, they traveled with friends Harold and Stella Youngman to Havana, Cuba. During a layover in Montgomery, Alabama, Harold spotted Mickey's face on the magazine cover at the airport newsstand. He nudged him and asked, "Hey, Mickey, isn't that your picture?" Mantle panicked, fearing Merlyn would see it too. He and Harold rushed to purchase every copy on display and tossed them into the nearest trashcan. But it was no use. When they returned home from Havana, a stack of issues awaited them at the front door.[9]

Mickey was no longer just a famous baseball player; he was a celebrity and, as such, a victim of the new rules of celebrity culture. In the past, cultural critic Neal Gabler noted, "the rich, the powerful, the famous and the privileged had always governed their own images." Prominent baseball players were protected by the sportswriters who crafted their public personas. Although sports reporters undoubtedly saw Mantle out on the town with Brooke and other women, they were not willing to jeopardize their chummy relationship with the Yankees by commenting on it. But in the 1950s gossip columnists treated everyone as a commodity; the private lives of "personalities"—actors, musicians, and now athletes—became sources of real-life drama that appeared to mimic Hollywood productions. At a time when Americans craved more revealing entertainment, scandal magazines like *Confidential* wallowed in sensationalism. And after 1956, Mickey Mantle was an ideal subject, not only because he was famous, but because he appeared so innocent and pure.[10]

IT WAS AN UNFORGETTABLE night, but when reporters asked the Yankees exactly what happened at the Copacabana in the early hours of May 16, 1957, they learned little. On the eve of Billy Martin's twenty-ninth birthday, he and five of his teammates—Mickey, Yogi, Whitey Ford, Hank Bauer, and Johnny Kucks—celebrated over dinner at Danny's Hideaway. Afterward the group enjoyed more drinks and a show featuring Johnnie Ray at the Waldorf-Astoria. Finally, the players and their wives packed into three taxis and headed for the Copacabana, where, according to the nightclub's motto, "every night was New Year's eve."[11]

It was about 2:00 a.m. when the taxis reached their destination on East 60th Street near Central Park. Mobsters, celebrities, casting agents, gossip columnists, and athletes made the Copa the "hottest club North of Havana." The biggest stars of the stage and screen—Frank Sinatra, Dean Martin, Jerry Lewis, Elizabeth Taylor, Marilyn

Monroe, Bette Davis, and many more—could be found there luxuri-ating in the glow of celebrity. Surrounded by electric blue and pink palm trees, the players told stories and cracked jokes, while Sammy Davis Jr. sang in the background. The Copa staff seated the Yankees players and their wives at a prominent table near the stage, treating them like royalty. "We were the kings and queens of New York," Car-men Berra beamed.

Suddenly a loud, drunken group of men celebrating a champion-ship in their local bowling league staggered into the club. From that moment on, there is no consensus on the exact order of events. To be sure, several of the men, who were from the Bronx, began to ride Da-vis, referring to him as a "jungle bunny" and "little black Sambo." The Yankees' Elston Howard had suffered similar indignities in American League ballparks, and Bauer, his roommate, became furious. The play-ers told the men to shut up. Martin, who even sober had a short fuse, insisted that the loudest racists follow him outside for a "talk."

Moments after Martin left the table, Mickey told Merlyn that he had to make sure that Billy didn't get into trouble. "Billy, Billy, Billy!" he shouted, searching for his best friend. At that point several people in the club, including reporters, followed the commotion toward the cloakroom. By that time one of the Bronx men, a delicatessen owner named Ed Jones, was stretched out on the floor with a broken nose, a bruised face, and a large knot on his chin. Mantle was so drunk that he hardly knew what had happened. "A body came flying out and landed at my feet," he testified about a month later before a grand jury. "At first I thought it was Billy, so I picked him up. But when I saw it wasn't, I dropped him back down. It looked like Roy Rogers rode through the Copa on Trigger and Trigger kicked the guy in the face."

"L'Affaire Copa" received front-page treatment in the New York tabloids. The next morning the *Journal-American*'s bold headline screamed, "Yanks Star in Copa Brawl." The *Daily Mirror* featured a front-page photograph of Ed Jones pointing to a discolored lump on his chin. His brother, Leonard Jones, claimed that Bauer had coldcocked him, though Ed couldn't recall who threw the knockout punch. "The Bruiser" denied it. He claimed that one of the club's bouncers hit Jones. Ultimately, conflicting testimony and insufficient evidence allowed Bauer to escape a criminal trial. The "Battle of the Copa," however, proved consequential to the future of the team.[12]

The "Copa Six," Roger Kahn wrote, had violated the Yankees' corporate code of personnel conduct: "Shun scandal. Keep your name out of the gossip columns. Be courteous, but reserved. Act kindly toward small boys and puppies. Keep your public drinking to a minimum. Remember your dignity. Treat your superiors with a touch of reverence. Watch your romantic life; girls have a place, but don't forget to keep them in it." Kahn and the New York beat writers knew that Mantle, Martin, and Ford regularly broke these sacred rules—but that only one of them would pay for it.[13]

Before the season began George Weiss reminded Martin of the Yankee code. Weiss had of course read about him in the tabloids and disapproved of Martin's carousing. Pictures of him with his arm around chorus girls and Broadway dancers conveyed the wrong message in the general manager's view. A Yankee should be a button-down family man, but Martin, a divorced father, flaunted his bachelor lifestyle. Weiss had warned him that if he caused any more trouble, if he did anything that embarrassed the club, he would be gone.[14]

The Copa incident disturbed Weiss. He sensed a deeper problem, one that threatened the Yankee franchise and possibly professional baseball. He understood the value of an unblemished Mickey Mantle. He pored over daily gate receipts, fully aware that Mantle's spectacular performance in 1956 added significantly to the revenues of the Yankees and every American League team. His soaring home runs were as much a part of the New York skyline as the Empire State Building.

Weiss also knew that Mantle was immature and easily influenced by others—especially Martin. He didn't care who threw the punch that floored Ed Jones. It was enough that Martin was there, that he had shot off his mouth and was certainly willing to slug someone.

More importantly, when Martin left the table—Billy later gave a benign reason for that decision—Mickey followed, ready for whatever came next.

The event prompted Weiss to do a little baseball math. Martin was expendable. The Yankees already had the squeaky-clean Bobby Richardson, a talented twenty-one-year-old, who could take his place at second. Mantle, however, was irreplaceable. He was the franchise's crown jewel.

Soon the press was reporting that Weiss had tried to trade Martin to the Washington Senators, but the deal had fallen through. Billy knew his days with the Yankees were over. Yet Weiss never even considered trading Mantle's other mischievous partner, Whitey Ford. The son of a bartender, Ford was known as a "playboy" who never skipped a party, but somehow he was able to avoid the same notoriety as Martin. Of course, the main difference between him and Martin was that he was the best starting pitcher in the American League, while Billy was an average player.[15]

Weiss's bottom line: Billy had to go. In Kansas City, on June 15, 1957, the last day of the trading period, Casey Stengel delivered the news. "You're gone," he told Martin. One hour and nine minutes before the trade deadline, Weiss dumped Martin, as part of a trade involving multiple players, on the woeful Kansas City Athletics.

The careers of the M&M boys were far from over, but this moment brought a sense of finality, signaling the end of an era. They all knew that this was it. Mickey, Whitey, and Billy spent their last night together as teammates, Three Musketeers drinking into the early morning, raising their glasses for one last toast.

FOR MICKEY LIFE IN professional baseball would never be as good again. Emotionally, Martin was irreplaceable. "It's like losing a brother," he said. Mantle went on to enjoy a few more spectacular seasons, winning the MVP Award in 1957 and 1962. In 1961, he again chased Babe Ruth's single-season home run record, though he fell short after being sidelined with an abscess in his hip joint. Instead he watched teammate Roger Maris break the record that season. New Yorkers rooted hard for Mantle that year; they wanted "a real Yankee" to break the record, not Maris, who came to the team via a trade with the Kansas City Athletics.

After 1956, though, Mantle struggled to fulfill the unreasonable demands of baseball fans. His fragile body repeatedly betrayed him. He suffered a rosary of injuries—a torn tendon in his right shoulder, a fractured right index finger, a broken bone in his right foot, and assorted pulled and strained muscles. Surgeons repaired his knees and shoulders until there weren't enough pins to hold his body together. The most remarkable aspect of his career is that it lasted eighteen seasons.[16]

Despite persistent injuries, he compiled a Hall of Fame resume. His career numbers tell part of the story: 2,415 hits, 536 home runs, and a .298 batting average. More than those impressive statistics, fans appreciated him for the thrills he delivered year after year. On June 8, 1969, when the Yankees retired his number, seven, a packed Yankee Stadium honored him with a standing ovation. They cheered for what seemed like an hour, growing louder and louder as Mantle waved for them to quiet down. "I always wondered how a man who knew he was going to die could stand here and say he was the luckiest man in the world," he said of Lou Gehrig. "But now I can understand."[17]

That was how he wanted to be remembered. That was how the Yankee organization wanted him to be remembered.

But life didn't follow the script.

In 1970, he was living in Dallas, far from the New York spotlight. His name had all but disappeared from the sports pages. He socialized mostly with his golfing partners at the local club. "It was like Mickey Mantle had died," he recalled. Later that year former teammate Jim Bouton resurrected him. In his exposé *Ball Four*, Bouton shattered Mantle's heroic image and the country's faith in the purity of the Great American Game. Grown men who once idolized him learned that many of the baseballs with Mantle's signature were actually forged by clubhouse attendant Pete Previte. And Bouton revealed what sportswriters concealed during the 1950s: Mickey caroused late into the night, played with hangovers, and peered into hotel room windows, leering at undressed women.[18]

Although Bouton's book chronicled his own experiences during the 1969 season, his portrait of Mantle turned *Ball Four* into the best-selling sports book of the time. Critics denounced the mediocre pitcher as attention starved, a traitor who wanted to ruin the reputation of America's pastime and the men who played the game. Commissioner Bowie Kuhn tried to force Bouton into admitting that the book was fiction. His former teammates and other players shunned him for betraying the game's most treasured, long-standing rule: "What you see here, what you say here, what you do here, let it stay here."[19]

Ball Four marked the beginning of a new era in sports. During the Vietnam War, reporters challenged the authority of American institutions: government, military, church, corporations, and even sports. Fewer sportswriters aimed to write about athletes as heroes in the manner of Red Smith and Jimmy Cannon. Instead, they wanted to be more like Bob Woodward and Carl Bernstein, investigative journalists puncturing sacred American myths.

Mickey Mantle became the most prominent victim of the new ambition to reveal the truth. In the process, who he was and what he meant to America in 1956 became lost. When Mantle hung up his spikes, it signaled the end of an era—not just for the Yankees but for baseball as well. The spring of pinstripe legends—Ruth, Gehrig, DiMaggio, Mantle—ran dry. The Yankees anointed Bobby Murcer, a handsome center fielder from Oklahoma, as their next great, but he was no Mickey Mantle. It took a decade for the Yankees to find a player who came close to Mantle as a slugger and a draw, but Reggie Jackson never won over the nation. By that time, too, baseball had been replaced by football, which dominated television as baseball once did the radio. Joe Namath emerged as the face of the new American game. If any athlete replaced Mantle in New York, it was Broadway Joe, as much a product of the 1960s as Mantle was of the 1950s. As the journalist Mary McGrory noted, "Baseball is what we were, football is what we have become."[20]

In 1969, the year Namath led the New York Jets to a stunning victory over the Baltimore Colts in Super Bowl III, the Yankees turned Mantle into a monument, a relic of the past. During his retirement ceremony, they honored him with a plaque in center field. Columnist Jim Murray recognized that there would never be another athlete like Mickey Mantle. "He's the last of the Yankees," Murray wrote. "He might have been the best of them, considering the night games, the slider, the big parks, the trappers' mitts, and the fact that he would have been a certified cripple in any other industry. He was rejected four times by the military, afraid he couldn't keep up with a Fourth of July parade."[21]

"I know one thing," Murray added, "those monuments in center field are going to be awfully lonely this summer. Their last link to the present is gone."

Yet, in the seasons that followed, the cheers for Mantle continued to echo throughout Yankee Stadium. Whenever his name was announced at the Old-Timers' Day celebrations, fans rose to their feet, honoring the man who was the closest link to Yankee glory of years past. He connected the fans to another age, a time before players let their hair fall to their shoulders and wore fur coats when they went out on the town. The revelations of his personal troubles, his drinking, carousing, and occasional boorishness, did not diminish his aura. Perhaps his faults made him even more human, strengthening his connection to his legion of admirers. Even younger Yankees fans who never saw him play learned to love him.

OZZIE SWEET PERFECTLY captured the essence of Mickey Mantle and his times. In the 1950s the photographer became well known for his memorable portraits for the cover of *Sport*, the first general-interest sports magazine. Featuring profiles of famous athletes written by the best writers of the era, *Sport* emphasized the stories off the field, making athletes more accessible to readers. As distinctive as the *Saturday Evening Post*, it published colorful photographs that brought athletes to life. A self-proclaimed "photographic illustrator," Sweet posed his subjects in revealing close-ups and simulated-action scenes. Using color film, he turned full-page photos of baseball's biggest stars into posters, perfect for tacking onto bedroom walls.[22]

In early April 1957, after spring training ended in St. Petersburg, Florida, Sweet invited Mickey—one of his favorite subjects—along with Billy Martin, Whitey Ford, and Bob Grim for a photo shoot on a fishing boat off the coast of Madeira Beach. Ozzie snapped candid shots of the men, four teammates in their prime, a fraternity of brothers basking in the sunshine without a care in the world. Sweet's roll of black-and-white film reveals an animated and happy Mantle: reeling in a big catch; recounting a hunting story with an imaginary rifle in his hand; eating a bucket of fried chicken; laughing at Billy, who smiles right back at him. It's the sweetest moment between the men caught on camera.[23]

Another picture, a colorful Rockwellian portrait reminiscent of a Technicolor movie frame, captured the essence of the men and their times. Sweet caught the foursome in the back of the boat: Grim and Ford sitting on the railing, Mickey and Billy lounging in chairs fastened to the deck. Surrounded by the clear emerald-turquoise water, a trail of waves behind them, Grim, wearing a white sleeveless undershirt, his tan arms exposed, turns his head portside, looking into the distance. Dressed in a wrinkled white T-shirt and khaki pants, Ford, the only one looking directly at the camera, eases a broad grin across his face. Turning away from Sweet, Martin and Mantle sit at an angle, holding bottles of Coca-Cola, which many famous ballplayers pedaled as their preferred beverage. Leaning back in his chair, sporting brown pants and a short-sleeve buttoned shirt, Martin casts his eyes downward. Mantle leans forward, dressed in a white golf shirt and blue pants, the sun warming his handsome face.

That photograph, taken after Mantle's magnificent Triple Crown season, when the Yankees were the defending World Series champions, but prior to the Copa brawl—before George Weiss sent Billy Martin to baseball purgatory—preserves an image of youthful innocence. It's a snapshot of the good times, a scene that evokes Mantle's and Martin's glory days when they were untouchable and the world belonged to them.

Mickey would never forget the joy of 1956. He was the toast of New York, the champion of the boroughs, winner of the last Subway Series of the era, when the city was still baseball's epicenter. That season crowds cheered his name in every stadium in the American League. As he clobbered majestic home runs, spectators honored him with standing ovations, chanting his alliterative name. *Mickey Mantle*. The name evoked power and poetry, arousing the kind of admiration reserved for baseball immortals.

Long after he retired, Mantle could still feel the thrill of hitting a home run—rounding the bases, his head down, the crowd roaring, his teammates jubilant in the dugout. No drink or drug could produce such a high. There was no greater sensation, he said, than to hear the fans cheering just for him. "I wish everybody in America could have that feeling just once."[24]

ACKNOWLEDGMENTS

From beginning to end, writing our second book together has proved as rewarding as it did the first time. But we could not have done it without the generosity of many people. Throughout our journey we have benefitted from a great team at Fletcher & Company. Sylvie Greenberg, Don Lamm, and Christy Fletcher helped us transform the proposal into a finished manuscript, offering endless support and sage advice along the way. We are especially thankful for the continued enthusiasm of our publisher, Lara Heimert, who has made Basic Books an ideal home. Her expertise and extraordinary trust in us has made our publishing experience thoroughly enjoyable. Basic's stellar supporting cast, particularly Dan Gerstle, Betsy DeJesu, and Alia Massoud, have helped us in countless ways. Nate Corzine, who knows more about the history of baseball than just about anyone, offered a close reading of the manuscript. His suggestions helped us situate Mickey Mantle's career in the broader history of the game. We also wish to thank Aram Goudsouzian for taking the time to carefully read parts of the manuscript as well. We are grateful to both for their insight and friendship.

A number of people and institutions made our research for this book possible. In particular we wish to thank the staff at the National Baseball Hall of Fame's A. Bartlett Giamatti Research Center, especially John Horne with the photo archives; the staffs at the Library of Congress Newspaper and Periodical Reading Room and the New

ACKNOWLEDGMENTS

York Public Library; George Rugg at the University of Notre Dame Special Collections; and Barbara Becker of the Miami, Oklahoma, Public Library. In Commerce, Oklahoma, conversations with the encyclopedic Charles Duboise proved enormously helpful on subjects ranging from Mickey's childhood to the history of mining in Oklahoma.

Our home universities have enabled us to write *A Season in the Sun*. At Purdue University, Randy Roberts's distinguished professorship funded research trips and many of the images used in this book. He is especially thankful for the support department head R. Douglas Hurt has shown him throughout his career. Over the years Purdue has done everything possible to facilitate his research. At Georgia Tech, the School of History and Sociology and the Julius C. "Bud" Shaw Professorship provided research and travel aid to Johnny Smith. He wishes to thank his colleagues in the School, especially Chair Steve Usselman, and Ivan Allen College of Liberal Arts dean Jacqueline Royster for their incredible support.

Finally, we wish to thank both of our wives for putting up with our occasional absences from home and our frequent mental absences from daily life. We owe Marjorie Traylor Roberts and Rebecca Smith for all that they do and all that they tolerate. We can only offer our love and gratitude.

ABBREVIATIONS USED IN NOTES

BD	*Baseball Digest*
BG	*Boston Globe*
BH	*Boston Herald*
BM	*Baseball Magazine*
DFP	*Detroit Free Press*
DN	*Detroit News*
NYDM	*New York Daily Mirror*
NYDN	*New York Daily News*
NYHT	*New York Herald-Tribune*
NYJA	*New York Journal-American*
NYP	*New York Post*
NYT	*New York Times*
NYTM	*New York Times Magazine*
NYWTS	*New York World-Telegram and Sun*
RD	*Reader's Digest*
SEP	*Saturday Evening Post*
SI	*Sports Illustrated*
TSN	*The Sporting News*
WP	*Washington Post*
WTH	*Washington Times-Herald*

NOTES

INTRODUCTION

1. Falkner, *The Last Hero*, jacket; Leavy, *The Last Boy*, xviii.

2. Barra, *Mickey and Willie*, 185–186; Castro, *Mickey Mantle*, 128–129; Leavy, *The Last Boy*, 84; Nuttall, *Mickey Mantle's Greatest Hits*, 34.

3. For examples of Mantle telling the story about throwing Jackie Robinson out during the 1952 World Series, see Mantle with Gluck, *The Mick*, 90; Mantle with Herskowitz, *All My Octobers*, 30.

4. *NYT*, October 4, 1952; Milton Gross, "New Pride of the Yankees," *Sport*, April 1953, 36.

5. *NYP*, September 23, 2015.

6. Richard Hoffer, "Mickey Mantle," *SI*, August 21, 1995, 25; Mantle and Pepe, *Mickey Mantle*, xiv.

7. David Halberstam, "American Notes: Baseball and the National Mythology," *Harper's Magazine*, September 1970, 22.

8. Bruce Catton, "The Yankees," in Jackson and Dunbar, *Empire City*, 789.

9. Halberstam, "American Notes," 54.

10. Bruce Catton, "The Great American Game," *American Heritage*, April 1959, 16–20, 86; Jacque Barzun, "America at Play," *Atlantic*, February 1954, 38–41; Roger Angell, "Baseball—the Perfect Game," *Holiday*, May 1954, 81; Robert Creamer, "The Great American Game—1956," *SI*, April 9, 1956.

11. Jay, *More Than Just a Game*, 11–13.

12. Gilbert, *A Cycle of Outrage*, 1–10.

13. Jay, *More Than Just a Game*, 40–44; Sullivan, *Rocky Marciano*, 206.

14. Oshinsky, *A Conspiracy So Immense*, 132.

15. Elias, *The Empire Strikes Out*, 187–188.

16. Jay, *More Than Just a Game*, 54, 59.

17. Patterson, *Grand Expectations*, 79–81.

18. Angell, "Baseball—the Perfect Game," 86; Creamer, *Baseball and Other Matters in 1941*, 5–6.

19. *NYP*, August 12, 1956.

20. *TSN*, July 4, 1956.

CHAPTER 1

1. For the speed of the ball, see Adair, *The Physics of Baseball*, 39–46; *Fastball* (Legendary Entertainment, 2015), written and directed by Jonathan Hock.

2. Williams and Underwood, *The Science of Hitting*, 1.

3. *TSN*, October 3, 1956, March 15, 1952.

4. Tim Kurkjian, "It's Really Not Great to Be a Switch-Hitter," *ESPN The Magazine*, September 3, 2010, http://www.espn.com/mlb/columns/story?columnist=kurkjian _tim&id=5524029.

5. Hall, *Mickey Mantle*, 1–58; Leavy, *The Last Boy*, 38–70; Castro, *Mickey Mantle*, 3–28.

6. "Community Assessment," Miami Library Commerce files; Leavy, *The Last Boy*, 38–39.

7. For information about daily work in the mines, we thank Charles Duboise.

8. Leavy, *The Last Boy*, 40–43.

9. Mantle with Gluck, *The Mick*, 12.

10. Schoor, *Mickey Mantle of the Yankees*, 31.

11. Mickey Mantle as told to Ben Epstein, "How My Dad Made Me a Switch-Hitter," *RD*, September 1956, 56.

12. Mantle with Gluck, *The Mick*, 7–8.

13. Mantle as told to Epstein, "How My Dad Made Me a Switch-Hitter," 57.

14. Schoor, *Mickey Mantle of the Yankees*, 31.

15. For Mantle's osteomyelitis, see Castro, *Mickey Mantle*, 25–27; Leavy, *The Last Boy*, 61–63; Hall, *Mickey Mantle*, 61–64,

16. Barra, *Mickey and Willie*, 98.

17. Mickey Mantle as told to Charles Dexter, "A Year I'll Never Forget," *Sport*, December 1951, 82.

18. Dexter, "A Year I'll Never Forget," 82; Schaap, *Mickey Mantle*, 50–51.

CHAPTER 2

1. Cramer, *Joe DiMaggio*, 296; *WP*, May 23, 1951; Halberstam, *October 1964*, 89.

2. Castro, *Mickey Mantle*, 54–55.

3. "What About DiMaggio Now?," *Sport*, November 1950, 18; Jimmy Cannon, "The Joe DiMaggio I Remember," *Sport*, September 1956, 65; *NYT*, December 12, 1951; Halberstam, *Summer of '49*, 47.

4. "What About DiMaggio Now?," 20; O'Toole, *Strangers in the Bronx*, 38.

5. Halberstam, *Summer of '49*, 50–54.

6. *TSN*, March 14, 1951; Arch Murray, "Mickey Mantle: Gold Plated Rookie," *Sport*, June 1951, 72; Cramer, *Joe DiMaggio*, 298–299.

7. Mantle with Gluck, *The Mick*, 44, 53; *TSN*, April 4, 1951.

8. *TSN*, April 4, 1951; Cramer, *Joe DiMaggio*, 301.

9. Dan Daniel, "Mickey Mantle," *BM*, August 1951, 10; *NYDM*, March 20, 1951.

10. Schaap, *Mickey Mantle*, 53; Leavy, *The Last Boy*, 13–14.

11. *TSN*, April 25, 1951; Tim Cohane, "Mantle: Will He Become Game's Greatest Switch Hitter?" *BD*, October 1952, 16.

12. "Mickey Makes It," *Life*, April 30, 1951, 105; *NYT*, April 8, 1951; *WP*, April 3, 1951; Leavy, *The Last Boy*, 11.

13. O'Toole, *Strangers in the Bronx*, 27, 70; Tom Meany, "That Man Mantle," *Collier's*, June 2, 1951, 73.

14. "Mickey Makes It," 105.

15. Mantle with Gluck, *The Mick*, 1, 59; *TSN*, April 25, 1951.

16. *NYDM*, April 5, 1951; Mantle with Gluck, *The Mick*, 56; Leavy, *The Last Boy*, 61–62.

17. Oakley, *God's Country*, 83–88; Patterson, *Grand Expectations*, 225–228.

18. Creamer, *Stengel*, 244; *NYT*, April 12, 1951.

19. *NYT*, April 14, 1951.

20. *NYDM*, April 6; *TSN*, April 11, 1951; O'Toole, *Strangers in the Bronx*, 73–74; *NYJA*, April 14, 1951.

21. Cramer, *Joe DiMaggio*, 207–214.

22. For the conversation between Casey and Weiss, see Mantle with Gluck, *The Mick*, 1.

23. Stanley Frank, "Yankee Kingmaker," *SEP*, July 24, 1948, 23; Tom Meany, "George Weiss—the Real Yankee Clipper," *Sport*, December 1947, 16, 78.

24. Halberstam, *Summer of '49*, 201–202; Mantle with Gluck, *The Mick*, 2.

25. White, *Here Is New York*, 19; Mantle et al., *A Hero All His Life*, 9; Mantle and Pepe, *Mickey Mantle*, 31.

26. John Steinbeck, "Autobiography: Making of a New Yorker," *NYTM*, February 1, 1953, 27.

27. For Mantle's memories of the Bronx in 1951, see Mantle with Gluck, *The Mick*, 61.

28. Mantle with Gluck, *The Mick*, 69–70; "Manhattan: City of Lights and Towers," *Time*, March 28, 1955, 20–26; Brooks Atkinson, "This Is New York," *RD*, November 1951, 35.

29. Meyer Berger, "Our Town: Open Letter to a Visitor," *NYTM*, April 29, 1956, 9.

30. White, *Here Is New York*, 51–52.

31. Montville, *The Big Bam*, 124; Cramer, *Joe DiMaggio*, 78–96.

32. Noel Busch, "Joe DiMaggio: Baseball's Most Sensational Big-League Star Starts What Should Be His Best Year So Far," *Life*, May 1, 1939, 63, 69.

33. Gems, *Sport and the Shaping of Italian-American Identity*, 135–136.

34. Cramer, *Joe DiMaggio*, 100–102.

35. Halberstam, *Summer of '49*, 14.

36. Gilbert Millstein, "Case History of a Rookie," *NYTM*, June 3, 1951, 23; Murray, "Mickey Mantle: Gold-Plated Rookie," 71.

37. Meany, "That Man Mantle," 72.

38. Barra, *Mickey and Willie*, 158–159; O'Toole, *Strangers in the Bronx*, 116–117; Shirley Povich, "Mickey Mantle, Incorporated," *SEP*, February 2, 1957, 19, 21, 72.

39. Mickey Mantle as told to Charles Dexter, "A Year I'll Never Forget," *Sport*, December 1951, 82.

40. Mantle with Gluck, *The Mick*, 61.

41. Castro, *Mickey Mantle*, 88–89.

42. *TSN*, July 25, 1951; Mantle with Gluck, *The Mick*, 64.

43. Mantle as told to Epstein, *The Mickey Mantle Story*, 66–67.

44. Schaap, *Mickey Mantle*, 75; Leavy, *The Last Boy*, 26.

45. The exchange between Mantle and Mutt is drawn from Mantle with Gluck, *The Mick*, 66–67; Schoor, *Mickey Mantle of the Yankees*, 92–93; Mantle as told to Epstein, *The Mickey Mantle Story*, 67–68; Mantle, *The Quality of Courage*, 6–7.

46. Castro, *Mickey Mantle*, 100.

47. *NYT*, August 21, 1951; *TSN*, August 29, 1951.

48. Unless otherwise noted, for Mantle's collision with DiMaggio and subsequent injury during the 1951 World Series, see Harold Kaese, "Too Big a Mantle," *BD*, January 1952, 81; Cramer, *Joe DiMaggio*, 300–301, 310–311; Leavy, *The Last Boy*, 32–35; Mantle with Herskowitz, *All My Octobers*, 6; Schoor, *Mickey Mantle of the Yankees*, 94–95; Mantle as told to Epstein, *The Mickey Mantle Story*, 76–77.

49. *NYT*, October 6, 1951; Tullius, *I'd Rather Be a Yankee*, 218.

50. Mantle with Herskowitz, *All My Octobers*, 8; Leavy, *The Last Boy*, 36; Mantle with Gluck, *The Mick*, 78.

51. Mantle with Gluck, *The Mick*, 78–79.

52. Mantle with Gluck, *The Mick*, 79.

CHAPTER 3

1. Leavy, *The Last Boy*, 72–73, 76–77, 104–105.

2. Mantle as told to Epstein, *The Mickey Mantle Story*, 82; *NYT*, December 1 and 5, 1951, February 23, 1952; Mantle with Gluck, *The Mick*, 78–79.

3. *NYT*, April 17, 1952; Leavy, *The Last Boy*, 77–78.

4. Mantle with Gluck, *The Mick*, 83–84.

5. Mantle with Gluck, *The Mick*, 83–84; Mantle et al., *A Hero All His Life*, 58.

6. Leavy, *The Last Boy*, 53; Mantle et al., *A Hero All His Life*, 54, 58.

7. Shirley Povich, "Can Yanks Lean on Mantle?" *BD*, March 1952, 55.

8. *WP*, July 4, 1952 (emphasis ours).

9. *NYHT*, October 7, 1952; *NYP*, October 7, 1952.

10. *NYHT*, October 8, 1952; World Series television broadcast, NBC, October 7, 1952.

11. *WP*, October 8, 1952.

12. *WP*, October 8, 1952; *NYHT*, October 8, 1952.

13. Leavy, *The Last Boy*, 85–89; *WTH*, April 18, 1953; *WP*, April 18, 1953.

14. Leavy, *The Last Boy*, 89; *NYT*, April 18, 1953.

15. *WP*, April 18, 1953; Barra, *Mickey and Willie*, 192–193.

16. Kahn, *The Era*, 165.

17. Kahn, *The Era*, 166.

18. Schaap, *Mickey Mantle*, 101; Schoor, *Mickey Mantle of the Yankees*, 123; *NYT*, April 19, 1953.

19. See Malamud, *The Natural*; Castro, *Mickey Mantle*, 37, 45; Ben Epstein, "What Manner of a Man Is Mantle?" *Look*, July 24, 1956, 31; Tom Meany, "Wham! Whoosh— Mantle's Away!" *Collier's*, July 4, 1953.

20. *NYT*, June 9, 1953; Charles Dexter, "Can Mickey Carry the Big Load?" *BD*, April 1953, 5–6; "Young Man on Olympus," *Time*, June 15, 1953; Milton Gross, "New Pride of the Yankees," *Sport*, April 1953, 75.

21. *NYT*, August 9, 1953, August 15, 1953; Barra, *Mickey and Willie*, 198.

22. Schaap, *Mickey Mantle*, 101; Leavy, *The Last Boy*, 104; Barra, *Mickey and Willie*, 198; Milton Gross, "Is Mantle Another Pete Reiser?" *Sport*, January 1954, 63.

23. Milton Gross, "Rebuilding the Mantle," *BD*, January 1954, 24; Creamer, *Stengel*, 258.

24. Falkner, *The Last Hero*, 110.

25. Falkner, *The Last Hero*, 110.

26. Gross, "Is Mantle Another Reiser?" 63; Creamer, *Stengel*, 258.

27. Gross, "Is Mantle Another Reiser?" 63, 65; Joe Trimble, "The Yankees' Troubled Ace," *SEP*, April 18, 1953, 203.

28. Schaap, *Mickey Mantle*, 103–104; Leavy, *The Last Boy*, 104, 106–107; *NYT*, November 10, 1953, February 4, 1953.

29. Leavy, *The Last Boy*, 106.

30. Castro, *Mickey Mantle*, 126–127; Tullius, *I'd Rather Be a Yankee*, 219.

31. Leavy, *The Last Boy*, 114–115; Pennington, *Billy Martin*, 107; Mantle et al., *A Hero All His Life*, 60, 63; Jim Scott, "Billy Martin's Story," *Sport*, May 1954, 35–36.

32. Scott, "Billy Martin's Story," 36–37.

33. In *Mickey Mantle: My Favorite Summer, 1956*, Mantle mistakenly recalled that the hotel incident took place in 1956, but an article in *Sport* proves otherwise. See Mantle and Pepe, *Mickey Mantle*, 151–152; Scott, "Billy Martin's Story," 37.

34. Scott, "Billy Martin's Story," 37; Roger Kahn, "Why They Broke Up Billy Martin's Gang," *Sport*, October 1957, 21.

35. Leavy, *The Last Boy*, 115; Mantle with Gluck, *The Mick*, 108–111.

36. Mickey Mantle with Jill Lieber, "Time in a Bottle," *SI*, April 18, 1994, 74, http://www.si.com/vault/1994/04/18/130871/time-in-a-bottle-after-42-years-of-alcohol-abuse-a-legendary-ballplayer-describes-his-life-of-self-destructive-behavior-and-hopes-his-recovery-will-finally-make-him-a-true-role-model.

37. Mantle with Gluck, *The Mick*, 117; Mantle with Lieber, "Time in a Bottle," 74.

38. *NYT*, February 4, 1954; Leavy, *The Last Boy*, 118; Castro, *Mickey Mantle*, 132–133.

39. Creamer, *Stengel*, 259.

40. Halberstam, *October 1964*, 79–80; Falkner, *The Last Hero*, 107.

41. Barra, *Mickey and Willie*, 200.

42. *NYT*, February 27, 1955; *WP*, April 7, 1955.

43. Trimble, "The Yankees' Troubled Ace," 204.

44. Milton Gross, "They'll Always Boo Mickey Mantle," *Sport*, February 1956, 66.

45. Gross, "They'll Always Boo Mickey Mantle," 35.

46. Gross, "They'll Always Boo Mickey Mantle," 66.

47. Epstein, "What Manner of a Man Is Mantle?," 27–28.

48. Gross, "They'll Always Boo Mickey Mantle," 67.

49. Gross, "They'll Always Boo Mickey Mantle," 67.

50. Franklin Lewis, "The Yankees Were Dis-Mantled," *BD*, November–December 1955, 49–50.

51. Gross, "They'll Always Boo Mickey Mantle," 67.

52. Schoor, *Mickey Mantle of the Yankees*, 168–169.

53. Gerald Holland, "All Hail the Hero Mighty Mickey," *SI*, March 4, 1957, 55.

54. Frank Graham, "Everybody Loves Yogi," *BD*, January–February 1956, 60; Ed Fitzgerald, "The Fabulous Yogi Berra," *Sport*, August 1951, 42–43, 70; Irv Goodman, "The Other Yogi Berra," *Sport*, May 1958, 53.

55. Fitzgerald, "The Fabulous Yogi Berra," 42.

56. Fitzgerald, "The Fabulous Yogi Berra," 42; David Halberstam, "Baseball and the National Mythology," *Harper's Magazine*, September 1970, 25.

57. Holland, "All Hail the Hero Mighty Mickey," 55.

58. Roger Kahn, "Oklahoma's Mickey Mantle: Can the Young Yankee Beat the Babe?" *Newsweek*, June 25, 1956, 66–67 (emphasis in the original).

59. Roger Angell, "The Short Season," *New Yorker*, April 13, 1968, 129; "It'll Be Dodgers—and Yanks Again!" *BD*, April 1956, 20–21; *TSN*, April 18, 1956; *WP*, April 8, 1956; Dan Parker, "Baseball Forecast for 1956," *American Weekly*, April 15, 1956, 6.

60. Ed Linn, "The Last Days of Brooklyn's Old Gang," *Sport*, October 1956, 54.

61. *NYDN*, March 3, 1956; *NYT*, March 31, 1956; *NYP*, March 21, 1956, March 28, 1956; Robert Creamer, "How to Do It Again," *SI*, March 19, 1956, 22, 24.

62. "New York Yankees," *SI*, April 9, 1956, 39.

63. Schoor, *Mickey Mantle of the Yankees*, 170–173; Mantle, *My Batting Secret*.

64. *NYJA*, March 21, 1956; *NYDN*, March 22, 1956.

65. *WP*, March 25, 1956; *NYP*, April 13, 1956.

CHAPTER 4

1. Gerald A. Behn to U. E. Baughman, chief of US Secret Service, Protective Security Report, April 13, 1956, US Treasury, Secret Service, Presidential Protection Unit: Papers, Box 5, Folder: 602.111 Griffith Stadium, National Archives, Dwight D. Eisenhower Presidential Library.

2. George C. Rable, "Patriotism, Platitudes and Politics: Baseball and the American Presidency," *Presidential Studies Quarterly* 19, no. 2 (spring 1989): 363; Kirsch, *Baseball in Blue and Gray*, 135.

3. *TSN*, April 18, 1956; Rable, "Patriotism, Platitudes and Politics," 364.

4. Rable, "Patriotism, Platitudes and Politics," 364–365.

5. *TSN*, April 18, 1956.

6. Rable, "Patriotism, Platitudes and Politics," 368.

7. Franklin D. Roosevelt to Kenesaw Mountain Landis, January 15, 1942, in *Inside the Baseball Hall of Fame*, 97.

8. Rable, "Patriotism, Platitudes and Politics," 369.

9. *NYDM*, April 18, 1956; *NYJA*, April 18, 1965; *NYT*, April 18, 1956.

10. *NYDP*, April 17, 1956; *NYDN*, April 18, 1956; *NYDM*, April 18, 1956.

11. *NYDM*, April 17, 1956.

12. *NYDM*, April 18, 1956; *WP*, April 18, 1956.

13. *NYJA*, April 18, 1956; *NYP*, April 18, 1956.

14. *WP*, April 18, 1956; *NYJA*, April 18, 1956; *NYDM*, April 19, 1956.

15. *NYDM*, April 19, 1956.

16. Rader, *Baseball*, 190; Tygiel, *Past Time*, 148–149.

17. Michael Bein, "A Graphic History of Baseball," Michael Bein's Home Plate, http://michaelbein.com/baseball.html.

18. Surdam, *The Postwar Yankees*, 89.

19. Rader, *Baseball*, 191–192.

20. Surdam, *The Postwar Yankees*, 87–90.

21. James Murray, "The Case for the Suffering Fan," *SI*, August 20, 1956.

22. Murray, "The Case for the Suffering Fan."

23. For stories on the weather, see "April Chill Kills Flowers—and Gates," *TSN*, May 2, 1956; Joe King, "TV, Parking or Weather to Blame? Attendance Sags for Three N.Y. Clubs," *TSN*, May 2, 1956.

24. Grantland Rice, "Is Baseball Afraid of Television?," *Sport*, April 1951, 12–13, 90.

25. Halberstam, *Summer of '49*, 233–135.

26. Roberts and Olson, *Winning Is the Only Thing*, 96; Dan Daniel, "TV Must Go—or Baseball Will!," *BM*, November 1952, 6–7, 36–37.

27. *NYDN*, March 3, 1956; *TSN*, March 14, 1956; *TSN*, May 23, 1956.

28. *NYHT*, June 19, 1956.

29. Rader, *Baseball*, 191.

30. Sullivan, *The Diamond in the Bronx*, 102–104; Gonzalez, *The Bronx*, 1; *NYT*, July 11, 1955 (emphasis in the original).

31. Creamer, *Stengel*, 282; Halberstam, *October 1964*, 231.

32. Rampersad, *Jackie Robinson*, 253.

33. Tygiel, *Baseball's Great Experiment*, 295, 291.

34. Mantle with Gluck, *The Mick*, 123; Castro, *Mickey Mantle*, 129; telephone interview with Charles Duboise.

35. *WP*, October 14, 1953; Kahn, *Boys of Summer*, 164.

36. Tygiel, *Baseball's Great Experiment*, 296–297; Halberstam, *October 1964*, 233–234; *NYT*, April 1, 1955.

37. Tygiel, *Baseball's Great Experiment*, 288; *NYT*, April 1, 1955; Howard with Wimbush, *Elston and Me*, 39.

38. *TSN*, September 19, 1956; Roger Kahn, "The Ten Years of Jackie Robinson," *Sport*, October 1955, 77.

39. "Are There Too Many Negroes in Baseball?," *Our World*, August 1954, 43; John Lardner, "The Old Emancipator—II," *Newsweek*, April 9, 1956, 84.

40. *DFP*, June 20, 1995.

41. Jerome Weidman, "Nobody Goes to the Bronx," *Holiday*, October 1955, 58–59.

42. Riess, *Touching Base*, 108.

43. Stout, *Yankees Century*, 97.

44. Frommer, *New York City Baseball*, 126–127; Stout, *Yankees Century*, 104–105; Frommer, *Remembering Yankee Stadium*, 5–6; Weintraub, *The House That Ruth Built*, 29.

45. Margolick, *Beyond Glory*, 7.

46. *NYHT*, April 21, 1956.

47. *NYJA*, April 21, 1956.

48. *NYDM*, April 21, 1956; *NYHT*, April 21, 1956.

49. *NYDM*, April 21, 1956.

50. *NYDM*, April 21, 1956; *NYHT*, April 21, 1956.

51. *NYDM*, April 22, 1956; *NYWTS*, April 24, 1956.

52. *NYP*, April 24, 1956, April 25, 1956, April 28, 1956.

53. Lipsyte, *SportsWorld*, 170.

54. Berkow, *Red*, 98; Holtzman, *No Cheering in the Press Box*, 259.

55. Holtzman, *No Cheering in the Press Box*, 259.

CHAPTER 5

1. Ribowsky, *The Complete History of the Home Run*, 3–58.

2. Bryson, *One Summer*, 124.

3. Marshall Smelser, "The Babe on Balance," *American Scholar*, Spring 1975, 301.

4. For Babe Ruth's 1927 season, see Creamer, *Babe*, 307–310; Montville, *The Big Bam*, 252–259; Smelser, *The Life That Ruth Built*, 346–357; William Nack, "The Colossus," *SI*, August 24, 1998, http://www.si.com/vault/1998/08/24/247910/the-colossus-in-the-

late-summer-of-1927-babe-ruth-who-died-50-years-ago-this-week-went-on-a-historic
-home-run-hitting-spree-to-set-the-record-that-would-seal-his-immortality; Bryson, *One Summer*, 353–354, 410–412, 419–424.

5. Nack, "The Colossus."

6. Bryson, *One Summer*, 421; Nack, "The Colossus"; Creamer, *Babe*, 309.

7. Creamer, *Babe*, 309.

8. "April Chills Kill Flowers—and Gates," *TSN*, May 2, 1956.

9. *NYDN*, May 2, 1956; *NYP*, May 2, 1956; *NYDN*, May 3, 1956.

10. *NYDN*, May 3, 1956; Mantle and Pepe, *Mickey Mantle*, 60–63.

11. *NYDM*, May 6, 1956; *NYHT*, May 6, 1956; *NYT*, May 6, 1956; *NYDN*, May 6, 1956.

12. *WP*, May 7, 1956.

13. *NYT*, May 6, 1956.

14. *BG*, May 8, 1956.

15. *NYDM*, May 9, 1956, May 10, 1956.

16. Pennington, *Billy Martin*, 110–115.

17. Jackson, *The Encyclopedia of New York*, 1036.

18. Mantle and Pepe, *Mickey Mantle*, 69–70.

19. Frommer and Frommer, *Manhattan at Mid-Century*, 213–214.

20. Frommer and Frommer, *Manhattan at Mid-Century*, 209–210.

21. John Bainbridge, "Toots's World: II—Friendship," *New Yorker*, November 18, 1950, 54.

22. Michael Hainey, "Everybody Went to Toots's Place," *GQ*, October 2001, 198 (emphasis in the original).

23. Bainbridge, "Toots's World: II—Friendship," 53.

24. Bainbridge, "Toots's World: II—Friendship," 53; Frommer and Frommer, *Manhattan at Mid-Century*, 210.

25. John Bainbridge, "Toots's World: I—How Far Can We Go," *New Yorker*, November 11, 1950, 50.

26. Hainey, "Everybody Went to Toots's Place," 200.

27. Corzine, *Team Chemistry*, 14.

28. Bainbridge, "Toots's World: II—Friendship," 69–70 (emphasis in the original).

29. Mantle and Pepe, *Mickey Mantle*, 74.

30. Corzine, *Team Chemistry*, 11.

31. Mantle et al., *A Hero All His Life*, 16, 5.

32. *NYP*, May 11, 1956; *NYP*, May 14, 1956.

33. *NYWTS*, May 14, 1956; *NYP*, May 14, 1956.

34. *NYP*, May 14, 1956.

35. *NYDM*, May 17, 1956; *TSN*, May 16, 1956.

36. Mantle and Pepe, *Mickey Mantle*, 77.

37. *NYWTS*, May 22, 1956; Pennington, *Billy Martin*, 121.

38. *NYHT*, May 19, 1956.

39. *NYHT*, May 19, 1956; *NYP* May 22, 1956.

40. *NYWTS*, May 23, 1956.

41. *NYWTS*, May 23, 1956.

42. *NYP*, May 23, 1956.

43. *NYP*, May 23, 1956; Mantle et al., *A Hero All His Life*, 65–66.

44. *NYHT*, May 25, 1956; *NYJA*, May 25, 1956.
45. *NYJA*, May 26, 1956.
46. *BG*, May 30, 1956; *NYDM*, May 30, 1956.

CHAPTER 6

1. Unless noted otherwise, this section is drawn from Crystal, *700 Sundays*, 69–72.
2. Robert Creamer, "The Mantle of the Babe," *SI*, June 18, 1956; Roger Kahn, "Oklahoma's Mickey Mantle: Can the Young Yankee Beat the Babe?" *Newsweek*, June 25, 1956, 63.
3. Creamer, "The Mantle of the Babe"; *TSN*, June 20, 1956; *NYT*, May 31, 1956; *NYDM*, May 31, 1956.
4. *NYDM*, May 31, 1956; *BG*, May 31, 1956.
5. *NYT*, June 6, 1956; *TSN*, June 13, 1956.
6. Montville, *Ted Williams*, 128–129; Seidel, *Ted Williams*, 154–155.
7. *NYJA*, June 1, 1956.
8. *TSN*, June 6, 1956; Ed Linn, "If You Were Mickey Mantle," *Sport*, August 1957, 60; *NYT*, May 31, 1956; *NYJA*, June 1, 1956.
9. "A Prodigy of Power," *Life*, June 25, 1956, 100.
10. Whyte, *The Organization Man*; K. A. Cuordileone, "'Politics in an Age of Anxiety': Cold War Political Culture and the Crisis in American Masculinity, 1949–1960," *Journal of American History* 96 (September 2000): 522–526; Arthur Schlesinger Jr., "The Crisis of American Masculinity," *Esquire*, November 1958, 246.
11. Kimmel, *Manhood in America*, 223, 241; Dan Wakefield, "In the Defense of the Fullback," *Dissent* 4 (summer 1957): 313–314.
12. *NYJA*, May 27, 1956; George Roy, dir., *Mantle: The Definitive Story of Mickey Mantle*, DVD (New York: Home Box Office, 2005).
13. Leavy, *The Last Boy*, 156; United Press International news clipping, August 13, 1995.
14. Kahn, "Oklahoma's Mickey Mantle," 64; Shirley Povich, "Mickey Mantle, Incorporated," *SEP*, February 2, 1957, 20, 72; *TSN*, April 18, 1956.
15. Linn, "If You Were Mickey Mantle," 60; Joan Flynn Dreyspool, "Breakfast with Mickey," *SI*, June 18, 1956; Gerald Holland, "All Hail the Hero Mighty Mickey," *SI*, March 4, 1957, 54.
16. Dick Young, "The Man Who Handles Maris and Mantle," *Sport*, May 1962, 52.
17. *TSN*, April 18, 1956; Young, "The Man Who Handles Maris and Mantle," 52, 101–102.
18. *TSN*, October 24, 1956.
19. Young, "The Man Who Handles Maris and Mantle," 103; Povich, "Mickey Mantle, Incorporated," 20.
20. Ogilvy, *The Confessions of an Advertising Man*, 13.
21. Schaap, *Mickey Mantle*, 120.
22. *NYJA*, May 31, 1956.
23. Mantle et al., *A Hero All His Life*, 6.
24. *TSN*, July 4, 1956; *NYJA*, May 31, 1956; *NYHT*, June 2, 1956; *NYWTS*, June 4, 1956; "A Prodigy of Power," 102; Povich, "Mickey Mantle, Incorporated," 73.
25. *NYWTS*, June 4, 1956.

26. Mickey Mantle, Federal Bureau of Information file.

27. Surdam, *The Postwar Yankees*, 94–95; *NYT*, June 10, 1956.

28. *NYJA*, June 11, 1956.

29. For Larsen's early career, see Frank Graham Jr., "The Great Larsen," *Sport*, April 1957, 55; Mantle and Pepe, *Mickey Mantle*, 219; Arthur Richman and Milton Richman, "Is Larsen a One-Game Wonder?" *SEP*, March 30, 1957, 25; *NYT*, April 4, 1956; Paper, *Perfect*, 16.

30. Kahn, *The Era*, 331.

31. Graham, "The Great Larsen," 55–56; Paper, *Perfect*, 17.

32. *NYJA*, June 4, 1956; Povich, "Mickey Mantle, Incorporated," 73.

33. Kahn, *The Era*, 285; Surdam, *The Postwar Yankees*, 128.

34. *TSN*, April 18, 1956; Povich, "Mickey Mantle, Incorporated," 73.

35. Linn, "If You Were Mickey Mantle," 58; Povich, "Mickey Mantle, Incorporated," 20; Bill Bryson, "Whopping Salaries Usually Are Part 'Paper' Money," *BD*, April 1956, 61–62; Hirsch, *Willie Mays*, 241.

36. Jamieson, *Mint Condition*, 89–100; Burgos, *Playing America's Game*, 223–224.

37. Tygiel, *Baseball's Great Experiment*, 337.

38. Mantle and Pepe, *Mickey Mantle*, 101.

39. "Damn Yankees," I:i, in Dawidoff, *Baseball*, 269–274; Wolcott Gibbs, "Beelzebub Blanks Yanks," *New Yorker*, May 14, 1955, 132, 134.

40. Wallop, *The Year the Yankees Lost the Pennant*; Douglass Wallop, "How the Yankees Get That Way," *NYTM*, September 30, 1956, 78.

41. Creamer, *Baseball and Other Matters in 1941*, 20–23; Milton Gross, "Why They Hate the Yankees," *Sport*, September 1953, 10.

42. James Murray, "I Hate the Yankees," *Life*, April 17, 1950, 25–36.

43. Burk, *Much More Than a Game*, 110–111; Surdam, *The Postwar Yankees*, 170–177.

44. Gross, "Why They Hate the Yankees," 81; Helyar, *Lords of the Realm*, 365.

45. Wallop, "How the Yankees Get That Way," 26; Charles Einstein, "The Yankees: There Oughta Be a Law," *NYTM*, September 8, 1957, 96; Gay Talese, "There Are Fans—and Yankee Fans," *NYTM*, June 29, 1958, 18.

46. Charles Dexter, "New Reign of Terror," *Sport*, February 1954, 90.

47. *TSN*, June 27, 1956.

48. *SI*, June 18, 1956; *NYJA*, June 19, 1956.

49. *DN*, June 19, 1956; *NYWTS*, June 19, 1956.

50. *DN*, June 19, 1956; *DFP*, June 19, 1956; *NYDN*, June 19, 1956.

51. *DFP*, June 21, 1956; *NYJA*, June 21, 1956.

52. "Mantle's Marauding," *Newsweek*, July 2, 1956, 51.

53. *NYJA*, June 23, 1956; *NYT*, June 22, 1956; *NYP*, June 19, 1956.

54. *NYWTS*, June 25, 1956; *TSN*, June 27, 1956, July 4, 1956.

55. *NYT*, June 22, 1956; *NYDM*, June 22, 1956.

56. *NYDM*, June 22, 1956.

57. James, *The New Bill James Historical Baseball Abstract*, 220–221; *NYT*, June 29, 1956; "The Growing Boys," *Time*, July 9, 1956, 46; Dave Grote, "Livelier Ball? No, Heftier Hitters!" *BD*, August 1956, 26–28.

58. *NYT*, June 29, 1956; Creamer, "The Mantle of the Babe"; Montville, *The Big Bam*, 261.

59. *NYT*, July 4, 1956.

60. "League by League Totals for Home Runs," Baseball Almanac, http://www.base ball-almanac.com/hitting/hihr6.shtml; *TSN*, July 4, 1956; *NYT*, July 4, 1956.

61. James, *The New Bill James Historical Baseball Abstract*, 148, 224; "League by League Totals for Batting Average," Baseball Almanac, http://www.baseball-almanac.com/hitting /hibavg4.shtml; Grote, "Livelier Ball?," 28.

62. *NYWTS*, July 2, 1956.

63. *NYP*, July 2, 1956.

CHAPTER 7

1. Roger Kahn, "Oklahoma's Mickey Mantle: Can the Young Yankee Beat the Babe?" *Newsweek*, June 25, 1956, 63.

2. *NYT*, June 29, 1956; *TSN*, July 4, 1956.

3. Shirley Povich, "As High and as Far as Ruth," *BD*, July 1956, 14; *NYP*, July 10, 1956; *NYJA*, April 25, 1956; *NYT*, May 25, 1956; *NYWTS*, July 10, 1956.

4. Halberstam, *The Fifties*, 496–497, 506.

5. "Why Do Our Cars Look the Way They Do?" *Popular Mechanics*, January 1959, 282, 284.

6. John Updike, "Hub Fans Bid Kid Adieu," *New Yorker*, October 22, 1960, http:// www.newyorker.com/magazine/1960/10/22/hub-fans-bid-kid-adieu.

7. Bradlee, *The Kid*, 370, 401; Robert Creamer, "Ted Is Hope," *SI*, March 12, 1956, 41.

8. Ted Williams as told to Joe Reichler and Joe Trimble, "This Is My Last Year," *SEP*, April 10, 1954, 17; Al Hirshberg, "Handsome Bad Boy of the Boston Red Sox," *Cosmopolitan*, July 1956, 126; "A Question of Age," *Newsweek*, March 19, 1956, 68.

9. Halberstam, *Summer of '49*, 181; "A Question of Age," 68.

10. "A Question of Age," 68. On Williams's hitting approach, see Williams and Underwood, *The Science of Hitting*.

11. Seidel, *Ted Williams*, 277.

12. Updike, "Hub Fans Bid Kid Adieu."

13. Seidel, *Ted Williams*, xvi.

14. *BG*, July 4, 1956; *NYT*, June 6, 1956; Hirshberg, "Handsome Bad Boy of the Boston Red Sox," 123.

15. *BG*, July 5, 1956; *NYT*, July 6, 2002; Bradlee, *The Kid*, 23.

16. Joan Flynn Dreyspool, "Conversation Piece: Subject: Ted Williams," *SI*, August 1, 1955, 58.

17. *BG*, July 5, 1956; *NYJA*, July 6, 1956.

18. *NYDN*, July 5, 1956; *BG*, July 5, 1956.

19. *NYT*, July 6, 1956; *BG*, July 6, 1956; *NYDN*, July 6, 1956.

20. *NYWTS*, July 2, 1956; *NYDN*, July 7, 1956; *TSN*, July 4, 1956; *NYJA*, July 7, 1956, July 9, 1956.

21. *NYT*, July 9, 1956; *WP*, July 9, 1956.

22. *WP*, July 11, 1956; Mantle and Pepe, *Mickey Mantle*, 124.

23. Hirshberg, "Handsome Bad Boy of the Boston Red Sox," 127; Richard Ben Cramer, "What Do You Think of Ted Williams Now?" *Esquire*, June 1986, http://www .esquire.com/features/biography-ted-williams-0686; Bradlee, *The Kid*, 300–304; Halberstam, *Summer of '49*, 189–191.

24. Cramer, "What Do You Think of Ted Williams Now?"; Bradlee, *The Kid*, 344.

25. Mantle with Gluck, *The Mick*, 131–132; Mickey Mantle FBI file.

26. Cleveland Amory, "I Wanna Be an Immortal," *SEP*, January 10, 1942, 74.

27. Mickey Mantle with Jill Lieber, "Time in a Bottle," *SI*, April 18, 1994, http://www.si.com/vault/1994/04/18/130871/time-in-a-bottle-after-42-years-of-alcohol-abuse-a-legendary-ballplayer-describes-his-life-of-self-destructive-behavior-and-hopes-his-recovery-will-finally-make-him-a-true-role-model.

28. Ed Linn, "Ted Williams: The Kid Comes of Age," *Sport*, August 1954, 61; Halberstam, *Summer of '49*, 189; Dreyspool, "Conversation Piece," 29.

29. Arthur Daley, "A Prideful Man," *BD*, August 1956, 58; Dan Daniel, "Mickey Mantle," *BM*, August 1951, 11.

30. Bradlee, *The Kid*, 423; Shirley Povich, "Ted's Big Itch: To Outhit Mantle," *BD*, September 1956, 44.

31. Mantle and Pepe, *Mickey Mantle*, 125.

32. Williams and Prime, *Ted Williams' Hit List*, 67; Tom Meany, "As Casey Stengel Sees Mickey Mantle," *Collier's*, July 20, 1956, 76.

33. *WP*, July 11, 1956; Robert Creamer, "The All-Star Idea," *SI*, July 9, 1956, http://www.si.com/vault/1956/07/09/582286/the-all-star-idea.

34. Rader, *Baseball*, 153–154; White, *Creating the National Pastime*, 118–122.

35. *NYDM*, July 11, 1956; *NYHT*, July 11, 1956.

36. *TSN*, July 18, 1956; *NYT*, July 11, 1956.

37. *NYP*, July 11, 1956.

38. *NYHT*, July 12, 1956.

39. *NYHT*, July 12, 1956.

40. *NYT*, July 15, 1956.

41. *NYT*, July 15, 1956; *NYDM*, July 15, 1956.

42. Robert Creamer, "Casey Puts It on Ice," *SI*, July 23, 1956.

43. *NYDM*, July 19, 1956.

44. *NYDM*, July 19, 1956.

45. Creamer, "Casey Puts It on Ice."

46. Douglass Wallop, "How the Yankees Get That Way," *NYTM*, September 30, 1956, 26.

47. *NYWTS*, July 19, 1956.

48. *NYWTS*, July 19, 1956.

49. *BG*, August 5, 1956; Ben Epstein, "What Manner of a Man Is Mantle?" *Look*, July 24, 1956, 27–28.

50. Creamer, *Stengel*, 265.

51. Creamer, *Stengel*, 263; "The Language of Casey Stengel," ESPN.com, November 19, 2003, http://espn.go.com/classic/s/Stengelese.html.

52. Tom Meany, "Stengel—the Ol' Perfesser," *BD*, June 1952, 76; Arthur Daley, "Philosophy of C. Stengel," *NYTM*, July 26, 1953, SM14; Creamer, *Stengel*, 262.

53. Creamer, *Stengel*, 12; Meany, "Stengel—the Ol' Perfesser," 77.

54. Meany, "As Casey Stengel Sees Mickey Mantle," 75.

55. Meany, "As Casey Stengel Sees Mickey Mantle," 77.

56. Meany, "As Casey Stengel Sees Mickey Mantle," 77.

57. *TSN*, August 1, 1956.

58. *TSN*, August 1, 1956; *BG*, August 5, 1956.

59. *NYT*, July 31, 1956; *NYP*, July 31, 1956.
60. *TSN*, July 18, 1956.
61. *NYT*, August 6, 1956; *TSN*, July 18, 1956.

CHAPTER 8

1. "N.C." to Jackie Robinson, October 6, 1947; Robinson to "N.C.," October 15, 1947, Jules Tygiel Papers, Box 2, Folder 3, National Baseball Hall of Fame Library, Cooperstown, New York.
2. Mrs. Mickey Mantle as told to Christy Munro, "Mickey Mantle's Private World," *Look*, August 6, 1957, 38.
3. For the background of Mantle's affair with Brooke, see Holly Brooke, "I Own 25% of Mickey Mantle," *Confidential*, March 1957, 32–33, 52, 54, 56; Castro, *DiMag and Mick*, 19–26; Castro, *Mickey Mantle*, 82–83.
4. Brooke, "I Own 25% of Mickey Mantle," 52.
5. Brooke, "I Own 25% of Mickey Mantle," 54 (emphasis in the original).
6. Brooke, "I Own 25% of Mickey Mantle," 65.
7. Bradlee, *The Kid*, 417; Montville, *Ted Williams*, 200.
8. For the spitting incident, see *NYT*, August 8, 1956; *TSN*, August 15, 1956; *NYP*, August 8, 1956; Bradlee, *The Kid*, 417–421; Montville, *Ted Williams*, 196–201.
9. Bradlee, *The Kid*, 418.
10. *NYHT*, August 10, 1956; Montville, *Ted Williams*, 197.
11. Bradlee, *The Kid*, 419; *BG*, August 8, 1956; *NYP*, August 8, 1956.
12. Joan Flynn Dreyspool, "Ted Williams Defies His Critics," *SI*, August 20, 1956, 23; *BG*, August 11, 1956.
13. *BG*, August 9, 1956.
14. Bradlee, *The Kid*, 421; *NYJA*, August 18, 1956.
15. *NYJA*, August 10, 1956.
16. *NYHT*, August 12, 1956; *BG*, August 13, 1956; *TSN*, August 29, 1956.
17. Barnouw, *Tube of Plenty*, 198.
18. Gay Talese, "Platter Up," *NYTM*, October 7, 1956, 259.
19. Mickey Mantle as told to John Ross, "My Hits—and My Errors," *American Weekly*, September 9, 1956, 12.
20. Ross, "My Hits," 13.
21. *BG*, October 4, 1956.
22. *NYP*, October 5, 1956; *NYHT*, September 9, 1956.
23. *TSN*, October 10, 1956.
24. Cleveland Amory, "I Wanna Be an Immortal," *SEP*, January 10, 1941, 74; *NYP*, August 15, 1956.
25. Dreyspool, "Ted Williams Defies His Critics," 25.
26. *NYP*, August 15, 1956.
27. *NYP*, August 15, 1956.
28. *NYP*, August 15, 1956; *BG*, August 15, 1956.
29. *NYHT*, September 12, 1956.
30. Interview with Carl Erskine.
31. *NYJA*, August 15, 1956; *NYWTS*, August 17, 1956.

32. *NYT*, August 16, 1956.

33. *NYP*, August, 15, 1956.

34. *NYJA*, August 17, 1956.

35. *NYJA*, August 17, 1956; *DN*, August 18, 1956; *TSN*, August 22, 1956.

36. Mantle and Pepe, *Mickey Mantle*, 159.

37. Ed Linn, "If You Were Mickey Mantle," *Sport*, August 1957, 55.

38. Shecter, *The Jocks*, 136.

39. Shecter, *The Jocks*, 137.

40. Pennington, *Billy Martin*, 79.

41. Gerald Astor, "Mickey Mantle: Oklahoma to Olympus," *Look*, February 23, 1965, 73.

42. Astor, "Mickey Mantle."

43. Al Stump, "He's Never Out of Trouble," *SEP*, August 18, 1956, 19.

44. Stump, "He's Never Out of Trouble," 44.

45. Corzine, *Team Chemistry*, 61–62.

46. Corzine, *Team Chemistry*, 61–62.

47. Corzine, *Team Chemistry*, 64.

48. Goldman with Bush and Klatz, *Death in the Locker Room*, 77.

49. Stump, "He's Never Out of Trouble," *SEP*, 44; Leavy, *The Last Boy*, 210–212, 225–226.

50. Leavy, *The Last Boy*, 173.

51. *NYDN*, August 22, 1956; Roger Kahn, "Why They Broke Up Billy Martin's Gang," *Sport*, October 1957, 20.

CHAPTER 9

1. "A Real Rap Session," *SI*, April 14, 1986, http://www.si.com/vault/1986/04/14/633776/a-real-rap-session.

2. *NYJA*, August 23, 1956; *NYWTS*, August 24, 1956.

3. *NYP*, August, 24, 1956.

4. *NYP*, August, 24, 1956.

5. "Blackout at Home," *Newsweek*, August 27, 1956, 63; *NYT*, August 30, 1956; *NYP*, August 31, 1956.

6. *NYP*, August 30, 1956.

7. *BG*, September 9, 1956.

8. *TSN*, September 12, 1956; *BG*, September 1, 1956; *NYT*, September 1, 1956.

9. *NYT*, September 1, 1956.

10. *NYT*, September 1, 1956.

11. *NYP*, August 19, 1956.

12. *NYP*, August 19, 1956.

13. *DFP*, September 1, 1956.

14. For Al Kaline, see Jack Olsen, "The Torments of Excellence," *SI*, May 11, 1964, http://www.si.com/vault/1964/05/11/607197/the-torments-of-excellence; Robert Shaplen, "On the Lookout for a Kaline," *SI*, May 14, 1956, 32–39; H. C. Butler, "The Tigers' Million-Dollar Kid," *SEP*, September 3, 1955, 66–69; Tommy Devine, "Kaline Can Be King in Detroit," *Sport*, August 1955, 34–35, 60–62. Some sources list Kaline's batting average at Southern High as .462.

15. Olsen, "The Torments of Excellence"; Shaplen, "On the Lookout for a Kaline," 32–34.

16. Shaplen, "On the Lookout for a Kaline," 32–34.

17. Olsen, "The Torments of Excellence"; Shaplen, "On the Lookout for a Kaline," 32–34; Devine, "Kaline Can Be King in Detroit," 62.

18. Bradlee, *The Kid*, 423.

19. *NYHT*, September 12, 1956.

20. *BG*, September 10, 1956.

21. *BG*, September 10, 1956.

22. Mantle and Pepe, *Mickey Mantle*, 169, 173.

23. *DFP*, September 4, 1956; *BH*, September 4, 1956; *NYP*, September 4, 1956; *NYHT*, September 5, 1956.

24. *NYWTS*, August 6, 1956; Mantle and Pepe, *Mickey Mantle*, 174.

25. *NYWTS*, October 3, 1956.

26. *DFP*, September 12, 1956; *BG*, September 10, 1956.

27. *BG*, September 14, 1956; *TSN*, October 10, 1956.

28. *DFP*, September 15, 1956, September 16, 1956.

29. *DFP*, September 16, 1956.

30. *BH*, September 14, 1956; *BH*, September 20, 1956; Bradlee, *The Kid*, 423.

31. *TSN*, September 26, 1956; Williams and Underwood, *The Science of Hitting*, 26.

32. Mantle and Pepe, *Mickey Mantle*, 176–177.

33. *NYHT*, September 19, 1956; *NYT*, September 19, 1956.

34. *NYHT*, September 19, 1956.

35. *NYHT*, September 19, 1956.

36. *TSN*, September 26, 1956.

37. *Cincinnati Post*, October 2, 1956; *NYDN*, September 20, 1956.

38. *BH*, September 20, 1956; *NYDN*, September 21, 1956; Williams and Underwood, *The Science of Hitting*, 14–15, 24.

39. *NYT*, September 21, 1956.

40. *BG*, September 24, 1956.

41. *NYT*, September 22, 1956.

42. *DFP*, September 20, 1956.

43. *NYDN*, September 20, 1956.

44. *NYP*, September 23, 1956.

45. *NYT*, September 22, 1956; *BH*, September 22, 1956.

46. *BH*, September 23, 1956.

47. *BH*, September 23, 1956; *NYHT*, September 23, 1956.

48. *NYT*, September 22, 1956; *NYHT*, September 23, 1956; *NYP*, September 23, 1956.

49. *NYHT*, September 24, 1956.

50. *NYHT*, September 24, 1956; *BH*, September 24, 1956.

51. Mantle and Pepe, *Mickey Mantle*, 181–184.

52. Halberstam, *Summer of '49*, 266.

53. *NYP*, September 27, 1956.

54. *NYHT*, September 29, 1956.

55. Bradlee, *The Kid*, 423.

56. *NYDN*, October 1, 1956.

57. For the clubhouse scene, see *TSN*, October 10, 1956; *NYP*, October 1, 1956; *NYWTS*, October 1, 1956; *NYHT*, October 1, 1956.

CHAPTER 10

1. Pennington, *Billy Martin*, 114; Paul O'Neil, "The Damndest Yankee of Them All," *SI*, April 23, 1956, 69.

2. *NYP*, October 3, 1956; Roy Campanella as told to Milton Gross, "How I Catch a Ball Game," *SEP*, May 26, 1956, 118.

3. Lanctot, *Campy*, 335.

4. *NYP*, October 3, 1956.

5. Prince, *Brooklyn's Dodgers*, 57; Golenbock, *Bums*, 394.

6. Hughes, *Literary Brooklyn*, 2, 105.

7. Hughes, *Literary Brooklyn*, 233.

8. Golenbock, *Bums*, 440; "Brooklyn Rolls, the U.S. Rocks," *Life*, October 17, 1955, 38–39.

9. Golenbock, *In the Country of Brooklyn*, 193; Frommer and Frommer, *It Happened in Brooklyn*, 38–39; D'Antonio, *Forever Blue*, 39–40.

10. Prince, *Brooklyn's Dodgers*, 102, 106–107; Gay Talese, "There Are Fans—and Yankee Fans," *NYTM*, June 29, 1958, 18; Golenbock, *Bums*, 65, 387.

11. Goodwin, *Wait Till Next Year*, 61.

12. *NYT*, October 8, 1952.

13. *NYDN*, October 3, 1956; *NYHT*, October 3, 1956; *NYP*, October 3, 1956.

14. *NYT*, October 2, 1956; *NYHT*, October 2, 1956.

15. *NYHT*, October 3, 1956; *NYP*, October 3, 1956.

16. "New York Yankees," *SI*, October 1, 1956, 18.

17. *NYP*, October 3, 1956.

18. *NYT*, October 3, 1956; *NYWTS*, October 3, 1956.

19. Goodwin, *Wait Till Next Year*, 45–49; Frommer and Frommer, *It Happened in Brooklyn*, 36.

20. *NYT*, October 4, 1956; *NYDN*, October 4, 1956; *NYWTS*, October 4, 1956.

21. Jay, *More Than Just a Game*, 20.

22. *NYWTS*, October 4, 1956; *NYHT*, October 4, 1956.

23. *NYWTS*, October 4, 1956; *NYHT*, October 4, 1956.

24. *NYP*, October 5, 1956.

25. *NYWTS*, October 4, 1956; *NYDN*, October 5, 1956; *NYT*, October 5, 1956.

26. "He Throws Hard," *Time*, September 19, 1956, 52; Robert Creamer, "Subject: Don Newcombe," *SI*, August 22, 1955, 51.

27. Don Newcombe as told to Milton Gross, "I'm No Quitter," *SEP*, March 9, 1957, 27, 90; *BG*, October 2, 1956.

28. *NYDN*, October 5, 1956.

29. Arthur Richman and Milton Richman, "Is Larsen a One-Game Wonder?" *SEP*, March 30, 1957, 83.

30. *NYDN*, October 6, 1956.

31. *NYWTS*, October 5, 1956.

32. Mantle and Pepe, *Mickey Mantle*, 230; *NYWTS*, October 6, 1956.

33. *NYT*, October 6, 1956; Roger Kahn, "Whitey Ford Is His Own Boss," *Sport*, December 1958, 54; Robert Creamer, "The Pitcher Who Could Win the Series," *SI*, September 10, 1956, 14.

34. *NYHT*, October 7, 1956; *NYDN*, October 7, 1956.

35. *NYHT*, October 8, 1956.

36. Robert Creamer, "The Name Is Yogi," *SI*, October 22, 1956, https://www.si.com/vault/1956/10/22/670462/the-name-is-yogi.

37. Paper, *Perfect*, 5; Larsen with Shaw, *The Perfect Yankee*, 33–35.

38. Larsen with Shaw, *The Perfect Yankee*, 27–30; Kahn, *The Era*, 331–332.

39. Mantle and Pepe, *Mickey Mantle*, 262–263; Corzine, *Team Chemistry*, 19–26.

40. Creamer, "The Name Is Yogi"; Barra, *Yogi Berra*, 218.

41. Larsen with Shaw, *The Perfect Yankee*, 162–163.

42. Frank Graham Jr., "The Great Larsen," *Sport*, April 1957, 54; Barra, *Yogi Berra*, 218.

43. Larsen with Shaw, *The Perfect Yankee*, 179.

44. Graham, "The Great Larsen," 54; Richman, "Is Larsen a One-Game Wonder?" 83; *NYWTS*, October 9, 1956.

45. Richman, "Is Larsen a One-Game Wonder?" 83.

46. *NYT*, October 9, 1956; Graham, "The Great Larsen," 54.

47. Mantle and Pepe, *Mickey Mantle*, 275; Richman, "Is Larsen a One-Game Wonder?" 83; Larsen with Shaw, *The Perfect Yankee*, 181; Robert Creamer, "The Curtain Rises," *SI*, October 15, 1956; *NYT*, October 9, 1956; Graham, "The Great Larsen," 54.

48. Barra, *Yogi Berra*, 223.

49. Graham, "The Great Larsen," 55.

50. *NYT*, October 9, 1956; *NYDN*, October 9, 1956; *NYHT*, October 9, 1956.

51. Creamer, "The Name Is Yogi."

52. Barra, *Yogi Berra*, 226.

53. *NYHT*, October 10, 1956.

54. Mantle and Pepe, *Mickey Mantle*, 293; Golenbock, *Dynasty*, 188.

55. Golenbock, *Dynasty*, 188.

56. Barra, *Yogi Berra*, 227.

57. Gross, "I'm No Quitter," 90.

58. *NYHT*, October 11, 1956.

59. Golenbock, *Dynasty*, 189–190; *NYDN*, October 11, 1956.

60. *NYHT*, October 11, 1956; *NYDN*, October 11, 1956.

61. *NYHT*, October 11, 1956.

62. *NYHT*, October 11, 1956.

63. *NYP*, October 11, 1956.

EPILOGUE

1. Gerald Holland, "All Hail Mighty Mickey," *SI*, March 4, 1957, 53.

2. Holland, "All Hail Mighty Mickey," 53.

3. Holland, "All Hail Mighty Mickey," 54 (emphasis in the original).

4. Mantle with Gluck, *The Mick*, 143–145.

5. Mantle with Gluck, *The Mick*, 143–145.

6. Mantle with Gluck, *The Mick*, 143–145.

7. Mantle with Gluck, *The Mick*, 146–147; "Penthouse Interview: Mickey Mantle," *Penthouse*, September 1986, 86.

8. Holly Brooke, "I Own 25% of Mickey Mantle," *Confidential*, March 1957, 32; Gabler, *Winchell*, 468.

9. Castro, *Mickey Mantle*, 150.

10. Alfred Garvey, "There Was No Umpire Around When These Yankees Had a Ball," *Confidential*, September 1957, 29–30; Jim Hanks, "Have Those 'Damn Yankees' Ruined Mickey Mantle?" *Suppressed*, October 1957, 15–17, 50; Gabler, *Winchell*, 81.

11. Unless noted otherwise, this section on the Copacabana incident and its aftermath is drawn from Corzine, *Team Chemistry*, 14–16; Barra, *Yogi Berra*, 235–239; Leavy, *The Last Boy*, 163–167, 180–181; Pennington, *Billy Martin*, 126–129.

12. *NYJA*, May 16, 1957, June 24, 1957; *NYDM*, May 17, 1957.

13. Roger Kahn, "Why They Broke Up Billy Martin's Gang," *Sport*, October 1957, 20.

14. *NYP*, June 24, 1957; Irv Goodman, "You Think You Know Billy Martin?" *Sport*, August 1958, 57.

15. *NYP*, May 17, 1956; Stanley Frank, "The Yankees' Southpaw Wizard," *SEP*, May 12, 1956, 33, 101; Roger Kahn, "Whitey Ford Is His Own Boss," *Sport*, December 1958, 55.

16. "Mantle's Breaks and Yours," *Popular Science*, October 1964, 100.

17. *NYT*, June 9, 1969.

18. Castro, *Mickey Mantle*, 238; Bouton, *Ball Four*, 30, 37–39.

19. Bouton, *Ball Four*, ix.

20. Elias, *The Empire Strikes Out*, 263.

21. Falkner, *The Last Hero*, 188–189.

22. Canale, *Mickey Mantle: The Yankee Years*, 22.

23. This description of the fishing trip is drawn from Canale, *Mickey Mantle: The Yankee Years*, 80–95; Canale, *Mickey Mantle: Memories and Memorabilia*, 11; "Sweet Memories," *SI*, October 16, 1991, 27–28; Pennington, *Billy Martin*, 130–131. A few of the photos were published in various issues of *Sport* in 1957. See Kahn, "Why They Broke Up Billy Martin's Gang," 19; Ed Linn, "If You Were Mickey Mantle," *Sport*, August 1957, 62.

24. Mantle with Gluck, *The Mick*, 161.

BIBLIOGRAPHY

Adair, Robert K. *The Physics of Baseball*. 3rd ed. New York: Harper-Perennial, 2002.

Barnouw, Eric. *Tube of Plenty: The Evolution of American Television*. Rev. ed. New York: Oxford University Press, 1982.

Barra, Allen. *Mickey and Willie: Mantle and Mays, the Parallel Lives of Baseball's Golden Age*. New York: Crown Archetype, 2013.

———. *Yogi Berra: Eternal Yankee*. New York: W. W. Norton & Company, 2010.

Berkow, Ira. *Red: A Biography of Red Smith*. Lincoln: University of Nebraska Press, 2007.

Bouton, Jim. *Ball Four*. New York: Wiley Publishing, 1990; orig. 1970.

Bradlee, Ben, Jr. *The Kid: The Immortal Life of Ted Williams*. New York: Little, Brown and Company, 2013.

Bryson, Bill. *One Summer: America, 1927*. New York: Doubleday, 2013.

Burgos, Adrian, Jr. *Playing America's Game: Baseball, Latinos, and the Color Line*. Berkeley: University of California Press, 2007.

Burk, Robert. *Much More Than a Game: Players, Owners, and American Baseball Since 1921*. Chapel Hill: University of North Carolina Press, 2001.

Canale, Larry. *Mickey Mantle: Memories and Memorabilia*. Iola, WI: Krause Publications, 2011.

———. *Mickey Mantle: The Yankee Years: The Classic Photography of Ozzie Sweet*. Richmond, VA: Tuff Stuff Books, 1998.

Castro, Tony. *DiMag and Mick: Sibling Rivals, Yankee Blood Brothers*. Guilford, CT: Lyons Press, 2016.

———. *Mickey Mantle: America's Prodigal Son*. Washington, DC: Brassey's, Inc., 2002.

Corzine, Nathan Michael. *Team Chemistry: The History of Drugs and Alcohol in Major League Baseball*. Urbana-Champaign: University of Illinois Press, 2016.

Cramer, Richard Ben. *Joe DiMaggio: The Hero's Life*. New York: Simon & Schuster, 2000.

Creamer, Robert W. *Babe: The Legend Comes to Life*. New York: Simon & Schuster, 1974

———. *Baseball and Other Matters in 1941*. Lincoln: University of Nebraska Press, 2000.

———. *Stengel: His Life and Times*. New York: Simon & Schuster, 1984.

Crystal, Billy. *700 Sundays*. New York: Grand Central Publishing, 2005.

D'Antonio, Michael. *Forever Blue: The Story of Walter O'Malley, Baseball's Most Controversial Owner, and the Dodgers of Brooklyn and Los Angeles*. New York: Riverhead Books, 2010.

Dawidoff, Nicholas, ed. *Baseball: A Literary Anthology*. New York: Library of America, 2002.

Elias, Robert. *The Empire Strikes Out: How Baseball Sold U.S. Foreign Policy and Promoted the American Way Abroad.* New York: New Press, 2010.

Falkner, David. *The Last Hero: The Life of Mickey Mantle.* New York: Simon & Schuster, 1995.

Frommer, Harvey. *Remembering Yankee Stadium: An Oral and Narrative History of "The House That Ruth Built."* Guilford, CT: Lyons Press, 2008.

———. *New York City Baseball: The Last Golden Age, 1947–1957.* Madison: University of Wisconsin Press, 2004.

Frommer, Myrna Katz, and Harvey Frommer. *It Happened in Brooklyn: An Oral History of Growing Up in the Borough in the 1940s, 1950s, and 1960s.* Albany: State University of New York Press, 1993.

———. *Manhattan at Mid-Century: An Oral History.* London and New York: Taylor Trade Publishing, 2013.

Gabler, Neal. *Winchell: Gossip, Power, and the Culture of Celebrity.* New York: Vintage, 1995.

Gems, Gerald. *Sport and the Shaping of Italian-American Identity.* Syracuse, NY: Syracuse University Press, 2013.

Gilbert, James. *A Cycle of Outrage: America's Reaction to the Juvenile Delinquent in the 1950s.* New York: Oxford University Press, 1986.

Goldman, Bob, with Patricia Bush and Ronald Klatz. *Death in the Locker Room: Steroids and Sports.* South Bend, IN: Icarus Press, 1984.

Golenbock, Peter. *Bums: An Oral History of the Brooklyn Dodgers.* Mineola, NY: Dover Books, 2010.

———. *Dynasty: The New York Yankees, 1949–1964.* Englewood Cliffs, NJ: Prentice Hall, Inc., 1975.

———. *In the Country of Brooklyn: Inspiration to the World.* New York: William Morrow, 2008.

Gonzalez, Evelyn. *The Bronx.* New York: Columbia University Press, 2004.

Goodwin, Doris Kearns. *Wait Till Next Year: A Memoir.* New York: Simon & Schuster, 1997.

Halberstam, David. *The Fifties.* New York: Ballantine Books, 1994.

———. *October 1964.* New York: Villard Books, 1994.

———. *Summer of '49.* New York: Perennial Classics, 2002.

Hall, John G. *Mickey Mantle: Before the Glory.* Keawood, KS: Leathers Publishing, 2005.

Helyar, John. *Lords of the Realm: The Real History of Baseball.* New York: Villard Books, 1994.

Hirsch, James S. *Willie Mays: The Life, the Legend.* New York: Scribner, 2010.

Holtzman, Jerome. *No Cheering in the Press Box.* New York: Holt, Rinehart, and Winston, 1974.

Howard, Arlene, and Ralph Wimbush. *Elston and Me: The Story of the First Black Yankee.* Columbia: University of Missouri Press, 2001.

Hughes, Evan. *Literary Brooklyn: The Writers of Brooklyn and the Story of American City Life.* New York: Holt Paperbacks, 2011.

Inside the Baseball Hall of Fame: The National Baseball Hall of Fame and Museum. New York: Simon & Schuster, 2013.

Jackson, Kenneth T., ed. *The Encyclopedia of New York City.* New Haven, CT: Yale University Press, 1995.

Jackson, Kenneth T., and David S. Dunbar, eds. *Empire City: New York Through the Centuries.* New York: Columbia University Press, 2002.

James, Bill. *The New Bill James Historical Baseball Abstract.* New York: Free Press, 2001.

Jamieson, Dave. *Mint Condition: How Baseball Cards Became an American Obsession*. New York: Atlantic Monthly Press, 2010.

Jay, Kathryn. *More Than Just a Game: Sports in American Life Since 1945*. New York: Columbia University Press, 2004.

Kahn, Roger. *The Boys of Summer*. New York: Perennial Classics, 2000; orig. 1972.

———. *The Era, 1947–1957: When the Yankees, the Giants, and the Dodgers Ruled the World*. Lincoln: University of Nebraska Press, 2002.

Kimmel, Michael. *Manhood in America: A Cultural History*. New York: Free Press, 1996.

Kirsch, *Baseball in Blue and Gray: The National Pastime During the Civil War*. Princeton, NJ: Princeton University Press, 2003.

Lanctot, Neil. *Campy: The Two Lives of Roy Campanella*. New York: Simon & Schuster, 2011.

Larsen, Don, with Mark Shaw. *The Perfect Yankee: The Incredible Story of the Greatest Miracle in Baseball History*. Champaign, IL: Sports Publishing, LLC, 2012.

Leavy, Jane. *The Last Boy: Mickey Mantle and the End of America's Childhood*. New York: HarperCollins, 2010.

Lipsyte, Robert. *SportsWorld: An American Dreamland*. New York: Quadrangle/New York Times Books Company, 1975.

Malamud, Bernard. *The Natural*. New York: Farrar, Straus and Giroux, 2003; orig. 1952.

Mantle, Merlyn, Mickey E. Mantle, David Mantle, and Dan Mantle. *A Hero All His Life: A Memoir by the Mantle Family*. New York: HarperCollins, 1996.

Mantle, Mickey. *My Batting Secret*. New York: Mickey Mantle Enterprises, 1956.

———. *The Quality of Courage*. New York: Bantam, 1970.

Mantle, Mickey, as told to Ben Epstein. *The Mickey Mantle Story*. New York: Henry Holt and Company, 1953.

Mantle, Mickey, with Herb Gluck. *The Mick*. New York: Doubleday & Company, Inc., 1985.

Mantle, Mickey, with Mickey Herskowitz. *All My Octobers: My Memories of Twelve World Series When the Yankees Ruled Baseball*. New York: HarperCollins, 1994.

Mantle, Mickey, and Phil Pepe. *Mickey Mantle: My Favorite Summer, 1956*. New York: Island Books, 1992.

Margolick, David. *Beyond Glory: Joe Louis vs. Max Schmeling, and the World on the Brink*. New York: Vintage, 2006.

Montville, Leigh. *The Big Bam: The Life and Times of Babe Ruth*. New York: Doubleday, 2006.

———. *Ted Williams: The Biography of an American Hero*. New York: Doubleday, 2004.

Nuttall, David S. *Mickey Mantle's Greatest Hits*. New York: S. P. I. Books, 1998.

Oakley, J. Ronald. *God's Country: America in the Fifties*. New York: Barricade Books, 1990.

Ogilvy, David. *Confessions of an Advertising Man*. London: Southbank Publishing, 2004; orig. 1963.

Oshinsky, David. *A Conspiracy So Immense: The World of Joe McCarthy*. New York: Oxford University Press, 2005.

O'Toole, Andrew. *Strangers in the Bronx: DiMaggio, Mantle, and the Changing of the Yankee Guard*. Chicago: Triumph Books, 2015.

Paper, Lew. *Perfect: Don Larsen's Miraculous World Series Game and the Men Who Made It Happen*. New York: New American Library, 2009.

Patterson, James T. *Grand Expectations: The United States, 1945–1974*. New York: Oxford University Press, 1996.

Pennington, Bill. *Billy Martin: Baseball's Flawed Genius*. Boston: Houghton Mifflin Harcourt, 2015.

Prince, Carl E. *Brooklyn's Dodgers: The Bums, the Borough, and the Best of Baseball.* New York: Oxford University Press, 1996.

Rader, Benjamin. *Baseball: A History of America's Game.* 3rd ed. Urbana-Champaign: University of Illinois Press, 2008.

Rampersad, Arnold. *Jackie Robinson: A Biography.* New York: Ballantine Books, 1997.

Ribowsky, Mark. *The Complete History of the Home Run.* New York: Citadel Press Books, 2003.

Riess, Steven. *Touching Base: Professional Baseball and American Culture During the Progressive Era.* Rev. ed. Urbana-Champaign: University of Illinois Press, 1999.

Roberts, Randy, and James Olson. *Winning Is the Only Thing: Sports in America Since 1945.* Baltimore: Johns Hopkins University Press, 1989.

Schaap, Dick. *Mickey Mantle: The Indispensable Yankee.* New York: Bartholomew House, 1961.

Schoor, Gene. *Mickey Mantle of the Yankees.* New York: G. P. Putnam's Sons, 1958.

Seidel, Michael. *Ted Williams: A Baseball Life.* Lincoln: University of Nebraska Press, 2000.

Shecter, Leonard. *The Jocks.* New York: Paperback Library, 1970.

Smelser, Marshall. *The Life That Ruth Built: A Biography.* New York: Quadrangle/New York Times Book Co., 1975.

Stout, Glenn. *Yankees Century: 100 Years of New York Yankees Baseball.* Boston: Houghton Mifflin Company, 2002.

Sullivan, Neil J. *The Diamond in the Bronx: Yankee Stadium and the Politics of New York.* New York: Oxford University Press, 2008.

Sullivan, Russell. *Rocky Marciano: The Rock of His Times.* Urbana-Champaign: University of Illinois Press, 2005.

Surdam, David G. *The Postwar Yankees: Baseball's Golden Age Revisited.* Lincoln: University of Nebraska Press, 2008.

Tullius, John. *I'd Rather Be a Yankee: An Oral History of America's Most Loved and Most Hated Baseball Team.* New York: MacMillan, 1986.

Tygiel, Jules. *Past Time: Baseball as History.* New York: Oxford University Press, 2000.

———. *Baseball's Great Experiment: Jackie Robinson and His Legacy.* New York: Oxford University Press, 1997.

Wallop, Douglass. *The Year the Yankees Lost the Pennant.* New York: W. W. Norton & Company, 1954.

Weintraub, Robert. *The House That Ruth Built: A New Stadium, the First Yankees Championship, and the Redemption of 1923.* New York: Little, Brown and Company, 2011.

White, E. B. *Here Is New York.* New York: Little Bookroom, 2005; orig. 1949.

White, G. Edward. *Creating the National Pastime: Baseball Transforms Itself, 1903–1953.* Princeton, NJ: Princeton University Press, 1996.

Whyte, William, Jr. *The Organization Man.* New York: Simon & Schuster, 1956.

Williams, Ted, and Jim Prime. *Ted Williams' Hit List.* Boston: McGraw-Hill, 1998.

Williams, Ted, and John Underwood. *The Science of Hitting.* New York: Simon & Schuster, 2013.

INDEX

Wertz, Vic, 153
White, E.B., 19, 22
Whyte, William H., 111
Williams, Ted, xv, xix, xx, 2, 11, 17, 63,
    77, 78, 81, 109-110, 126, 131, 132,
    133-136, 138, 139-144, 172, 179-180,
    187-188, 193, 204
  batting race with Mickey, 152-153,
    167-168, 170, 189, 192, 195-201
  spitting incident of, 159-162
Wilson, Hack, 97
Wilson, Woodrow, 59
Winchell, Walter, xiii, 11
Wolfe, Thomas, 209
Wolfe, Tom, 235
Wolff, Bob, 39
Woodward, Bob, 261

Woodward, Stanley, 80-81
World Series
  of 1951, 28-30
  of 1952, xi-xii, 37-38
  of 1953, 42-43
  of 1955, 49-51, 207, 209
  of 1956, 211-231
  Yankees dominance in, 19, 123-124
Wynn, Early, 44, 92, 171, 192

Yancey, Dan, 43, 46
Yankee Stadium, xx, 39, 69-70, 74-77, 91,
    107-108, 125, 133, 168, 200, 220, 240
Young, Dick, xiii, 230,
Youngman, Harold, 235

Zernial, Gus, xix

Randy Roberts is distinguished professor of history at Purdue University. An award-winning author, he focuses on the intersection of popular and political culture and has written or co-written biographies of such iconic athletes and celebrities as Jack Johnson, Jack Dempsey, Joe Louis, Bear Bryant, Oscar Robertson, John Wayne, and Muhammad Ali, as well as books on the Vietnam War, the Alamo, the 1973–1974 college basketball season, and West Point football during World War II. *A Season in the Sun* is the second book he has written with Johnny Smith. Roberts lives in Lafayette, Indiana.

Johnny Smith is the Julius C. "Bud" Shaw Professor in Sports, Society, and Technology and assistant professor of history at Georgia Tech. He is coauthor of *Blood Brothers: The Fatal Friendship Between Muhammad Ali and Malcolm X* (with Randy Roberts) and author of *The Sons of Westwood: John Wooden, UCLA, and the Dynasty That Changed College Basketball*. Smith lives in Atlanta, Georgia.